Primal Scenes of Communication

SUNY series in the Philosophy of the Social Sciences
Lenore Langsdorf, editor

Primal Scenes of Communication

COMMUNICATION, CONSUMERISM, AND SOCIAL MOVEMENTS

Ian Angus

STATE UNIVERSITY OF NEW YORK PRESS

Published by
State University of New York Press, Albany

For information, address State University of New York Press,
State University Plaza, Albany, N.Y., 12246

Production by Michael Haggett
Marketing by Fran Keneston

Library of Congress Cataloging-in-Publication Data

Angus, Ian H.
   Primal scenes of communication : communication, consumerism, and
social movements / Ian Angus.
      p. cm. — (SUNY series in the philosophy of the social sciences)
   Includes bibliographical references and index.
   ISBN 0-7914-4665-4 (alk. paper) — ISBN 0-7914-4666-2 (pbk. : alk. paper)
      1. Communication—Philosophy. 2. Communication—Social aspects. 3. Social
movements. I. Title. II. Series.

P91 .A55 2000
302.2′01—dc21
                                                                    99-054268

10 9 8 7 6 5 4 3 2 1

for Cassandra
who sparkles with the new

Contents

Acknowledgments

The perspective I utilize and explain in this book has been pursued in related directions in two other recent works, *A Border Within: National Identity, Cultural Plurality and Wilderness* (Montreal and Kingston: McGill-Queen's Press, 1997) and *(Dis)figurations* (London and New York: Verso, 2000). Some of the material was published in an earlier form in *Human Studies; Canadian Journal of Communication; Communication Theory; Cultural Politics in Contemporary America* (Routledge, 1989); *Communication Yearbook 15* (Sage, 1992); *Continuity and Change: The Cultural Life of Alberta's First Ukrainians* (Canadian Institute of Ukrainian Studies, 1988).

CHAPTER 1

Language and Institution
in the Human Sciences

Through the twentieth century, and with increasing urgency in recent years, there has been a persistent influence by an emergent and still controversial perspective which suggests that language use is the most fundamental phenomenon for the philosophy of the human sciences. Consequently, reflection on language has important implications for the method, results, historical location, and meaning for human life of the human sciences. This is the basic position that underlies most of the debates about postmodernism throughout the 1980s. Unlike the predominant modern philosophy of consciousness, which was focused on subject-object relations, critics of modernity turn toward language and culture, which is focused on intersubjective meaning. One way to express this perspective is to notice that recent language theories have been fused with earlier theories of the social construction of reality such that language has ceased to be understood as a distinct phenomenon but is rather taken to be the key to social processes outright. Thus, recently, hermeneutics, deconstruction, and speech act philosophy have converged on the proposal that language is the distinctively human component of social life. This emphasis on language has been overlaid on the previous position that "reality" is socially constructed—a trend in which

1

phenomenology, systems theory, and certain brands of Marxism were significant. Many other trends of thought could be mentioned, certainly. Nonetheless, it is possible to discern beyond specific intellectual traditions and innovations an emerging convergence on the notion that social reality is constructed in and through language and that, consequently, the proper activity of philosophy and the human sciences is the investigation of language use in various settings as well as its wider theoretical implications.

While modernity can be characterized through the predominance of a philosophy of consciousness stemming from Descartes, the dualism of this approach always contained the possibility of a degeneration into objectivism. The philosophical expression of modernity should be more accurately defined through the dualism of subjectivism and objectivism, or mentalism and behaviorism, and the continued attempt, but failure, to reconcile these positions. Postmodern philosophical expression thus begins when one ceases to argue from within the subject-object formulation and takes the articulation of this dualism itself as the problem requiring explanation. The Frankfurt School and phenomenology initiated this critique, but it is now pursued more commonly through language-based criticism.

The most distinctive nexus of substantive issues in this convergence is the suggestion that Western societies, and perhaps others also, have entered a new postmodern condition in which the "foundationalist" assumptions of intellectual and social life have been undermined. On the theoretical level, this suggestion pertains primarily to the status of the language of social inquiry: Whereas modern "science" was concerned with the *representation* of social life, and therefore raised questions of accuracy and methodology, postmodern "theory" emphasizes language-in-use as the *construction* of social relationships, which raises issues of institutional legitimacy and the rhetorical power of intellectual discourses. On the level of substantive social analysis, anti-foundationalism suggests that society is, or should be, constituted by a plurality of discourses, none of which can claim overriding legitimacy in the manner that the "grand narratives" (Lyotard) of progress and emancipation did for modernity. There can certainly be more subtle, and more extensive, characterizations of this shift. In particular, the very distinction between theoretical and substantive levels becomes questionable with the shift away from the modern *epistemological* warranting of inquiry toward the postmodern rhetorical emphasis on *what is done by* language rather than what is *said in* it. For this reason, questions concerning the "epistemology of the social sciences" have now largely been overtaken by contemporary issues of the "rhetoric of the human sciences," which focuses on what they do rather than on the adequacy of their representations. This entire new intellectual perspective, including its substantive claims, can be generally referred to as "discourse theory" due to the key role that language plays in it.

The discursive turn in philosophy and the human sciences thus stems from taking language use as especially significant in illuminating the whole of social praxis. Philosophical and scientific activity itself, after the turn, takes language as the metaphorical basis for understanding its own theoretical formation. Metaphors drawn from social life have allowed a reflexive conception of the formation and role of theory throughout the history of philosophy and the human sciences. Consider the (usually) conservative model of society as an organism, for example, or the liberal theory of society as an aggregate of atoms. Marxism has articulated its conception of theory mainly on the architectural metaphor of base and superstructure, though it has also at times used labor itself as a model in order to clarify the tasks and claims of theory. The basic metaphor in Harold Innis's communication theory of society is transportation, the traversal of space. The concept of metaphor is itself a metaphorical one, based on the Greek for "carrying-over." Metaphor carries over a meaning from one domain to another or, as we often say now, from one "level" to another. Thus, theoretical discourse is necessarily elaborated through metaphorical use of experiential materials. Innis's communication theory rediscovers—in his own sense, through the notion of carrying-over embedded in the concept of transportation as the traversal of space—the root metaphor from which the idea of metaphor began. Nowadays, theory is understood primarily through its expression in language. This reflexive application of the discursive turn to theory itself is one of the main sources of the power of the metaphor of language. It not only provokes interesting new descriptions of social praxis but also re-configures the relationship of theory to social praxis. Or, to state the issue somewhat more generally, when society is understood as a complex of expressive forms, it also encloses the social role of the particular expressive formation that is theory. The metaphor of language gives itself to a concise formulation of the recursive doubling that is always present in the project of self-knowledge in philosophy and the human sciences, since humanity is both known and knower. The project of self-knowledge in the human sciences produces a doubling of the subject which is characteristic of modernity since the anchoring of knowledge in subjectivity by Descartes. It is called by Foucault the empirical-transcendental doublet and by Husserl the transcendental and concrete egos.[1] This book addresses this issue through the notion of a medium of communication as both the transmission of a certain content and, more importantly, as the primal scene instituting social relations. Every communication is thus reflexive. Since humanity appears as both the subject and object of social representations, the reflexive capacity of language demands a theory of social praxis as a complex of expressive forms.

The term "expression" has, of course, a Romantic origin which tends to lead toward the notion of a deep inner experience that is pressed outward into external forms. It seems to imply an inner-outer dualism, similar to and based upon the subject-object dualism, that would be problematic in the context of the discursive turn. The metaphor of language has, perhaps above all, undermined the earlier presupposition that "subjective" human experience is inherently separate from "objective" social forms. By way of contrast, language occupies a middle realm in which human self-conceptions and social activities both emerge from cultural praxis. Language as metaphor has turned philosophy and the human sciences away from this subject-object, or representational, posing toward a conception of culture as its primary realm of investigation. But culture itself must be understood on this basis, not as a merely external or secondary activity, but as the process of formation of individual, group, and inter-group life. This process of formation of identities is expressive, albeit one shorn of inner-outer assumptions, in the sense of a socio-cultural praxis as the shaping of a distinct way of life. Such a self-shaping, or instituting, of a way of life requires a notion of expression, even if we must abandon the notion of an already-existing subjectivity hiding behind the forms of expression.

Expression can thus be understood as a primal scene of self-shaping through culture, indeed as the active component of the instituting of an order that gives rise to the unity of a subsequent history. This use of the term "institution" derives from Edmund Husserl's concept of *Urstiftung*, or sometimes simply *Stiftung*, which is normally translated into English as "instituting," "primal instituting," or "establishment" and which refers to the setting-into-play of a primal scene that founds a scientific or philosophical tradition—that is to say, a distinct formation of temporality.[2] In the context of describing the origin of geometry, Husserl used the term in this way: "Starting from what we know, from our geometry, or rather from the older handed-down forms (such as Euclidean geometry), there is an inquiry back [*Rückgang*] into the submerged original beginnings of geometry as they necessarily must have been in their 'primally establishing' [*urstiftende*] function."[3] An *Urstiftung* is thus not an event within history but is rather the founding moment of a way of knowing that allows a history to emerge. It can be discovered through an "inquiry back" or "regressive thinking" through the later history to the primal instituting that makes the history possible. Husserl's concept of *Urstiftung* was developed by Maurice Merleau-Ponty to refer to social institutions, who also suggested that it could provide the basis for a theory of culture. Claude Lefort took the concept further to include the notion of "regime" in political philosophy.[4] Martin Heidegger's concept of "the Open," or an "opening," is similar to "institution" and may well have been influenced by Husserl. He describes it this way in the context of the work of art: "The establishing of truth in the work is the bringing forth of a being such as never was before and will never come to be again. The bringing forth places this being in the Open [*Offene*] in such a way that what is to be brought forth first clears the openness of the Open [*die Offenheit des Offenen*] into which it comes forth." Heidegger mentions the act that founds a political state, essential sacrifice, the thinker's questioning, and the work of art as instances of opening.[5] While Husserl's use of the term "institution" refers to the institution of a tradition of science or knowledge, in this case the Galilean mathematical science that became definitive for modernity, Merleau-Ponty, Lefort, and Heidegger expand the use of the term to cover social institutions, political regimes, works of art, works of thought, and historical disclosures of epochs of Being. In other words, it is no longer confined to primal formations of knowledge, but applies also to social institutions and epochs of ontology. I will use this expanded meaning of "institution" in which it refers to the opening of a space from which a new temporal order comes forth and applies both to a formation of knowledge and an epoch of Being.

According to Husserl, every primal establishing also institutes a final establishment which culminates and clarifies the historical process brought into play by the opening. "But to every primal establishment [*Urstiftung*] essentially belongs a final establishment [*Endstiftung*] assigned as a task to the historical process. This final establishment is accomplished when the task is brought to consummate clarity and thus to an apodictic method which, in every step of achievement, is a constant avenue to new steps having the character of absolute success, i.e., the character of apodictic steps."[6] It is the aim of this book to fulfil the teleology of the concept of institution and opening in phenomenological philosophy with a theory of socio-cultural praxis based upon the primal scenes of media of communication. At the current moment of social movements in consumer society, which are primarily phenomena of communication, the final establishment of the instituting social role of media of communication becomes possible.

The shaping of a way of life in instituting praxis is, among other things, a process of self-convincing into a way of life, a rhetoric which establishes the identifications that constitute a social order. The term "rhetoric" is used in its theoretical sense here, and is to be distinguished from the popular usage in which "mere" rhetoric refers only to the outer presentation, or fashionable packaging, of an argument, rather than to its internal formulation—a formulation which also partakes in the inner-outer presupposition based on the philosophy of consciousness. Rhetoric originally referred to the persuasive component of any discourse, not in the common sense of mere decoration (though it can certainly degenerate into that), and as not necessarily opposed to "truth." Language in its rhetorical use is inherently connected to action because it deals, in Aristotle's words, "with such matters as we deliberate upon without arts or systems to guide us" and "to praise a man is in one respect akin to urging a course of action."[7] This classical formulation involves the notion that the speaker and hearer of a discourse are already formed as subjects prior to, or outside, the rhetorical discourse itself.[8] Once this presupposition of a subject already-there prior to rhetoric is abandoned, the constitutive function of rhetoric in forming subjects and interpellating them into the social formation can be recognized. In this way, the unfortunate Romantic associations of the term "expression" can be avoided.

Such a contemporary reformulation of the concept of rhetoric has been achieved through the concept of "identification" as developed by Kenneth Burke. Through the identificatory aspect of rhetoric, the "consubstantiality" of social actors is established; in short, they are formed into groups with common characteristics.[9] It is of the nature of humans that their social forms are not given directly by nature. Thus, the expressive formation of these social forms is an anthropological characteristic. As Hans Blumenberg has put it, rhetoric corresponds to the "immanent deficiency" of humans that they do not fit into pre-given structures of the world. Thus, "rhetoric means to be conscious both of being compelled to act and of the lack of norms in a finite situation."[10] The discursive turn in philosophy and the human sciences thus brings to the fore both the rhetorical effect of discourses themselves in the social formation as a whole and also the rhetorical formation of social actors. Anthropological incompleteness stirs rhetorical accomplishments.

The contemporary focus on language thus turns away from inner-outer, or consciousness-reality, dichotomies to the process "in-between" where instituting praxis is understood as the expression of a way of life that forms itself. Its most basic theoretical shift is thus to drop the assumption that the medium of communication could be a neutral channel for the passage between inner and outer, or consciousness and reality. Language, and thus communication more generally, is seen as an active process of the formation of expression.[11] Representation itself becomes questionable when the assumption that a social fact can be represented without being thereby altered is dropped. Terms such as "articulation" or "expression" seem to capture this active process more completely. Indeed, what becomes interesting is precisely the plurality of forms which the active process of expression can take. Philosophy and the human sciences after the discursive turn center precisely on the forming influence of language, and media of communication generally, in giving shape to the form of life that may later be distinguished into the extremes of consciousness and reality (which are constituted by the specific form of modern life). They are concerned with expressive culture, or "language as practical consciousness," as Marx and Engels said in *The German Ideology,* continuing to explain that "consciousness is, therefore, from the beginning a social product." Nietzsche also made this point in *The Gay Science,* where it is argued that "consciousness has developed only under the pressure of the need for communication."[12] The origin of the contemporary discursive turn is thus in the nineteenth century break with the philosophy of consciousness that was achieved by Marx and Nietzsche and confused with the end of philosophy as such.

The discursive turn in philosophy and the human sciences is a turn towards meaning as the central problem that requires understanding, explication and, perhaps, explanation. There were earlier forms of meaning-oriented inquiry, however, notably phenomenology. The current focus adds the notion that the investigation of meaning is best pursued through a focus on language, since language can be taken as the model for meaningful activity in general. Language has become the central phenomenon in both analytic and continental philosophical schools in the twentieth century, but the turn toward language taken by itself often does not arrive at the key phenomenon that can be called "discourse." If language remains understood as primarily representational, as a more or less adequate description of an extra-linguistic activity, and if one still regards language in a common sense way as opposed to other forms of social praxis, then the turn toward discourse has not yet been made. The status of language in discourse requires that language is not understood merely in the sense of speaking activity but rather that such speaking activity, insofar as it forms and conveys meaning, be taken as *exemplary* for all social action. Once language is regarded as exemplary, it achieves a status as the leading metaphor for all human action and thought. Other types of social action that don't obviously involve speaking, such as wearing clothing or jumping out of airplanes, can also be investigated as meaningful activities in which the characteristics of spoken language can be used to identify analogous characteristics. Moreover, this metaphorical extension of language to social action in general suggests that the primary function of language is not to describe social action scientifically but rather to constitute social action as meaningful. In other words, it should be understood as primarily constitutive rather than representational. If the understanding of language always includes these two co-present functions, then we may say that the *mode of expression* that animates a social action is modeled on discourse in its constitutive function. At this point, it is the constitutive character of expression that has become exemplary, or metaphorical, for philosophy and the human sciences and the main consequence is that the mode of expression, or medium of communication, can no longer be seen as a mere outer clothing of a pre-existing content. Rather, the medium of communication is understood to be a formation of meaning. Interest thus turns toward the particular characteristics of various formations of meaning, which can be called discursive formations. A discursive formation, which Foucault called a "regularity in dispersion,"[13] is concerned, not mainly with the characteristics of language in general, but rather with the constitutive character for social life of a specific form of expression. It consists of an indefinite plurality of related expressions, made from a number of subject-positions, that constitute an arrangement of social life and, thereby, an understanding of "what is," or reality in general.

Discourse as a metaphor for philosophy and the human sciences involves two main aspects. First, an expression is understood, not as a description of an extra-linguistic event, but as an action in its own right. Classic examples of language functioning in this way include, "I now call this meeting to order," and "I now pronounce you husband and wife." These language uses do not describe an event outside of language, but perform the event through an utterance, or expression. This active conception of language has been called text (Ricoeur), speech-act (Austin), and theme (Volosinov). While it may seem at first as if such speech acts refer only to a distinct class of utterances, further reflection suggests that performativity is rather a component of any discursive act.[14] The upshot of this shift has been described as a critique of "foundationalism," which is a critical term referring to the pre-discursive assumption that language acquires its meaning by describing an extra-linguistic reality upon which its truth and significance would be founded.

The second main aspect of the concept of discourse is that every utterance occurs within an organized but not closed system of related terms from which it takes its meaning. This system has been called a structure (Leví-Strauss), a system of differences (Saussure), a language game (Wittgenstein), and so forth. In the present introductory context the specific formulations of this system of meaning are not important. The point is that meaning is not produced by a single term in isolation but by the placing of the utterance within the context of an (at least partially organized) system of meaningful components. The turn to discourse thus replaces the question of the relation between words and things, which has been the main philosophical formulation of the problem of language since Plato and is probably unanswerable as such, with the construction of meaning through given acts within a system of difference-relationships. This shift has been described as a critique of "essentialism." Essentialism is a critical term referring to the pre-discursive notion that an expression has an internal meaning that could be determined without reference to the actual discursive formation in which it occurs. Human "subjects" are thus re-defined as subject-*positions*, as places within the field from which characteristic utterances originate. The field defines possible speakers through these subject-positions, as well as expressions, and the current critique of the "essentialist subject" is a rejection of the notion that the subject exists prior to expression and "enters into" language as a formed unity. Rather, it is suggested, the discursive formation itself encompasses expressions, speakers, and a field of discourse. Clearly, the determination of the limits and, therefore, definition of a given discursive formation is a key question for a specific discourse analysis. Based on these two aspects, discourse may be preliminarily defined as an act within a field of discriminations. Its primary model is an expression in language, but this is generalized into a whole approach to philosophy and the human sciences.

Several consequences of the discursive turn become immediately apparent. First, since discourse is seen as itself constituting the objects to which it refers, it implies abandoning a correspondence between expressions and reality as the criterion of truth, or correctness, of propositions. Second, the constitution of social action through discourse surpasses the fact-value distinction. Performances of social actions involve both factual and evaluative components, such that one can "derive" an obligation to perform certain acts in the future from promising to do so in the present, for example.[15] I propose to call this phenomenon the question of an "institutional ethic," in the sense that social institutions are constituted by speech acts which require further actions whose performance is neither a matter of individual proclivity nor universal human ethics but institutional obligation. If I am a teacher, for example, meeting my classes and discussing with my students is something required by my activity within the institution. It is not a matter of my individual characteristics nor of an obligation to which all humans would be subject. To the contrary, my individual integrity, for example, is given meaning and measured by my institutional position. Even further, evaluating my students' work on the basis of their intelligence and ability to express themselves, based on the evidence of essays or exams, is not a personal choice but an obligation. If other matters enter into the evaluation process—such as the race, gender, sexual orientation, disposition, etc. of the student—this is wrong not only because racism, sexism, etc. are wrong in general, but because these characteristics are irrelevant to the discursive formation of education. They are external considerations in the sense that they are based on extra-educational factors. An institutional ethic is immanent in the discursive practices of an institution. (This does not imply, however, that institutional ethics are a suffecent basis for the ethical component of social philosophy.) Third, the turn toward discourse implies that a social form is constituted by a plurality of discourses. If there were only one discourse, it would not be visible as a discourse but would seem to be the one and only reality. Any given discourse occurs within a field of discourses. While defining the boundaries of a given discourse is often quite difficult, and is normally pragmatically constituted by the aim of an inquiry, it is nonetheless clear that a discursive formation cannot extend to the entirety of a society. Whereas previous social forms could reconcile the plurality of discourses by establishing, or assuming, a super-discourse (meta-narrative) that could reconcile all the others into a hierarchical unity (thus making it appear as a non-discursive reality), for a discursive conception of society it is the interaction of discourses that constitutes the social totality. To this extent, a discursive turn in the human sciences and philosophy presupposes a loosening of the "discourse of the whole" that constitutes many societies and which is the basis for the sociological concept of "tradition." The fourth consequence of the discursive turn is that the plurality of discursive forms constitutes a world, or a culture, that is disclosed in historical epochs. Each epoch is an instituting of a certain relation between discursive forms. This has been described as a "form of life" (Wittgenstein) "in its characteristic style" (Husserl) such that "as individuals express their life, so they are" (Marx).

These consequences of the discursive turn are addressed in the various chapters of this book. At this point I want to mention certain critiques of the discursive turn in order to prepare the way for a conception of discourse that can avoid certain perceived problems. The critiques all center on the relation of discourse to the materiality of social life, and I address them not by abandoning discourse and retreating behind it to a presupposed and uncritical conception of reality, but by centering analysis on the materiality of discursive forms themselves: on what I call the primal scenes instituted by media of communication.

Criticisms of the discursive turn in philosophy and the human sciences are usually based on two distinct, although often related, concerns. One pertains to the epistemological issue of the relationship between discourse and the extra-discursive or, to put it as a question: Is social action reduced to language? Criticisms of this sort operate with a distinction between discursive and extra- or non-discursive in order to articulate their criticism. But that distinction is precisely what is rejected when language in use is taken as metaphorical. Thus, debates between these critics and their interlocutors give the reader a distinct sense that they are talking completely past each other, and that the real issue of the debate is simply assumed by both sides in a manner that precludes any real confrontation of ideas.

This sense also pervades the second criticism which concerns the political issue of the relations between deconstructive and reconstructive linguistic strategies in new social movements and the re-allocations of power, resources, and social organization which they propose. Again, the presupposition is generally that such resources are conceptually distinct from language, which implies that language is taken in the straightforward sense of spoken (or written) words as opposed to non-linguistic things like punches in the face or social labor. A further issue raised by Marxist critics is whether the plurality of the new social movements is an expression of the more deep-seated social conflict based in social class. Certainly, a discursive approach, insofar as it takes the specific object of a given discursive formation as itself constitutive, tends to set aside such criticisms as "foundationalist," as presupposing a "reality" behind its discursive manifestations.

The interesting thing about these criticisms and the subsequent debates is the extent to which they always seem to be about exactly the same issue—the discursive/extra-discursive problem—and the extent to which there is really no encounter between the two positions because the basic epistemological and theoretical divide is such as to preclude significant encounter. That the criticisms are theoretically naive from the viewpoint of discourse theory, I take as virtually self-evident. I do not propose to rehearse or enter these debates here, or to defend discourse theory from its critics. My present concern is quite different. Let me just state that the thrust of the criticisms points to a crucial issue, even though it is articulated in a language that does not appreciate what is has been accomplished by the discursive turn. When language is taken as metaphorical for philosophy and the human sciences outright, it must certainly be legitimate at some point to ask whether there is not something left out in this move. To ask that the something that is left out be formulated in terms accepted within discourse analysis is too much, especially in public debates with those who have not accepted discourse analysis as adequate to the whole of philosophy and the human sciences.

Ernesto Laclau and Chantal Mouffe respond to Norman Geras's criticisms of their discourse theory, for example, by restating their use of Wittgenstein's conception of a language game.[16] Wittgenstein considers the case of a builder's assistant who, when asked to, brings materials, brings things called blocks, pillars, slabs, and beams. He comments that the words one uses to provoke these actions can be called "a complete primitive language," thus suggesting that the blocks themselves, however, are not a part of the language even though any actual building will involve language.[17] Laclau and Mouffe suggest, following this line of thought, that putting bricks on the wall is extra-linguistic and bringing bricks at the command of another is linguistic. The totality of both acts, both of which are clearly necessary for the wall to be built, they call "discourse," which they understand to be prior to the linguistic/extra-linguistic distinction.[18] This distinction, then, refers to language in the ordinary sense in which language can be opposed to something other than speech, whereas discourse refers to meaningful activity (based on the metaphor of meaning drawn from language) that is prior to the issue of whether speaking occurs or not. In other words, building the wall, even if new blocks are not brought by an assistant who is commanded by words (but rather performed in silence by a single worker), is still a discursive action. This response clearly deals with the criticism made by Geras through outlining a conception of language as constitutive of social action rather than merely a representation of it. What it does not do, however, is allow a place for questioning the limits of the metaphor of discourse, i.e., the question whether something is lost in characterizing the activity of building a wall as discourse. Is the heaviness of the blocks, for example, adequately captured by the term discourse, or even the word "heavy"? Should it be? In the formulation of the discursive conception of meaningful activity, the question of whether a reduction of social life is so implied is often occluded. But this is a genuine issue, one which can only be held up to investigation if the metaphorical aspect of the discursive turn is emphasized. This metaphorical dimension occurs in any social theory and pertains to its capacity for universalization. It cannot be avoided (whatever one's model of theory) by a direct appeal to "reality."

These two major sources of criticism of the discursive turn—epistemological and political—can be addressed from within the discursive turn in philosophy and the human sciences if one develops the concept of language further in a direction that centers on the materiality of expressive forms themselves. The standpoint adopted in this book is to accept the discursive turn, at least in its general outline, as a productive root-metaphor for a contemporary philosophy of the human sciences but to look for an expression of the limits of the metaphor from within the formulations available after the discursive turn. I argue that a theory of the materiality of expressive forms can press the discursive turn toward a new philosophy of the human sciences. Its starting point is the primal institution [*Urstiftung*] of social reality and action by media of communication.

In order to emphasize the specificity of this approach through communication media, let me begin by sketching the alternative, and more widespread, content-oriented approach of "discourse theory" and indicating some of its limitations. From this perspective, to investigate a discourse is to focus on the interaction between arguments, the subject-positions from which these arguments can be produced, and the (dis)enablements of the linguistic resources of the discourse, in order to pin down the effects and silences produced by the discourse as a whole. The boundary of a discursive formation can be determined through the *meaning* which the discourse constitutes and the field of objects that it describes. For example, the current discourse of the "free market" consists of arguments pro and con an unregulated market society. From the "free market" position, the con arguments are labeled a priori as in league with some authoritarian (because "unfree") source, the activities of unrestricted buying and selling become emblematic for social practices as a whole, and the meaning of terms like "freedom," "regulation," "government intervention," and so forth, are key in constructing the limits of possible arguments concerning economic relations and social organization. The problem is not that one is automatically constrained to be in favor of free trade. The problem is, rather, that if one wishes to argue against it the terms in which one must do so are formed by the dominant terms, such as the "freeness" of "free trade." The discourse is such that alternative terms are inflected negatively, and thus have an automatic deficit to overcome. In other words, the *discourse* of free trade is such as to prefer the argumentative *position* in favor of free trade. One can argue in favor of a "certain amount" of government regulation of free trade, but a certain reluctance, a suggestion that this should not go "too far," necessarily accompanies the argument. Moreover, there is a deeper implication in that all other possible forms of economic and social organization are silently subsumed under the notion of "government regulation," resulting in a crippling of the public discourse concerning alternative forms of social organization. Opponents of free trade would thus be advised to shift the *discourse* itself and not remain within the discourse of free trade in arguing for the non–free trade position. If the discourse shifts to one of "responsibility" or "social justice" the non–free trade *position* is re-articulated as a pro-social justice *position* which has a much more positive relation to the *discourse* of social justice.

Such discursive formations are historical, thoroughly grounded in competing interests, and capable of important shifts in relation to strategic interventions. Nevertheless, they have sufficient stability to be studied as an articulation of the prevailing form of social relations. The relevant discourse can be circumscribed in relation to the question posed by the investigator and may be either very widely or quite narrowly conceived. For example, one might study the discourse concerning childcare in a local setting, the discourse concerning drugs in an urban or international setting, or the discourse concerning free market capitalism in either a contemporary setting or across three centuries and the entire globe. I mean to imply by the examples that I have chosen that such studies of discursive formations, whatever their relevant extent, can play an important role in political life, especially insofar as they are oriented toward the expansion of the horizon of political alternatives through the critique of the assumptions of dominant terms and the systemic silences within discourses. Uncovering the enabling possibilities of the discourses of alternative social movements is also a key aspect of this task. Thus, it is certainly not my intention to suggest that such discourse studies are irrelevant to the theoretical and political tasks of critical theory. When it comes to medium-range politics, they are often an important contribution to the widening of political vision. I do, however, want to suggest that such an approach has limitations when it comes to theorizing the field of discourse itself. While the content-oriented discursive approach is focused on intervention within prevailing common sense assumptions and thus orients itself to meaning, another approach is necessary to orient thought and action toward the horizons of those assumptions, toward the circumscription of the form of life as a whole.

Let me illustrate by returning to the example of the discourse concerning free trade. In studying this discourse, it would be necessary to collect relevant arguments, especially groundbreaking indexical interventions, from whatever domain in which they are articulated and circulated. It would not be particularly relevant for example, whether a key speech by a U. S. president was made on television or in a written document. Such differences would be considered as, at most, secondary variables dependent on the force and effects of the intervention in the discourse as a whole. To formulate the point more generally, the "materiality" of the medium of communication is, from the viewpoint of discourse studies in this sense, secondary to the content, or meaning, constructed in the discourse. The centrality of sense, or meaning-content, is the basis for the choice of object of study by the investigator, the circumscription of the relevant discourse, and the determination of its effects. This focus on meaning-content is precisely what confers the relevance of such studies to immediate or medium-range politics. However, two consequences follow from this focus which indicate the limitations of discourse analysis understood in this way. First, the materiality of the medium of communication is not regarded as important and gives rise to the poorly formulated but relevant issue of the relation of discourse to materiality. Second, there arises an intractable problem of the relation of the discourse to the totality of the social formation in which it occurs. What is the relation between the discourse of free trade and the economic practices of capitalist society, for example? It can hardly be denied that there is such a relation, and that it is an important one, but that relation cannot be formulated within the focus on meaning-content characteristic of discourse theory.

In more general terms we may say that rhetorical criticism comes upon its inherent limitation in its inability to determine the relation of rhetorical interventions either to "material reality" or to the social formation as a whole. I will argue throughout this book that a focus on the "materiality" of media of communication can address these issues without abandoning the advances made by the discursive turn in philosophy and the human sciences. This introduction has been concerned with establishing the linkage between the discursive turn and the concept of a medium of communication as a primal scene that institutes a world.

The basic philosophical formulation is of the role of the body as the root-phenomenon of expressive forms, a particular complex of expressive forms as the construction of a world, and the historical succession of such worlds as manifestations of Being.

A theory of communication must obviously provide analyses of communication processes in various settings, but it also needs to account for the conditions of its own enunciation. Since it is both a theory of enunciation and an enunciation, this self-referential constitution is unavoidable. Such a necessary reflexive self-reference renders a comprehensive theory of communication constitutively paradoxical. The three parts of this book attempt to fulfil this requirement. The first part outlines an approach to communication that I call comparative media theory. The second part establishes the point of origin of this theory in contemporary consumer society and outlines a communication theory of consumer society. The third part examines the social movements that destabilize the attempt at a closed circuit of communication in consumerism and thus outlines the point of emergence of reflexivity. This reflexivity is the condition for the emergence of a contemporary theory of communication and establishes the solidarity of a theory of communication with social criticism.

PART I

THE MATERIALITY
OF EXPRESSIVE FORMS

CHAPTER 2

Medium of Communication

The theory of media of communication can make a crucial contribution to the philosophy of language upon which the discursive turn in philosophy and the human sciences rests by virtue of its focus on the "materiality" of communication media rather than on the manifest content of language. In this chapter I will develop the idea of a medium of communication beginning from the work of Harold Innis in order to address the contemporary philosophy of the human sciences that can be generalized from his contribution.

In European thought, the critique of modernity in the twentieth century was developed primarily by the Frankfurt School and the phenomenology of Edmund Husserl and Martin Heidegger. They converge on the question of technology and the instrumentalizing of reason in modernity. This critique of a universalizing and mathematizing reason has been popularized and extended in the recent debates concerning postmodernism into a defence of local, particular, embodied articulations.[1] Such an emphasis is also characteristic of Harold Innis's communication theory of civilization and the critique of the civilizing project of "the West" from which it emerged.[2] The fundamental thesis underlying the media theory of Harold Innis is "that civilization has been dominated at different stages by various media of communication such as clay, papyrus, parchment, and paper produced first from rags and then

19

from wood. Each medium has its significance for the type of monopoly of knowledge which will be built and which will destroy the conditions suited to creative thought and be displaced by a new medium with its peculiar type of monopoly of knowledge."[3] His written work on communication tends to use the concepts (space, time, bias, medium, and so forth) through which his media theory is articulated in large-scale historical analyses rather than directly explaining or defining what they mean. Thus, there is plenty of room for interpretation. But while my interpretation of Innis may be controversial, in this book its main significance is as a way of introducing the materiality of expression into the discursive formation of contemporary philosophy and human science.

In *Empire and Communication* Innis introduces his focus on the materiality of media of communication through centrifugal and centripetal social forces—forces tending to make a society more integrated over a given area versus forces which tend to allow more independent peripheral areas. The concepts of time and space are used to describe the constitutive power of media of communication in constructing and maintaining society. Initially, it is clear that media that emphasize time are durable, such as clay and, especially, stone. Media that emphasize space, on the other hand, are light and easy to move over large areas, in particular papyrus and paper. He thus connects the latter media with administration and trade because of their space-orientation and the former with permanence and time. These characteristics are connected to aspects of institutions. "Materials that emphasize time favour decentralization and hierarchical types of institutions while those that emphasize space favor centralization and systems of government less hierarchical in character."[4] The centralization-decentralization axis refers to the manner and extent of coordination in space. To say that an organization is decentralized is to say that there is not much (or only very loose or difficult) coordination over a given area, implying that there are more dispersed centers of power. Innis's claim is that when there are more dispersed centers of power the tendency is for each of these centers of power to be more hierarchical. The axis of hierarchy, then, refers to the administrative chain of command. To say that an administrative organization is more hierarchical is to say that it is more or less continuous from bottom to top—that there are no equivalent but dispersed powers.

Time-oriented media promote means of social organization which are decentralized, involving more dispersed centers of power, but in each of these centers of power the administrative hierarchy is more direct from top to the bottom. By contrast, media that emphasize space favor centralization and less hierarchy. Centralization means coordination over a large area. Less hierarchy implies that in some of those administrative ladders, the relations of command overlap each other. There are equivalent ladders of power in different places, one of which does not necessarily subsume the rest. It is through these terms that Innis investigates what is for him the key subject matter of communication theory—the persistence of a society in the two dimensions of space and time, or *the constitution of a historico-geographical unity of a form of life*. Every society persists in both space and time, of course, but with different degrees of effectiveness dependent on the complex of media through which it is articulated. He introduces the term "empire" to describe a society that is persistent with a substantial degree of efficiency in both dimensions. That is, an empire covers a large area and it lasts a long time. Since every medium of communication has a tendency, or "bias," toward either space or time, an empire involves a co-existence of different media of communication. A society that manages to balance the influence of space-oriented media and time-oriented media will be successful in both space and time.

The dimensions of space and time might be interpreted in two different ways. One way is as a Kantian formal structure which is more or less filled out by media of communication in concrete cases. In this case, the space-time categorial schema would be pre-existent to media and there would be a distinction between the "real" (noumenal) space-time nexus and the (phenomenal) extent to which it is experienced within a given society. This interpretation poses several intractable problems since, while the distinction between the "real" (i.e., scientifically conceptualized) and the perceptual is necessary in this interpretation, they cannot *in principle* be related to each other. Thus, the space-time nexus would be split into a scientific version and one pertaining to social perception, which would lead back to the earlier dilemmas concerning the relation of discourse to an external "real" material world.

The alternative interpretation, which I believe to be truest to Innis's historical discussions, might be called phenomenological and Marxist. Space and time as they are experienced (in the widest sense) within any society are understood to be *constituted* through media of communication, and media of communication are formed and developed by human praxis. Space exists only insofar as it is traversed in some manner, and time exists only through the means of transmission between generations. Communication media thus constitute, through human labor, the limits of what is experienceable, and the *manner* in which it is experienced, in a social formation. We can thus say that, for Innis, communication media "set up," open, or constitute the limits of what is experienceable, and the manner in which it is experienced, in a social formation. In short, media of communication institute a social order, a regime. In this version there is no distinction between "real," or scientific, space-time and the social experience of space-time. Rather, one would have to interpret the scientific scheme as a specific cultural formation whose historico-spatial emergence in the Renaissance period of European society has its own conditions of existence in the complex of communication media emergent in modernity.

Let us explore in more detail the notion of medium utilized here. It is evident from Innis's historical discussions that he views pyramids and architecture in general as means of communication in addition to language and writing. A "medium of communication" is understood in a very wide sense as any kind of a formative and integrating social mechanism. Media of communication, understood in this way, are described as having intrinsic characteristics. Most straightforwardly, if one writes on stone it tends to last; if one writes on paper it can be easily transported. These characteristics are not given to the medium by its environment, though they are certainly used in a specific way in a given environment. At first blush, it may appear as if the characteristics of media are primarily, or even exclusively, directly physical. But the distinction between heavy and light media as media oriented toward time or space, even though it is used by Innis, is drastically oversimplified.[5]

A more thorough analysis of the structure and argument of *Empire and Communications* can clarify the relation between a medium and its object, or content. After the introductory chapter, the second chapter is on Egypt and the third on Babylonia. In both of these the main object that is at issue is water. But it is not the content "water" that is key in deciding the time or space bias in a medium of communication. In Egypt, there was a necessity to predict the annual flooding of the Nile. This concern with time led to calendars and exact methods of reckoning time. In Babylon, the problem was irrigation. There was lots of water but it wasn't in the right place. Irrigation solved this problem of space. Thus, the same content, water, in the case of Egypt led toward an emphasis on time, whereas in Babylon it led toward an emphasis on space. While water was the content at issue in both cases, the "medium" is different. Thus, it is not the object carried but the manner of carrying; it is not the flooding, but the construction of a manner of overcoming the problem of flooding. The characteristics of a medium of communication cannot be defined through the material characteristics of the object with which it is concerned but only the manner of dealing with that object. Thus, the intrinsic characteristics of a medium may include its durability or portability, but it is not confined to these. It is more fundamentally about the *manner of organization* that is constructed. It is not only a material resource and a technology (oriented to dealing with a particular object), but also a social relation constructed co-extensively with this technology. A medium of communication thus incorporates both a technology and a series of related social identities (or subject-positions).

We should notice that in Innis's historical discussions the social influence of a medium of communication is always analyzed in relation to the whole environment in which it operates. It is not an isolated thing but the central factor within a complex environment made up of many media of communication and the objects they carry or reckon with as contents. Its bias has to do with its influence on the whole of this environment. Thus, the *intrinsic characteristics* of the medium, which is a certain organization of perception, institutions and thought, lead in a *given environment* to effects of re-organization of that environment. It is this interplay between a medium's characteristics and the media environment that is the main domain of investigation for media theory. However, the conceptual relation between these two aspects of the influence of a medium of communication is not addressed by Innis and does not emerge clearly from his historical discussions.

Other writers concerned with the social influence of media of communication fall into two main camps with regards to this issue. The emphasis on the media environment is taken to its logical conclusion by Marshall McLuhan. He claims that there are no intrinsic characteristics to a medium of communication whatsoever, that the characteristics that it has in a given situation depend on its relation to the whole media environment and the given state of translations between media. Thus, the "content" of a medium is nothing intrinsic but only a previous medium on which it builds. If we follow the chain of contents back to its origin the implication is that the content of orality is thought and the content of thought is the world. This is a thoroughly rhetorical concept of the social influence of media insofar as the influence in question originates entirely from outside the medium in question and there is no intrinsic content of the medium *as such* at all.[6] The opposite view is taken by Don Ihde in his phenomenological investigations of the intrinsic characteristics of each medium considered as an alteration, or "inclination," of human perception.[7] This view might be characterized as "essentialist" insofar as each medium is investigated as such in isolation from its context, but it is not determinist insofar as the inclination can be resisted even though a certain degree of consciousness is required to do so.

Rather than accept either one of these two polarized interpretations, I suggest that further development of Innis's work in this respect needs to address what might be called the inside-outside relation of a specific medium to the complex media environment. It is in this inside-outside tension that the relation of particular local embodiments to the cultural horizon as a whole would have to be determined.

Innis introduced the notion of a "bias" of communication to refer to the specific social inclination inherent in the dominant expressive forms. Every medium of communication has a bias toward either space or time. By "bias" is meant the emphasizing of a certain aspect of experience, the time-oriented aspect or the space-oriented aspect, intrinsic to the medium of communication or through its relation to the media environment as a whole. Bias in Innis's sense is not a bad or distorting use of a medium. It is unavoidable. From this notion of bias follows the idea of "monopolies of knowledge." Innis's communication theory places a key stress on institutions as the constitution of an organization of human society. Institutions are based on a medium of communication that, within that institution, is the most significant and then monopolizes knowledge through monopolizing access to and use of that medium of communication. While Innis discusses the bias towards space or time, he also refers to a "concern," or a concern with the "problem," of space and time. This is best understood as a figure-ground shift. When a society has been reasonably successful in extending itself in space through utilizing media with a bias towards space, this success then comes to be taken for granted and the explicit concern, or thematization, of the social energy becomes directed toward time. Time becomes the problem which must be addressed on the basis of a presupposed success with space, or vice versa. The notion of bias is utilized also to articulate a relationship between the presupposed taken-for-granted organization of a society and the specific thematic projects that the society pursues.

Since every medium of communication is biased towards either space or time, it is not possible for a single medium to be complete. If the society was only oriented to space, for example, it would be unstable with respect to time. If a society was only oriented to time, it would have great difficulty in occupying a single area successfully. Innis introduces the notion of "balance" to suggest that a society is most successful when it is based not upon one predominant medium of communication but upon several, and especially, on a combination of several media which orient towards competing biases of space and time. This notion of balance is Innis's reformulation of the idea of disinterestedness in traditional humanism. Though it is no longer suggested that one can "rise above" the conflicts of social life and judge them from an "unbiased" perspective, it is argued that a balance of biases can allow a viewpoint which, in a sense, neutralizes the conflicting bias of each given medium. This theory of media of communication is, then, oriented to a twofold task. First of all, it attempts to present an historical theory of civilization which would incorporate and surpass previous theories by showing historical changes as emerging from shifting relations between competing media of communication. Second, Innis's media theory is oriented especially towards the present, towards answering the diagnostic question concerning the present state of civilization. This eventually also implies the reflexive question, Why does a communication theory of civilization arise now? What is it about our own society that motivates us to inquire into communication in a way that has not been done before? Innis suggests that our society has been extremely efficient in media oriented towards space. We have more and more organization over a larger and larger area, developing what is essentially a world system. What we do not do well is organize things in the dimension of time. While we have a very efficient and well-integrated world system, it is extremely sensitive to periodic shocks and dislocations. The critique is that it does not have stability over time despite a remarkable stability over space. In this respect, the emphasis on space is taken to be characteristic of industrialization, mechanization and modernity. In this critical vein, Innis stresses "the importance of the oral tradition in an age when the overpowering influence of mechanized communication makes it difficult even to recognize such a tradition. Indeed the role of the oral tradition can be studied only through an appraisal of the mechanized tradition for which the material is all too abundant."[8] The emphasis on time, by way of compensation, is a metonymic and synechdochic critique of industrial civilization. Innis claims that orality was a stabilizing influence in civilization in the past, though this has not been adequately enough understood.[9] In the present we need to recover and extend orality in order to develop greater stability in time and this is the healing intention of Innis's theory—to restore balance where balance has been disturbed. The diagnostic and therapeutic intention originating in the contemporary crisis of civilization ensures that media theory contains a reflexive, or recursively doubling, dimension that is characteristic of the project of self-knowledge of the human sciences.

Reflexive appraisal on one's own situation raises profound difficulties. In *Empire and Communications*, Innis states that the "significance of a basic medium to its civilization is difficult to appraise, since the means of appraisal are influenced by the media and indeed the fact of appraisal appears to be peculiar to certain types of media."[10] In other words, if our society is constituted through the biases inherent in media of communication, our social arrangements and therefore our manners of thinking are also constituted by these biases. How can we get a standpoint from which we can appraise or evaluate these biases? Aren't we so firmly inside the society as to be incapable of really seeing it? This was a continuing concern of Innis that is characteristic of the orientation of his communication theory.

> We must all be aware of the extraordinary, perhaps insuperable, difficulty of assessing the quality of a culture of which we are a part or of assessing the quality of a culture of which we are not a part. In using other cultures as mirrors in which we may see our own culture we are affected by the astigma of our own eyesight and the defects of the mirror, with the result that we are apt to see nothing in other cultures but the virtues of our own.[11]

It is in the context of this reflexive issue that Innis introduces the concept of empire in *Empire and Communications*. "I have attempted to meet these problems (the problems of reflexive assessment) by using the concept of empire as an indication of the efficiency of communication. It will reflect to an important extent the efficiency of particular media of communication and its possibilities in creating conditions favorable to creative thought."[12] Thus the concept of empire refers to the efficiency of the plurality of media of communication existing in a certain society to extend in both space and time. Efficient extension in both space and time constitutes an empire. And such efficiency has to do with the capacity for reflexive evaluation.

Innis suggests that writing has a centralizing effect that tends to promote bureaucratic organization due to its one-sided orientation to space.[13] It tends to promote analytic, abstract thought, and to isolate the writer and the reader from each other. Scientific thought, for example, whose cumulation of results depends on writing, continually liquidates its past to present an analytic, synchronic, theoretical summary of the current state of knowledge. Innis attempts to rescue and justify oral tradition in the context of a society which has been one-sidedly oriented toward the written. Two major aspects of orality are relevant to its contemporary critical function: the role of memory and the central importance of the concrete situation in the here and now.

Sound is essentially immediate and evanescent. Its immediacy connects it to action. Speech as action, though Innis does not seem to have recognized it, has been fundamental to the rhetorical tradition. To speak to someone is to act and to provoke an immediate reaction in a way that writing does not. Oral society is based upon the notion of speech as action, rather than language as description, and has evolved many strategies for overcoming the tendency of spoken words to be forgotten. Stories, rituals, and so forth are built upon formulas and mnemonics. Poetry has a key function in which the rhythmic meter makes things easier to remember and to put in place. Moreover, there is a high level of redundancy and of formulaic assemblage of pre-organized parts. The structure of speech in an oral society thereby tends to be additive rather than analytic. In analytic thought one subordinates the higher category to the lower, an example to the general theory, whereas within orality one tends to simply add on without any clear pattern of subordination or hierarchy. This key role of memory is extremely important in primary orality and exerts a formative influence on the whole of societies in which orality is the only, or major, medium of communication. Oral society is homeostatic due to the continuous incorporation of the past into the present.[14] There is no way for that which has really been forgotten to survive. Consequently, oral society orients much of its energy toward not forgetting, towards continuously re-enacting the past in the present.

Equally important to oral society, because speech is action, is the here and now situation in which an utterance takes place. Originality or creativity does not reside so much in making up new stories but in the quality of this enactment, or performance. The oral mind is oriented towards narrative accounts, stories rather than lists. Consequently, there is no neutrality but a standpoint with both a descriptive and an evaluative dimension. Orality is participatory and inclusive, not distant. It acts over small spaces and unites people in face-to-face encounters. Being situational rather than abstract, oral tradition is agonistic, or rhetorical, rather than epistemological—which is based on a separation of the knower from the known and proposes to warrant valid cases of their later coincidence.

Innis documents the unacknowledged importance of the oral tradition in maintaining Western civilization and he wishes, by acknowledging that importance, to promote greater orality in the present in order to increase time-consciousness and thereby to heal the one-sided emphasis of space-oriented bureaucratic society. The therapeutic goal of his communication theory is therefore oriented toward a greater "balance" between the competing biases of writing and orality. "Lack of interest in problems of duration in Western civilization suggests that the bias of paper and printing has persisted in a concern with space."[15] For Innis, the traditional humanist perspective outside competing interests is not possible since the biases inherent in media of communication extend throughout the material and intellectual formation of society. Nevetheless, the attempt at reflexive evaluation is not simply abandoned for interested polemic. Rather, it is to be sought in a balance between the differing biases of a plurality of media of communication. In this spirit Innis remarks that the power of Plato's dialogues is that they involve an encounter between two media of communication. They were written when oral society encountered a new literacy, and that it is the doublesidedness rooted in this moment of civilizational transformation that gives persistent relevance to Plato's philosophy.[16]

At this point, two criticisms of Innis's media theory can be made that will situate it as an attempt to continue the humanist tradition through its twilight. The first is with respect to the notion of empire as an index of the efficiency of communication. If we ask the question of what successful communication is, it is doubtful whether "extension" in either space or time, or both, can serve as an adequate measure. The term is introduced by Innis to describe a society which is persistent with a substantial degree of efficiency in the dimensions of both space and time. That is, an empire covers a large area and it lasts a long time. The apparent simplicity of the term "efficiency" expresses an apparent value-neutrality that is not tenable within Innis's own theory of bias and, consequently, Innis's communication theory itself incorporates an unacknowledged bias toward empire as the presupposed telos of communication. It is pervaded by resentment, in Nietzsche's sense, in that it retains an unacknowledged and unavoidable debt to the object of its critique. In this sense, Innis's dependency theory of communication is unable to imagine any possibility of independence for the ex-colony. For this reason, Innis's critique of colonialism remains a *dependent critique of dependency* in the sense that it does not contain the conceptual tools to imagine the possibility of independence. It remains tied to the imperial assumptions of European humanism. Innis's reliance on the concept of empire as a key term in his communication theory, and his attempt to avoid its normative implications, indicates his attempt to continue the ethical component of humanist tradition through its twilight. Insofar as extension in space or time is characteristic of a medium of communication, the most successful society is implied to be one that extends effectively in both space and time.[17] In order to pass beyond this assumption we need to ask whether there is any sense in which media theory might justify a restriction on the extent of communication and a defence of locality. Innis's theory suggests that the most successful communication, in both a descriptive and prescriptive sense, results in empire. Moreover, the most extensive reflexive evaluations can also be expected to emerge from such an imperial situation of balance. The concept of balance through which Innis's therapeutic intention is expressed thus seems replete with conservative political implications, and these cannot be removed from Innis's theory entirely even though recent ecological critiques of industrial capitalist society suggest that its instability over time is indeed important.[18]

The conservative implications of the term "balance" can, however, be overcome if we connect this critique of Innis's unacknowledged bias for empire to his notion of monopolies of knowledge. The relation between developed institutional knowledges and repressed or incipient ones is a main concern in this context. Innis spent great energy to argue that the unacknowledged influence of the oral tradition was essential to whatever remaining stability Western civilization contains. The idea of monopolies of knowledge necessarily involves conflict between knowledges, but not normally between equally constituted forms, since the resources commanded by powerful institutions allow their knowledges to be more developed and extensive. Rather, conflict is usually between instituted and emergent knowledges. The relation between undeveloped and incipient forms of knowledge and the developed and articulated knowledges of powerful institutions can be understood as a figure-ground relationship. In other words, the oppression of subaltern knowledges means that they are not articulated to a comparable degree as dominant monopolies. In addition to, in fact as a consequence of, the lesser social power they command, the knowledge they wield is less developed. While one need not agree with Gayatri Spivak that the subaltern cannot speak at all, it is nonetheless the case that voicing and articulation are radically problematic for emergent knowledges.[19] This is precisely why they are interesting in contrast to priorly constituted monopolies of knowledge: they problematize and investigate their own conditions of emergence, rather than hiding these conditions behind an ideology of universal applicability. To this extent, the theory of monopolies of knowledge can come to the aid of a critical social theory oriented to the emergent knowledges proposed by new social movements, and can aid in the critique of Innis's own central concept of balance.

My second criticism of Innis's theory has to do with the notion of oral tradition. I will argue that there are two incompatible accounts of oral tradition in Innis. In the first place, orality is understood as time-orientation and presented as a balance to the space-orientation of writing. This implies that orality, like any medium of communication, is a selection and coordination of human senses and an institutionalization of this selection founding a monopoly of knowledge. Therefore, in this version, orality is just as partial as any other medium of communication, such as writing, video, photography, sign language, architecture and so forth. Orality in this first sense is a medium of communication alongside of others. Its centrality derives from its capacity to balance the dominant space-orientation of contemporary society such that, in this specific situation, it may play a healing role. But there is another account of the conception of orality in Innis. Orality is also viewed as a fundamental synthesis, a basis coordinating all human senses, and incorporating both time and space in a unique manner. "In oral intercourse the eye, ear, and brain, the senses and the faculties acted together in busy co-operation and rivalry each eliciting, stimulating, and supplementing the other."[20] Orality understood in this manner is an integration of human capacities into a functioning whole from which all other media abstract partial selections and developments of human capacities. In this formulation, orality is not merely alongside other media of communication. It is the fundamental basis of all human communication from which other media derive and to which they are secondary.

This contradiction between two modes of understanding orality is embedded in Innis's theory and, more particularly, in the reflexive intention of his media theory of civilization—the intention of giving a historical account of the development of civilization based on media of communication and the intention of investigating and healing the problems of the present. This relationship between the history of civilization and its present crisis gives rise to the two manners of understanding orality that are densely intertwined in Innis's texts. We should resist any tendency to simply solve the contradiction between these two accounts of orality. This central contradiction motivates and animates his entire work, for it is itself symptomatic of the historical juncture that Harold Innis's communication theory seeks to address. The twentieth century may be described as the twilight of humanist civilization in which its normative commitments have become increasingly incredible while at the same time they are not replaced by any succeeding project of civilization. This is a situation of "decadence" in Niezsche's sense or a "crisis of legitimation" in Weber's derivative terms. In such a situation we are motivated to recover the fundamental notion of humanism—the unity of the human body as the origin of media of communication and human capacities and creativity—exactly in the moment when the present tendency of media is to shatter this unity, to fragment human capacities, and to fracture the conception of the self. The unity of the human body becomes very problematic and motivates a historical reflection on the origins of the conflicts of our own time that recovers the unity of the human body that is present in orality. By means of this conception of orality, one can criticize the contemporary development of media of communication. In this sense, the conception of orality is deeply reflexive since the motive for its recovery is rooted in the situation of its loss.

Nevertheless, it also may be the case that our present situation and the present fragmenting tendencies of media of communication show that this fundamental humanist notion of bodily integrity is simply no longer viable. It may have been simply a bias constructed by previous media of communication, not a *fundamentum* for media *sui generis*. The moment of recovery, due to its origin in the moment of endangerment, cannot erase the doubt inherent in its origin to embrace a humanist metaphysics of bodily integrity. While it recovers this conception, it is obliged to reconstruct it in the present, and thereby cannot simply rely on it as established. This reflexive situation, which leads to a contradiction between orality as the *fundamentum* to all media and orality as a balance to other media, is rooted in the contemporary situation for radical reflexion in which humanism is fading but is necessary to see what is emerging: a situation of twilight, not of definitive end or beginning. The key contemporary issue resides in the relation between technology and the human body as the root-phenomenon of expression.

The contemporary situation of the twilight of humanism has a further consequence for understanding the concepts of space and time as they are utilized by Innis. Innis criticizes the quantitative notion of time but not that of space. He contrasts time to mechanization and industrialization, thereby allowing the concept of space to stand, through the assumption of quantified space, for industrialism *per se*. Innis pointed out in "A Plea for Time," for example, that there are two ways of misunderstanding history.[21] We may misunderstand history as antiquarianism, as that which is simply finished, or on the other hand as that which remains and continues, implying that we understand those of the past as if they were just like us in the present. In both cases, we misunderstand history, which is change in continuity and continuity in change. Innis has done a great deal to resurrect the notion of history from this dilemma of reduction backward to the past or forward toward the present. We may term this, to utilize a Husserlian terminology, a critique of the mathematical substruction of experienced time.

However, there is no comparable critique of the mathematical substruction of lived space. As time can be misunderstood as a linear pro-gression which poses the apparent choice between discontinuity and continuity, so space can be misunderstood as simple location in a mathematical grid in which the opposition of here to there eradicates continuity in difference, or traversal. While in his concrete descriptions Innis uses the notion of space always as traversed space—that is, space that has been unified and differentiated through media of communication—he simultaneously conceptualizes space as already necessarily quantified. It is only on the basis of this quantified conception of space that the contrast between space and time can stand as emblematic of the problems of mechanization and industrialization as a whole. Thus, the contradiction in the conception of oral tradition enters the conception of space as well. If, however, one rejects Innis's substitution of an already quantified conception of space for the concrete experience and organization of traversal, an important connection to works in contemporary social theory which emphasize the concept of space as a critique of the historical emphasis of modernity can be made. It has been suggested that the emphasis on time and history is a consequence of the Eurocentric origins of social theory and that in order to theorize unequal development and imperialism one needs to uncover the spatial dimensions of dependency.[22] In an opposite emphasis to that of Innis, these works counter time with space. Both strategies reveal important aspects of the current social formation. Whereas Innis points to the increasing space-domination brought about by capitalism and technology, the space theorists point to the inequality inherent in such space-orientation such that *where one is* in the system is important—an emphasis which connects to the origins of Innis's theory in a political economy of dependency.

Instead of counterposing time to space, or vice versa, I suggest that the underlying issue may instead be the contrast between a mathematical, quantitative conception of space (or time) and the *social constitution of traversal* that allows the movements of goods and signs in some directions at the expense of their movements in others. Edmund Husserl, in his critique of modernity, argued that the possibility of technologically conquering space and time through social organization are a result of substituting an intellectual framework of mathematical concepts for the lived experience of space and time.[23] Science may well be aided by such a procedure, but we ought not to confuse what is precisely the result of a procedure with our ordinary experience of the world. For this reason, Husserl argues that contemporary criticism must return to the living body underneath mathematical substructions, whether they be substructions of space or time. His analysis thus suggests that the fundamental contradiction from which the crisis of humanism emerges is between mathematical scientific substruction, on the one hand, and the living body, on the other. The critique that is required, in this case, focuses on the relation between mathematical-formal substructions and lived experience in both spatial and temporal dimensions rather than the counterposing of time to space. From this perspective, Innis's descriptions capture the inscription of experience through the spatial and temporal components of media quite well, but there is a failure at the level of conceptualization that grounds the therapeutic and critical side of his theory.

The abstraction of various capacities from the unity of the living body has allowed them to be developed in a way which would not have been possible if their integration in orality had never been sundered. This development of separated capacities in the present time is allowing for a new coordination of the senses in the culture external to the individual body. Marshall McLuhan called this phenomenon the "global village." The socio-cultural coordination of abstracted and developed capacities is replacing the original coordination of capacities in the human body. We may define planetary culture as this emergent coordination of developed media of communication outside the human body. It is a systematic connection that originated from abstraction from the lived body, but now completes and reverses itself to construct a new synthetic body. Whereas the body used to be the ground for all the figures of the abstracted human capacities, now the synthesis of abstracted and developed capacities is creating a new media environment, a new planetary culture, which is the ground upon which the human body appears as a figure. This situation is not just another change within the continuum of history, but a change that brings this development between the human body and the abstraction of its capacities to some sort of conclusion or closure.

It is this situation that can be called the twilight of humanism. It implies a re-evaluation of the evaluative concept of civilization deployed by Innis in order to criticize the collapse of European civilization during the First World War. The first part of this re-evaluation was already undertaken by Innis through his concept of space.[24] Innis points us to the crisis situation of the present, but in a manner that differs from the Eurocentric version that is common to both Husserl and McLuhan. Despite the critique of Innis's conceptualization presented above, his counterposing of space and time, industrialization and orality, gives a marginal, post-colonial twist to the critique of modernity. For Innis, it is not just a story of abstraction-fracturing and synthetic recombination. The story must also include the fact that the abstraction-fracturing begins from a specific location which thereby gains power over other locations (becomes a center). Consequently, the planetary recombination, while it is a "whole," is a centered whole that skews all phenomena in the global context toward a Eurocentric bias. In this he is one with the social theorists of space and unequal development. It is to the post-colonial recuperation and extension of the critique of modernity that Innis makes his most profound contribution. The tension in Innis's work is exemplary of a pervasive tension in our historical-geographical configuration and cannot be simply resolved. In the present context, the tension between orality as fundamental and orality as alongside other media condenses the issue of whether the imperial domination of space can be surpassed or only limited. By linking orality with time-orientation, Innis developed a critique of the mathematical substruction of time and has been turned away from a similar critique of the mathematical substruction of space. In order to understand the contemporary tension between the unity of the living human body and the development of the capacities abstracted from this unity we require a critique of space as well as time. The therapeutic intention of communication theory cannot be properly fulfilled through the notion of balance. It is better served by a metaphor of excavation, of digging down to the fundamental unity from which communicative capacities have been abstracted, and at the same time a doubt that this excavation is uncovering a fundamental unity—a suspicion that perhaps this unity only appears as such through a historical bias that is in the process of disappearing, that the primal instituting [Urstiftung] only appears as such when its reign has begun to end [Endstiftung].

CHAPTER 3

Comparative Media Theory

The later work of Harold Innis incorporates a critique of modernity as space-dominating, or globalizing, and time-vulnerable, or temporally unstable, articulated through its focus on the biases inherent in the specific characteristics of media of communication. This approach can be generalized into a theory of media of communication as the primal instituting of social relations which I call a "comparative media theory" of society. From the standpoint of the relation between philosophy and the human sciences, the constitution of perception, institutions, and thought by media of communication is *the thesis proper to communication studies*, the thesis from which its larger significance derives. The study of communication is turned towards, in Innis's words, "Why do we attend to the things to which we attend?" understood not only in a psychological, but also in an institutional, historical, and intellectual, sense.[1] In my version, however, it is as important to ask, What might we be attending to? and even, Where are the limits of our attention? Through such questions, which in phenomenology are the topic of imaginative variations that lead to the definition of an essence of a phenomenon, comparative media theory becomes at once more philosophical and more political than in Innis's version.

The main characteristic of this approach is to view a form of life as an expressive complex of media forms which constitute social identities within a given configuration of culture. While Harold Innis is a major figure in this literature, there were several others who introduced a concern with the formative influence of media of communication into their disciplines. Developments in anthropology, especially, were important to reconsidering the influence of writing on the West's conception of itself and its relation to other societies. Consider, for example, the contribution of Jack Goody and Ian Watt to social anthropology, based on the key observation that oral and written modes of transmission affect differently the cultural heritage passed on. They argued that the "relative continuity of the categories of understanding from one generation to another is primarily ensured by language, which is the most direct and comprehensive expression of the social experience of the group" and, in particular, that "the intrinsic nature of oral communication has a considerable effect upon both the content and the transmission of the cultural repertoire."[2] Also, Claude Leví-Strauss has suggested that the existence of writing is the real difference between Western and so-called "primitive" societies—a difference that is constitutive of anthropology.[3] Similarly, scholars of classical Greek society, especially Eric Havelock and Francis Cornford, re-evaluated Greek philosophy through the influence of writing on its development and conceptuality.[4] In addition, Marshall McLuhan and contemporary media critics influenced by him have studied media from the viewpoint on the medium itself, rather than its content.[5] Whether it be in the context of a diagnosis of contemporary society, a re-thinking of its origins in ancient Greece, or a re-evaluation of modern views of non-Western, previously so-called primitive societies, the focus on media of communication marshalls a critical tendency through a focus on the materiality of forms of expression.

The notion that language and communication can be studied from the angle of its materiality has gained increasing recognition recently from other influences besides Innis.[6] Clearly, the meaning of the term "materiality" is key for any such interpretation. As I have argued in the previous chapter, Innis's focus on the medium of communication only apparently refers directly to physical characteristics such as heaviness or lightness. It refers primarily to the characteristics of expressive forms that determine a "bias" that emphasizes a certain perceptual and cognitive direction of a communication and makes another direction difficult, or even impossible, in that medium. If we compare Innis's conception of a bias in a medium of communication to Edmund Husserl's distinction between the living and the dead body, *Leib* versus *Körper*, my argument is that Innis's notion of medium refers to the expressive capacity of the living body rather than the dead materiality of straightforwardly physical characteristics. In Husserl's words, "these systems of 'exhibiting of' are related back to correlative multiplicities of kinaesthetic processes having the peculiar character of the 'I do,' 'I move' (to which even the 'I hold still' must be added)."[7] Media of communication may be understood as extended bodily kinaestheses whose materiality consists of animated modes of expression. This interpretation differs significantly from the main tendency to introduce materiality into communication through a focus on the "world of objects, products, goods."[8] The key difference here is exactly that referred to by Marx when he distinguished the reference of his materialism to "human sensuous activity, practice" from the "materialist doctrine that men are products of circumstances and upbringing, and that, therefore, changed men are products of other circumstances and changed upbringing" proposed by Feuerbach.[9] Language and communication can thus be taken in an active, practical, and constructive sense rather than a descriptive, or referential, sense referring to already-constituted objects.

The theory of media of communication that can be generalized from Innis's work gives the discursive turn in the human sciences another twist. The turn toward language is expanded into the notion of media of communication as a theory of expressive forms of life, and then analyzed from the viewpoint of the materiality of forms of expression. I give the name "comparative media theory" to this form of investigation derived from Innis and generalized into an approach to society as a complex of expressive forms and will follow it out in the succeeding chapters of this book. Let us look at the name for a moment. First, why "comparative"? Because the forming influence of a medium of communication on our perceptual, institutional and cognitive capacities is invisible as long as one "lives inside" it. Only by looking at it "from outside," as we say, can its influence be defined. But, if it is indeed true that our abilities to see, perceive, and think are formed by media of communication, then this "outside" cannot be outside media of communication as such, but only outside the medium which is at present being analyzed. Thus, every study of the forming influence of a medium of communication is always at least implicitly comparative, and often bringing this comparative dimension explicitly into concern sharpens the issues. Second, what does "media" mean? Though related to technology, a medium is not simply a technology, but the social relations within which a technology develops and which are re-arranged around it. A medium is thus a mode of social organization, defined not by its output or production, but by the relations obtaining within it. These two terms, medium and technology, while conceptually distinct are thus concretely closely bound together, and comparative media theory has the effect of emphasizing the role of technology not only in production, but in its perceptual, institutional, and cognitive consequences. Third, why "theory"? Primarily to emphasize that a descriptive focus on media is not sufficient. To the extent that the thesis holds up, the standpoint of the theorist is also formed by media. Thus, there is needed an explicit account of the reflexive dimensions opened up by this theory, of how the standpoint of analysis interacts with the phenomenon described. Comparative media theory is concerned with various dimensions of continuous translations in the media environment which, at any stage of relative fixity, define a culture through what it assumes as common sense and what it explicitly poses as problems to be addressed. Society is understood as a complex of expressive forms constituted by the materiality of media of communication in which is compacted a relationship of technology and social identities.

The study of media of communication in this form is in an undecided, perhaps undecidable, state with regards to its significance for the human sciences. In one respect, it appears as a specialized area of investigation which, although it has its own internal issues and perhaps even classics, is distinguished more widely primarily by the fact that it is a latecomer to the academic division of labor compared to sociology, anthropology, political science, or psychology. In another respect, it is often proposed as a synthetic approach to the human sciences outright, an interdisciplinary inquiry capable of linking the researches of specialized human sciences to the philosophical foundations of the project of human scientific inquiry itself. This characteristic oscillation is indicated in the predominant rhetoric by which a study is proposed first as concerned with a "neglected aspect" of a social formation or, more often, social change and second as the secret, or "organizing factor," behind it. The formative perceptual, institutional, and cognitive influence of media of communication are, by an increasing body of literature, first said to have been overlooked and then insinuated to be the key factor in the constitution of a social formation. *The thesis proper to communication studies* is the constitution of perception, institutions, and thought by media of communication. Innis asked, "Why do we attend to the things to which we attend?" in psychological, institutional, historical, and intellectual, senses.[10] Comparative media theory thus investigates the formation, limits, and alternatives of the direction of attention. It is at this point that Innis's communication theory converges with phenomenology as an analysis of modes of intentionality.

Let us consider two examples of this characteristic rhetoric of oscillation. Harold Innis wrote in the introduction to *Empire and Communications* that "the subject of communication offers possibilities in that
it occupies a crucial position in the organization and administration of
government and in turn of empires and Western civilization." Two pages
later he claimed that "We can conveniently divide the history of the West
into the writing and the printing periods" and four pages after that concluded the introduction by summarizing his general task as "to suggest
the roles of different media of communication with reference to civilizations and to contrast the civilizations."[11] In this argument communication begins as a "subject," albeit one with a "crucial position" among,
we may assume, a very large other number of subjects. The general intellectual value of this subject could only be determined by comparing it
with the contributions made by study of the other subjects. The argument very soon becomes a "convenient" manner of historical periodization for the "West" and, while it is not suggested that this is the only
periodization that may be relevant, it is insinuated that something crucial to the "West" is to be discovered thereby. Finally, when he suggests
that the "different roles" of media provide a standpoint from which to
"contrast civilizations," the expansion of significance is complete. Communication has become the most macroscopic study imaginable and the
presumption that it must be evaluated in relation to other intellectual
projects pales behind its claim to order all intellectual and practical projects as belonging to the civilizations that it studies. This rhetoric is made
possible by the focus on a previously ignored or undervalued subject-
matter in a manner that does not confine it to a specialized study but
syncretically expands to influence and, perhaps, integrate all specialized
studies into the most general, or even universal, evaluations.

It might be objected that Innis was eccentric in this regard, but it
seems to me that it is not only characteristic, but even constitutive, of
studies that focus on the role of "media of communication" in social formations and their transformation. This can be seen in as cautious a classical scholar as Eric Havelock in the foreword to his influential *Preface
to Plato*. While acknowledging that the transition from Homer to Plato
can be described in other terms, such as the contrast of shame and guilt
cultures, he nevertheless claims that "it remains true that the crux of the
matter lies in the transition from the oral to the written" and that related
changes are "generated by changes in the technology of preserved communication."[12] The oscillation begins by setting a new contribution
alongside many others and concludes by asserting that it is the founda-
tional, or generating, factor that can explain all the rest. However, when

forced to defend the latter universal claim, a counter-movement is often initiated through the defensive argument that this specific factor has not been well enough covered by existing studies.

Such an oscillation between particular and universal claims is an interesting feature of arguments for the constitutive role of media of communication in social formations and their transitions. It is rooted in the postmodern location of comparative media theory's reformulation of the relationship between philosophy and the human sciences.[13] Innis, for one, was aware of this constitutive paradox and he addressed it through his concept of "bias" by which societies are said to be oriented to space or time through their media of communication. "The significance of a basic medium to its civilization is difficult to appraise since the means of appraisal are influenced by the media, and indeed the fact of appraisal appears to be peculiar to certain types of media."[14] Thus, the rhetoric of oscillation is a characteristic of the reflexive explanatory power of the focus on media of communication. This suggests that the theoretical standpoint which selects media of communication as a, or the, focus for inquiry can, or should, be accounted for with the tools of the inquiry itself. The rhetoric of oscillation is thus rooted in the postmodern turning whereby the epochal form of awareness (opening, primal institution, *Urstiftung*), which is articulated through the primal scenes of media of communication, becomes "visible" as we turn at the end of one primal institution [*Endstiftung*], or epoch, toward another. Even deeper, it expresses the inevitability of expressing the forms of awareness, primal scenes, in terms drawn from the later history of expression based on the primal scene.

This constitutive paradox of communication stems from the fact that every "communication" as the meaning of an expression, or sense-content, is a metaphorical formation of the very possibility of "communication" as shaping a form of connection by a medium, or institution. This paradox produced by the reflexive, self-accounting role of a theory of communication media undercuts the conventional account of truth as a correspondence between knower and the known, as well as the concept of communication as the transmission of a content. The primal scene of a medium of communication sets into play, opens, a place where the knower and known co-exist and therefore can either correspond (truth) or not (falsity). In this sense, both truth and falsity co-exist within the opening of the primal scene. Similarly, the concept of communication as the transmission of a content requires the prior existence of the two places which can therefore be brought into connection by a transmission between them. Transmission thus relies on the prior institution of a space within which transmission can occur. The rhetoric of oscillation is thus produced by the constitutive paradox of communication that derives from its necessity to approach the primal institution through the later history of expression. This necessity is a consequence of the obligation of a communication theory to account reflexively for itself since it is both a theory of enunciation and an enunciation.

To state it somewhat differently, the representative and constitutive aspects of communication are interwoven in the same communicative act. In phenomenological terminology, every communication act is simultaneously a "mundane" act within the given world-horizon and a "transcendental" act of constitution of that horizon. This suggests that the medium of communication is actually the transcendental aspect of a communication act, always presented through a specific content, but never in it. A contemporary rhetoric thus has less to do with persuasion in the sense of yielding assent to a given content, than with a deeper persuasion, inherent in every expression, to assent to the form of awareness that is manifested through the content. It is a rhetoric of discursive forms. It is within the constitutive paradox of this loop that the postmodern connection between the human sciences and philosophy is to be found, which requires a thorough rethinking of the relation between rhetoric and philosophy—a relation whose terms had been largely settled since the Greek division of theoretical territory.

It is in this postmodern context of a newly unsettled relation between rhetoric and philosophy that the sphere of rhetoric can be expanded to deal with media forms, rather than just their contents. McLuhan's famous phrase, "the medium is the message," condenses this thought rather nicely, though I would really prefer it to be "the message is the medium," which also emphasizes that the rhetoric of media forms is only itself expressable as, or through, a content. The metaphorical, and even allusive, level at which discourse about the institution of historical forms of discourse is articulated remains tied to the contents of human expression—though in a reflexive manner. The thesis proper to communication in this expanded sense is that media of communication constitute human experience in its perceptual, institutional and cognitive aspects, which are elaborated in the dimensions of space and time, such that a specific cultural form is given to the lifeworld of a social group. Culture, in this usage, is not understood as distinct from society, economics, politics, and so forth, but in a more anthropological sense as the "specific pervasive style" (Husserl) that pervades these areas and unifies them into a "whole way of life" (Wittgenstein). Any communication, besides taking place within the horizon of this cultural form, contributes to the definition of the cultural form through its medium. If the thesis proper to rhetoric in its historical form concerns the persuasive power of language, comparative media theory is a "media rhetorics" insofar as it pertains to the institution of a cultural form—not the persuasion to see the world in this way or that, but the image-ing of the world as such— the opening of a space within which mundane communication, trans- mission, can occur.

In this context, the concept of a medium of communication is cen- tral, not only to what is conventionally understood as media studies— or even "communication" more widely—but to the wide-ranging refor- mulations presently underway in philosophy and politics. I would like to develop this key concept in comparative media theory in another way here, independently of Innis, through a certain convergence between the media theory of Marshall McLuhan, the phenomenological account of the relation between consciousness and world, and the systems theory of Gregory Bateson. Such a convergence on the space where comparative media theory can be elaborated also suggests certain revisions of each of these contributions. Thus, the mutual elaboration and critique of these approaches is to be understood in relation to the phenomenon that they clarify, not from a presupposed internal semantic integrity—obviously the intellectual lineages and conceptual elaborations differ significantly and provide the motivation for further work.

We may provisionally define a medium of communication as the "materiality," or outside, of meaning-content that is necessary for mean- ing to be expressed. All communication is about something and in that sense is an imparting of meaning. A medium of communication is the sup- port, or carrier, of this meaning—not the meaning itself. Thus, orality is a medium of communication that connects the vocal chords, sound waves, and the ear. Writing, by way of contrast, requires pen and paper and emphasizes the eye. A medium has specific characteristics distinct from its content. For example, the impermanence of expression in oral communi- cation motivates the use of mnemonic formulae, poetic and rhythmic forms to enable the perdurance of meaning. Also, writing separates author and reader in time and space in comparison to the reciprocal character of orality. A medium of communication has implications for perception, social relations, institutions, and thought. Comparative media theory is based on the formation of human experience by media of communication, focuses on comparisons between different media, and is concerned to elaborate its implications through its extension into social theory and phi- losophy. The most general way of referring to these reformulations is as a new understanding of the relation between whole and part.

According to Marshall McLuhan, the content of a medium of communication is another, previous, medium of communication. For example, the content of television is the play, the public announcement or town crier, and the hawker of goods or the snake-oil salesman. Thus, there is a certain regression set up when we inquire into the content of a medium of communication. The content of film is the novel; the content of writing is speech; the content of speech is thought. What, then, is the content of thought? One must say that the content of thought is, simply, the world—though the way we understand the "world" is a central issue at this point.

Modern philosophy has understood the world in two main ways: In the empiricist tradition, the world is understood as an aggregate of distinct objects of experience; in the rationalist tradition, the world is understood as actively constructed by thought in its experience of these objects. The division between these two traditions is characteristic of modern philosophy, due to its origin in the universalization of mathematical natural science. Thus, as Edmund Husserl has shown, modern philosophy must be understood, not as one or the other of these traditions, but as the discourse instituted by the mathematization of nature which makes both of these interpretations possible.[15] In this manner, the phenomenological critique of modern philosophy uncovers the experienced world presupposed by both the rationalist and empiricist "substructions" and argues that its systematic description must be the task of a new philosophy and human science.

In a similar vein, for McLuhan the world is understood as the cultural environment as a whole. The specific prevailing configuration of this cultural environment is defined by a continuous translation between a plurality of media. In short, when one investigates the content of a medium of communication, one initiates a regressive procedure which devolves back onto the relationship between culture and medium. Any question of content ultimately resolves itself back in to what is, for McLuhan, the fundamental question—the relationship between media and culture. This formulation does not fall into either of the two main epistemological traditions of modern philosophy. In fact, it reformulates the presupposition which both traditions have in common and which is therefore characteristic of the institution of modern philosophy itself from the universalization of the mathematical science of nature. Empiricism interprets conscious experience of the world as a pure openness to already existent objects, whereas rationalism interprets experience as an active appropriation. Modern philosophy thus situates "experience" as a meeting of objective and subjective elements in which either can be polemically emphasized as against the other. McLuhan's media theory aims at a more fundamental level below this polemic and is directed at the formation of experience itself. Therefore, we may see a relationship between medium and cultural environment in McLuhan's media theory that bears comparison to the phenomenological account of consciousness and world.

In the phenomenological approach, "world" is not understood in opposition to consciousness, but, rather, as the "surrounding world" (*Umwelt*), or environment, toward which consciousness is directed. The relationship of consciousness and world is, in phenomenological terminology, a relation of "intentionality"—that is, a relationship of direction of attention. This does not imply "deliberate orientation" as ordinary usage might suggest, but refers only to the characteristic of "directedness." Every experience is an experience *of the world*. It is this "of" that is most interesting to phenomenologists and which brings them close to communication theorists who are also concerned with the "connection between" subjectivity and objectivity. Intentionality is thus not a relationship between two separate types of things such as "subject" and "object"—whose connection must always remain mysterious—but is located *between* two essentially related phenomena. But it is not the two terms of consciousness and world that are most important here, rather the middle term that establishes their connection. The relation between consciousness and world occurs through intentionality and, for this reason, it is the explication of intentionality itself that is most characteristic of the phenomenological approach and is the basis for anything that may be said about the other two terms.

Within the intellectual development of phenomenology, the issue of socio-historical determinacy generally has been addressed through the turn away from Husserl's transcendental phenomenology toward existential and hermeneutic phenomenology. While this has led to specific analyses of considerable value, the problem of socio-historical (and cultural) specificity cannot be solved in this way by a rejection of the transcendental reduction that was for Husserl the key discovery of phenomenology. It would lead to an abandonment of the unprecedented reflexive dimenions opened up by Husserl and lead to a "mundanizing" of the transcendental subject that would leave it open to the charge that it postulates a "meaning-giving subject." Laclau and Mouffe share the common misconception about Husserl that he traced cultural practice back to a "meaning-giving subject."[16] Such constitution of meaning, in Husserl, can be addressed only transcendentally; the concrete, or mundane, ego does not confer meaning in this manner. It is clear that, for

Husserl, concrete egos encounter a world already permeated by cultural meaning, which is what discourse theory clarifies when it defines a concrete subject as constituted by the relational meaning of a discourse rather than from a pre-existing subject standing behind or above the concrete, empirical subject. Thus, while the dynamics of the discursive, cultural, constitution of the mundane ego can be clarified through a fusion of phenomenology and discourse theory, the rejection of the transcendental dimension that normally accompanies this fusion is not warranted. Similarly, in order to investigate the specific dynamics of the changing socio-historical formation of the experienced world, phenomenology may be supplemented by the media-culture relation described by Marshall McLuhan which, like discourse theory, is oriented to the relational constitution of the concrete subject.

There is also an important comparison to the work of Gregory Bateson at this point of cultural description beyond the subject-object dualism. His systems approach to communication puts the individual in the context of the relationships in which the individual is enmeshed. Indeed, one could say that, from a systems theory standpoint, an "individual" *is* precisely no more and no less than the complex of social relationships into which it enters. This applies not only to a biological individual, but to any "self," or identity, whatever the level of abstraction at which it is considered. For example, against traditional evolutionary theory Bateson insists that the unit of evolution is not the species alone, but the species along with its environment.[17] By thoroughly enmeshing the individual within its social relationships, this systems approach poses the question of how it is possible for the individual to know itself. Bateson diagnosed many dilemmas of contemporary culture by pointing out the disfunctional effects of human action when the acting human individual or group thinks of itself as independent of its context. Such action tends to destroy the environment it needs to survive. Thus, for example, industrialism tends to destroy the balance of nature on which it depends. The Versailles peace treaty that ended the First World War destroyed the common understanding of peaceful discourse as discontinuous from moves within the war game, thereby undermining the possibility of its own success.[18] This behavior by the individual is self-destructive of the necessary systemic, or environmental, context for individual survival and, in that sense, is pathological. Insofar as such self-destructive behavior is avoidable, the actor *within a system* must get a perspective *on the system* of which it is a part.

This reflexive relation is the core of Bateson's approach to communication. Enlightened action, or "systemic wisdom" in Bateson's terminology, requires that the actor within the system benefit from an under-standing which in some manner transcends the perspective internal to the system. This understanding requires a distinction between the "self" that is within a system and a "self" which observes the system. It is char-acteristic of human communication, indeed, of communication between mammals and perhaps of non-mammals also, that there are always at least two levels of communication simultaneously in operation. At one level of communication the actor acts within the system and, at a "higher" level of communication, observes the whole system of which the actor is a part. The reflexive relation between action and observation is key for a systemic view of communication which focuses on identity-formation within its relevant context, although in practice it is often much more difficult to achieve the viewpoint of an observer of the sys-tem of which one is a part than may be implied by this simple distinc-tion. Nevertheless, for Bateson, shifting to the level of observation, the next "higher" level, allows a perspective on action in relation to its envi-ronment such that action can take into account the entire system of which it is part, rather than simply acting within the restraints of the given system. Thus, while the acting and observing "selves" are distin-guished, they are nevertheless related as well.

This is exactly the paradoxical relationship between the "concrete" ego and the "transcendental" ego that is described in phenomenology. Husserl refers to the "difference and identity" of the concrete and tran-scendental egos. This terminology unfortunately obscures the difference between the transcendental, systemic viewpoint and the mundane, con-crete, intra-systemic viewpoint, though he does say that the transcen-dental ego "is actually called 'I' only by equivocation."[19] It would be clearer to follow Merleau-Ponty here and regard the transcendental as a "dimension" of experience, a "transcendental field," otherwise it tends to seem to be "another" subjectivity, but one isolated and protected from the world (as Sartre supposed). As Ludwig Landgrebe has remarked, the transcendental reduction that is key to phenomenological philosophy is "nothing other than a meditation upon reflection as a recursive relationship."[20] For this reason, the rigorous reflection on reflexivity characteristic of phenomenology is fundamental to the philo-sophical justification of an approach to communication that centers on systemic wisdom and is concerned that this wisdom address the prag-matics of social change.

Bateson de-emphasizes consciousness in the following sense: From a systems viewpoint, that part of a system which is conscious is only a part of the system as a whole. The attempt to control any system involves an increase in the conscious part. Thus, the attempt at controlling a system creates a multiplication of its complexity. The attempt at control promotes a consequent and greater increase in the system which is being monitored. Thus, the attempt at control, paradoxically, by virtue of the system in which the attempt at control occurs, creates a more complex system that cannot be monitored. Bateson's analysis of war, of the arms race, and of the ecological crisis all rest on this idea. Thus, for Bateson, we must set aside the urge for control. We must learn humility, that is, the fact that we are always part of a system and never able to control that system in its totality. As actors, we are always part of the system. We must also learn spontaneity. Spontaneity is immediate connection with the other parts of the system without that connection being brought to consciousness, therefore, without it being subjected to attempts at control. These two lessons, humility and spontaneity, are lessons for actors—that is, for those within the system.[21] In phenomenological terminology, they are applicable to the socio-historical determinacy of the mundane, or worldly, ego. But they are dependent on the main thrust of systems theory, which is the move to observation at a higher systemic level, a reflexive move toward the transcendental, non-worldly or non-imbedded, field of experience uncovered by Husserl.

These three contributions—McLuhan's media theory, the phenomenological intentionality of consciousness toward the world, and Bateson's reflexive theory of communication—all help to clarify the theoretical space of comparative media theory. McLuhan understands culture as the interaction of media of communication whose content is always another medium of communication. It is these modes of interaction that constitute cultural change. Phenomenology treats the conscious moment of human culture as a relation to the world, not as a supposedly enclosed "subjectivity." Systems theory diagnoses the source of pathologies in the consciousness-world relationship and suggests that a more encompassing perspective is both possible and necessary. From these clues, we can begin to discern the outlines of a comparative media theory that can address the contemporary transformations of modern philosophy and politics. Such a perspective centers on the relationship between the determinate context of an identity in relation to its environment and the reflexive relation whereby this determinate context can be surveyed.

Certain parts of this outline clearly reinforce each other. First, the rigorous phenomenological account of reflexivity and its philosophical consequences through the transcendental reduction can buttress Bateson's rather allusive notion of systemic wisdom. Both of these combine to suggest the key role of reflexivity in communication media—a theme almost entirely absent from McLuhan. Second, the emphasis on "environment" by both McLuhan and Bateson serves to expand the significance of communication theory from a delimited domain within the human sciences toward the philosophical dimensions of a social theory that reaches beyond the subject-object dualism. This emphasis dovetails nicely with the phenomenological critique of the dualism of modern philosophy and its reformulation of the task of philosophical reflection. Third, McLuhan's notion of the "translation" of one medium by another understands human experience as continuously transformed by the process of communication. It is reinforced by Bateson's conception of consciousness (both human and otherwise) as a *part* of a larger *whole* that it ignores to its own detriment. We may see both of these in terms of a phenomenological relation between theme and horizon, which converges with the Gestalt foreground-background relation, in which an element of the cultural environment stands forth as the conscious part that illuminates the background whole.

The convergence of Husserl's notion of theme-horizon and part-whole with the Gestalt conception was accomplished by Aron Gurwitsch and is extremely important for the subsequent development of phenomenology. It involves a critique of Husserl on the intra-thematic organization of wholes and parts which puts to rest a certain residual empiricism in Husserl's work. This development significantly influenced Merleau-Ponty, due to his attendance at Gurwitsch's lectures in Paris. It is the basis for Merleau-Ponty's "most radical attempt to break with the essentialism inherent in every form of dualism" mentioned by Laclau and Mouffe.[22] McLuhan makes particularly wide use of the figure/ground relationship throughout his work.

These mutual reinforcements suggest that comparative media theory must be centrally concerned with the components of *reflexivity, environment* and *translation* in the construction of cultural identities. Moreover, they indicate that the relation between determinate context and reflexive awareness central to current philosophical and political transformations can be formulated through the notion of a "medium of communication" and the translations between a plurality of media that define a cultural environment. The importance of communication studies to the human sciences and to social change is centered on this concept.

In following out the idea of a medium of communication and the media environment, we have thus seen a connection between McLuhan's media theory, phenomenology, and systems theory. This relationship poses many more detailed questions and conceptual clarifications that must be followed up in further work. For the present purpose, it is possible simply to draw one central conclusion. A key question for communication theory has been posed in contemporary discussions as the relationship between discursive formations and non-discursive "reality." But this posing of the question makes the question unanswerable. It is a non-productive posing which is ideological in the sense that it obscures other posings that illuminate better the fundamental question of the relation between communication media and the world. The problem of the effectivity of discursive practices, including a critical circumscription of this range of activity of effectivity, should not be posed in relationship to a "reality" that has been somehow stripped of all of its discursive, that is to say, cultural, aspects. This posing of the question is a legacy of a simplified Cartesianism which separates the material world from the "mental" or cultural world. This separation is the product of the *construction* of a notion of the "purely" material world through the mathematical substruction of nature. The distinction between material and cultural worlds is thus not a fundamental distinction but a historical artifact.

From this we may conclude that the question of the effectivity of discursive practices is not productively posed in terms of an opposition between discursive and non-discursive. Rather, it should be posed as a question of the relationship between a particular discursive practice and the wider cultural world. Once the question is posed in this way, we can see that all three of the traditions of thinking about communication discussed above understand a "medium" (McLuhan), or "intentionality" (phenomenology), or "information" (Bateson), as thoroughly cultural, or "discursive," and as effective in constituting the world—not as confined to social representations only. Communicative actions are particular representations which crystalize and consequently affect the whole of the cultural environment. The effectivity of discursive practices is understood more productively in terms of such a part-whole relationship rather than a dualism.

Certain mutual corrections thus emerge from the convergence described here. The phenomenological posing of the relationship between consciousness and world is often stated as if consciousness is understood to be completely "unmediated," in the sense of having no prior cultural structuring, no prior cultural formation. The previous discussion indicates that this is an incorrect understanding, for consciousness is at any moment the product of a previous cultural formation.

Nevertheless, it would be incorrect to reject the notion of immediacy on these grounds. Even though consciousness is formed by a previous cultural formation, it is experienced as a contact with the world. Through intentionality, consciousness is "immediate" in the sense that it has the sense of "reality" due to its encounter with a unique configuration of social representations and constitutions of the world. Conscious experience of the world is immediate while being simultaneously formed by a prior cultural formation, a cultural environment. Consciousness in its present immediacy will effect the translation of this prior cultural environment to a future cultural environment. Similar to the rejection of the dualism between discursive and extra-discursive reality above, we may also reject a dualism between mediation and immediacy. The part-whole relation implies that every conscious experience, every cultural formation, is both thoroughly mediated (in the sense of prior cultural formation) and immediate (in the sense of a unique present configuration) experience of the world.

The phenomenological account of consciousness can thus become central to comparative media theory if intentionality is interpreted as a part-whole relationship within culture. Concrete consciousness is not in ultimate opposition to the world but is, rather, that part of the environment that is taken at a given moment to represent the environment as a whole. Consciousness is, therefore, a constitutive part of the world which takes on a reflexive or representative function in a certain specific case and, thereby, is directed towards the whole. Intentionality, as we have described it here, is the part that, by representing the whole, sets up an intentional relation between the two. Consciousness is, in this sense, a mediation of a prior cultural environment with a subsequent cultural environment. It is the moment of consciousness, or representation, of the prior environment which will come to define and exercise an influence on the future environment. For this reason it is fundamental to an account of cultural change.

The part-whole relation that is explicit in Bateson's work can also be productively connected to McLuhan's media theory. McLuhan does not make a distinction between a "medium of communication" and a "technology"—terms which are used in his texts as rough equivalents. The source of this is probably the influence on McLuhan of the communication theory of Harold Innis where, similarly, a distinction between the two is not made. I will attempt to fill this lacuna in comparative communication theory in the next chapter. Indeed, a "medium" in McLuhan's usage refers to almost anything—for example, a chair, a highway, and a refrigerator (among many others) are all analyzed as media of communication in his work. A medium of communication is not, fundamentally, a *type* of object but a relationship that mediates a social identity with the world. From this perspective, anything can be *viewed* as such a mediation, especially insofar as it is the rhetorical effect of the thing that is emphasized. McLuhan's media theory is, in this sense, more a new epistemology of the socio-cultural world than the investigation of a certain delimited set of objects. He defines technology as "explicitness."[23] We may therefore say that a medium of communication is an explicitness. Or, to extrapolate slightly in a manner that makes the parallel with phenomenology clear, a "medium" of communication mediates one background state of the environment to another background state of the environment through thematizing some aspect of this presupposed cultural environment. In being thematized the background becomes explicit, becomes the possible object of purposeful human action. It is the moment of conscious purpose which mediates one cultural state with another and thereby provokes temporal changes in the cultural environment.

There is a related comment that should be made with regards to Bateson's theory. Bateson regards any analysis of power as being oriented to conscious control, that is, the attempted conscious control of a system by a part of the system—which he regards as in principle impossible, and therefore rejects any analysis of communication in which power is a central factor. Bateson regards any focus on power as part of a behaviouristic social science which talks about one stimulus giving one effect, unlike the systemic view which relies on negative explanation of constraints.[24] However, it is possible to view power differently from this behavioristic form. Power can be seen as itself a systemic relationship, rather than simply an attempt at control by the more dominant of the two in the relationship. Power, in this view, is something that the dominated play into; it is part of their social relationships as much as the social relationships of the dominant. This poses much more difficult questions for the analysis of power, but it does allow the connection of Bateson's systems theory to a critical theory of communication. The key question here is the extent to which the move up to observation at the next highest systemic level, which Bateson's writing always attempts to encourage, is limited or discouraged by the systemic relations of dominance within the system. This is the same issue that arises within phenomenology: While the transcendental reduction is always in principle possible, its actual performance is thoroughly enmeshed in the constraints of a given culture. It is for this reason that phenomenology needs a theory of ideology.

It may even be possible to say, following a line of thought opened up by Karl Marx, that at certain times and places the position of a key dominated group *calls forth* the reflexive move to a higher systemic level. The position of the dominated would be a strategic location in that case. It calls forth a reflection, however, not only on its own condition but on the condition of the system as a whole. This is the strategic role of the proletariat in Marxism. Marxism is not simply a propagandizing for the viewpoint of the proletariat, but an argument that the viewpoint of the proletariat is strategic for understanding and transforming the system as a whole. If one places the question of power and ideology at this point in a systemic analysis, Bateson's rejection of power is not a necessary consequence of the systemic viewpoint. More generally, through the development of this key role of power, comparative media theory can become a critical theory of communication.

The basic thesis of comparative communication theory is that the instituting of a historical epoch of culture occurs through a given complex of media of communication. It is crucial that the development of this thought in comparative media theory is tied to the contemporary situation in which it has emerged. Eric Havelock has claimed that the literature that argues for a focus on media of communication sprang onto the stage in 1963 and has grown by leaps and bounds ever since.[25] This must refer mainly to popularization, however, since it ignores the prior work of Innis. The rediscovery of orality that characterized this literature emerged in the contemporary historical shift away from a predominantly literate civilization under the influence of new electronic media such as radio and television, and which has accelerated more recently with the introduction of computers, satellites, and so forth. His appreciation of the prior oral culture of Homeric Greece led Havelock to suggest that philosophy itself was formed by the shift from orality to writing. The separation of the knower from the known, the condition for the emergence of philosophy, lies in the new conception of language as descriptive, material, and visual rather than rhetorical, agonistic, and acoustic. From this shift emerged both the Socratic practice of "essential definition," whereby an answer to the "What is x?" question was sought, and the Socratic conception of the self which, through the process of dialectic, formed itself in the image of justice.[26] It was thus suggested that the very form of knowledge in the culture of the West was initiated by a civilizational shift which was not itself fully comprehended by those who underwent it. It suggests an affinity with the nineteenth-century critique of philosophy by Marx, Nietzsche, and Freud, who suggested that the project of knowing could only be formulated under conditions that prevented its adequate self-knowledge. For this reason the inception of comparative media theory is a key theme in the story that has been called the "end of philosophy" and which underlies the contemporary reformulation of social and political philosophy.

The separation of knower and known emerges with the decline of mythic narrative and provokes the philosophical attempt to close the gap. Plato likened knowledge to vision and pointed out that the seer and the seen could only coincide in the presence of light. Similarly, the co-presence of knower and known can only occur in the presence of a medium of connection that Plato called the Good.[27] When the philosopher emerges from the cave and gazes on the sun, the soul is formed to resemble the order of the cosmos.[28] But the sight of the sun is not "another" knowledge, however exalted. It is the point of coincidence between the ability to see and the source of light that makes any and all connections between knower and known possible. Philosophy thus grounds the very possibility of rational civilization through the encounter with the origin of connection between human perception and extra-human order. Comparative media theory, if it is to be more than a catalogue of technological inventions, must link historical changes in media of communication to human perception of Being. Insofar as a given medium becomes metaphorically illuminative of the ground of this connection between humanity and Being it circumscribes an epoch of awareness. The history of Being, in Heidegger's phrase, is thus the history of these media of connection that open the possibility of, and assign a characteristic form to, the web of meaning that characterizes the world in a given epoch—which includes the constitution of a relation between knower and known. Communication, in this sense, is not a question of the transmission of a priorly articulated thought. It is the form of awareness that shapes the articulation of thought. Thought itself is understood less as an "internal" activity than as the multiplicity of connections that is spread out throughout the material forms of social communication. From this perspective, the media of communication that have been developed throughout human culture are expressions of the socio-historical Being of human life. They are the embodied rhetorical form that institutes, or establishes, a world.[29]

If philosophical thought was inaugurated by the attempt to close the gap between knower and known, the institution of the separation opens the space which inaugurates the discourse of philosophy itself. Such a discourse, although it attempts to close the gap, must simultaneously re-institute the gap in order for its own discourse to proceed. There are many different speeches which formulate different approaches to closing the gap, but, from the viewpoint adopted here, the opening and the gap define the similarity of these speeches such that they belong in a single discourse. This discourse constitutes a tradition built upon the institution of a world. Philosophy, if it can be called the most comprehensive discourse of closing, still remains within this gap of which it cannot speak. To the extent that philosophy pushes itself beyond this definition, by discarding a speech "progressively" oriented to the closing of a discourse from within itself, it must adopt a new procedure that forms a speech about the instituting of traditions. Phenomenology produced this speech through the transcendental reduction—which is a form of thinking in reverse that steps back from what is given to what allows the given to appear as such. If it can step back far enough from worldly involvements to clarify how such involvements open a world of a definite style or form, it begins to speak of the opening of historical epochs. This is the point where phenomenological philosophy becomes essential to comparative media theory.[30]

The basic philosophical formulation of the role of media of communication in the human sciences that I am proposing here is of the body as the root-phenomenon of expressive forms, media of communication as material expressions, a particular complex of expressive forms as the construction of a world, and the historical succession of worlds as manifestations of Being. This conception is an extension of the phenomenological concept of institution [*Urstiftung*]. A medium of communication initially appears to be simply the manifest form in which a communication content occurs, from which derives the conventional lineage of media forms—orality, writing, print, photograph, phonograph, and so forth. But, in the version outlined here, a medium is also understood as that which makes a communication possible. That is to say, while there is an immanent history of media forms, there is also a transcendental history of the constitution of media forms themselves—which is the version from within comparative media theory of the doubling that produces a constitutive paradox necessary to the project of self-knowledge constitutive of philosophy and the human sciences.

Put another way, that every speech act occurs *within* a medium of communication but also *through* its medium of communication, amplifies the notion of expression that is constitutive of human Being itself. This notion of expression, though it is manifested within the immanent history of media forms, is, in a certain sense, the *presupposition* of the immanent history. Every determinate history of media forms is expressible due to the phenomenon of expression itself. Thus, while every immanent history tends toward systematic formulation, it also presupposes a transcendental history that undoes its systematicity. Through this doubling, immanent history is turned "outside" toward a wonder at the phenomenon of expression itself. A theory of media of communication as human science is concerned with the immanent history of media forms, but it presupposes a philosophy of media forms in which the possibility of expression itself is manifested. To make the same point in rather a different way, every communication act is an "institution" in a double sense. It is an act within a given communication medium through which it is situated in the cultural complex of institutions that defines a world. It is also an *instituting act*, whereby a given form of expression is brought into being and sustained as such. In this sense, it is a rhetoric of media forms in which one is persuaded not primarily to a given content, but to see the world with a certain perceptual, social, and cognitive emphasis. Every communication act occurs within a given cultural complex but is also a persuasion to alter or sustain that complex and is thus a "choice" to promote a certain view of expression, and therefore involves a manifestation of expression as such.

This doubling is situated within the human body that is the origin of the phenomenon of expression and the priviliged medium of communication manifested in orality. The body, in the same double sense of institution, is both an origin of expression and is enfolded within an immanent cultural complex. Within the latter it may be disciplined in Foucault's sense, but it always contains the possibility of an original manifestation of the world in Husserl's sense. The expressive body is thus a "folding," whereby an expressive origin is folded within an immanent cultural complex. Every cultural world is constituted by such a folding-in of its origin, a making-systematic of what originates every system. This immanent closure is achieved through inscribing within the immanent of the manifestation of immanence itself. Such a turning inward constitutes a certain cultural form as the closure of the unboundedness of the manifestation of expression itself.

The reflexivity of the theory of media of communication from which doubling and folding stem is a central component of the discursive turn in the human sciences and philosophy. While the discursive turn by itself tends to focus on the manifest content of communication acts, comparative media theory can shift the issue toward the materiality of expressive forms themselves. This materiality constitutes a "form of life" (Wittgenstein) "in its characteristic style" (Husserl) such that "as men produce their life, so they are" (Marx). Comparative media theory can investigate an immanent history of media forms oriented to the rhetorical construction of a cultural complex that is the mirror-image, as it

were, of the transcendental manifestation that is the philosophical constitution of the phenomenon of expression itself. Manfestation enters
into immanent history only in glimpses. It is these glimpses that institute
monopolies of knowledge, and which social movements re-figure when
they rediscover the unbounded in order to confront existing institutions
with their incipient forms of instituting anew.

CHAPTER 4

Technology and Social Identity

I have argued that the discursive turn of philosophy and the human sciences requires a further twist to recognize that the root-phenomenon of meaning is the medium of communication which compacts a relation between technology and the human body. Furthermore, I argued that the concept of a medium of communication as used by Innis conflates the related, but not identical, notions of technology and social relations, or identities. The relationship between these two concepts is rooted in the deeper question of the humanist side of Innis's communication theory which is based in the notion that orality is an expression of the unity of the human body. It is through this meaning of orality that Innis attempted to resurrect the humanist subject in a time of its transformation and endangerment due to the splitting and discomposition of the body by contemporary technologies. In the present situation of the twilight of humanism the relationship between technology and social relations must be explicitly developed by considering, first, the standpoint of contemporary critique of technology and, second, the historical preconditions of the politics of social identity. From this philosophical core, I will develop my analyses of consumerism and social movements in the subsequent parts of this book. The concept of medium of communication as a complex of technology and social identities is intended as a continuation of the metaphor of language as the paradigm for expressive forms in general.

It was shown above that as a diagnosis and critique of modernity Innis's communication theory merits comparison with the better-known critiques by the Frankfurt School and Edmund Husserl's work *The Crisis of European Sciences and Transcendental Phenomenology*. In this latter work the loss of meaning of science for human life was diagnosed as a result of the separation of specialized scientific inquiry from its universal and reflexive foundation in philosophy due to the modern instrumental ideal of knowledge that has prevailed since the Renaissance. The cultural and historical concept of instrumental reason comprises two components: The formal-mathematical mode of thought deriving from the seventeenth-century scientific revolution and the technical form of action that has become widespread with industrial production processes. The importance of this unprecedented connection between scientific thought and technical action can be illustrated by, on the one hand, the new centrality of instrumentation (especially the telescope) to science in Galileo's workshop and, on the other, the novel impetus to technical and scientific innovation in industrial production processes.[1] The advancement of science and the increasing scope and scale of technology have occurred in tandem, though not of course in precise equilibrium, since this unprecedented connection.

The traditional humanist approach to the criticism of technology began by asserting a conception of reason as ethical. Thus, it was argued that specific sciences and technologies must be evaluated with regard to a higher conception of human culture centering on an ethical concern with the whole of human life. Humanist evaluation of technology gains its intellectual credentials from such antecedents as Aristotle's distinction of *praxis* from *techne* and his conception of practical wisdom [*phronesis*], Kant's distinction of reason [*Vernunft*] from understanding [*Verstand*], and Hegel's surpassing of Enlightenment science by histori-cal-cultural reason. The fundamental intellectual strategy is to draw a distinction between instrumental, merely technical, reason and a wider, more encompassing conception from which specific techniques, and even instrumental reason itself, can be evaluated, criticized, and perhaps displaced from their centrality to current social organization. It thus nec-essarily involves the supposition that instrumental reason has not under-mined the validity of pre-, extra-, or super-instrumental world views from which the evaluation can proceed. In a manner characteristic of this approach, Edward Ballard, even though he wishes to avoid a simply external standard for criticizing technology, nevertheless suggests that

> we proceed by determining whether technological culture or technological man effectively accept the obligation coura-

geously to pursue the truth about the self to which Western world-symbols point and the guiding recognition of his dependency, finiteness, and non-identity. To this end we have first to determine what a technological culture is like and whether or not it invites or at least renders possible the discharge of the first human obligation, the inquiry into oneself.[2]

In such an assertion of a wider ethical conception of reason, or first human obligation, the humanist approach requires an *external denial* of the claims of instrumental reason to universality. Another conception is differentiated, put "alongside" as it were, and then argued to be "more fundamental," and taken as the basis for evaluation. This is also the standpoint of the early work of Jurgen Habermas, as well as that of Hannah Arendt and Hans-Georg Gadamer from whom he derived it.[3] But in our present postmodern condition, there is no independently subsisting basis for public debate and evaluation that is not thoroughly permeated by specialist discourses. The humanist critique of technology must therefore be supplanted by a theory based on an integration of technology and social identities.

Overcoming the dominant instrumental conception of reason requires rethinking the relation between totality and particularity in order to show how particular inquiries can be imbued with universal concerns and how the articulation of universality in philosophy remains tied to its local origins. Such a postmodern connection between specific inquiry and universalizing theory, which is both reflexive and situated, I initially termed "judgment" to retain a connection to the appropriation of this term from Kant's *Critique of Judgment* by Max Horkheimer, Hans-Georg Gadamer, and Hannah Arendt to describe the key interest of twentieth-century philosophy in a singular judgment that cannot be subsumed under a rule.[4] "To mark this expansion of the constitution of self and world beyond the delimited and assumed domains of tradition and instrumental reason, self-world constitution can be substituted as the wider judgmental relationship formerly designated as subject-object. Each thematic constitution of self-world in explicit judgments unthematically transforms the entirety of life-world experience."[5] After the discursive turn, this constitution of a world of meaning can be formulated as a rhetoric of forms of expression centering on media of communication.

"World," in the phenomenological sense that I am using it here, does not refer in an objectivist sense to a reality presupposed as existing prior to human meaning nor in a subjectivist sense as a projection of mental acts, but rather to the totality of meaning that is immanent in practical involvements.[6] It is a contemporary formulation of the relation between humanity and nature sketched by the early Marx, in which the externality of nature and humanity produced by modern alienation— what I am here reformulating as instrumental reason—is replaced by a conception in which "nature is man's body."[7]

In recent years, this world of meaning has been investigated through the metaphor of language, since language-use is the most characteristic activity enacting human meaning. In taking discourse as exemplary for meaning in this way, the possibility of understanding a complex of media of communication as expressions of a human world emerges and, even more, one may become attuned to the historical disclosure of a succession of these worlds—what we might call the embodied history of human Being. It is important that the institution of a world be understood as an articulation of a complex of media of communication. Since a world does not derive from a single primal scene but from a complex of such scenes, the possible misunderstanding that it has a singular and overriding origin or destiny is dispelled—a notion that seems to be operative in the singular and overweening character of "destiny" in Heidegger's philosophy. Only through the plurality of its scenes in a historical instituting can the embodied history of human Being escape being enclosed between an unchanging origin and destiny.

Instrumental reason is a critical concept in the sense that it attempts to conceptualize the relationship between formal reason and technical action from outside, as it were, in order to *circumscribe the limits* of instrumental reason and thereby show its inadequacy in addressing larger social and cultural issues. Instrumental reason is the mode of thought and action whereby humanity dominates nature for its own ends. For this reason, its origins lead back deeply into the formation of the human species. But, in the late Renaissance reforming of both reason and action, and consequently their relationship, instrumental reason achieves a conceptual clarity and cultural centrality that are unprecedented. Many aspects of these new formations took a considerable period of time to develop; however, their origins can be traced back to the "freeing" of capital from wider social constraint that occurs when labor power becomes a commodity and to the "freeing" of science from substantive metaphysical world views. The critique of instrumental reason is thus a critique of the post-Renaissance period that we may call capitalism or modernity depending on the inflection toward the development of industrial society or the new scientific paradigm. The contemporary issues that arise with respect to the formal-mathematical mode of thought that predominates in instrumental reason have often been discussed in terms of the relation between science and ethics, or fact and value. But this formulation supposes that there is such an entity as a "value," and this supposition is itself a consequence of instrumental reason: the very idea of a value involves the wresting of an abstracted end from its practical context and the conception of this practical context as devoid of substantive meaning. The critique of instrumental reason addresses this same issue, but from a deeper perspective that shows how the fact-value dichotomy has come into being. Formal abstraction leads to unprecedentedly universal dimensions for thought; thus modern science and philosophy can easily criticize the local and arbitrary components of pre-modern substantive world views and religions. But this entails the consequence that *any substantive content* appears arbitrary from the standpoint of formal universalization, which leads to what Edmund Husserl has called "the crisis of science as the loss of its meaning for life."[8] The problem of values is thus more fundamentally a problem of how a conception of reason deriving from rigorous formal-universal abstraction can at the same time have meaning for human life. It seems equally indifferent to all contents and thus severs reason altogether from the practical, ethical conduct of life. In order to overcome the predominance of the instrumental concept of reason, one must recover the metaphorical origin of all theory and rethink its teleological orientation toward redesigning the world. Both of these retrospective and prospective dimensions are implicated in the relation of theory to the socio-historical life-world as a whole—called, in the Marxist tradition, the mode of production. In this respect, judgment is a critique of theory rooted in a more fundamental experience-world relationship that constitutes social formations.

These two problems—of values/ethics and the metaphorical nature of theory—constitute a crisis of reason that cannot be resolved until the instrumental concept of reason is displaced from its centrality to social and cultural life. Judgment includes both a dimension of human action and a dimension of reason and theory. First, judgment is concerned with the *practical context* of the functioning technology from which techniques are abstracted and which is altered as a whole by the plurality of techniques. Second, it involves a post-formal, material notion of reason that is formed through interaction with the content to which it is directed. Thus judgment sets up a new relationship between reason and action in which each judgment, in interaction with a given topic, involves a co-constitution of self and world through the interaction of technology and social identity.[9] This co-constitution of social identities in relation to the technological transformation of their environments depends upon the *specific configuration* of the practical context in contemporary capitalism from which this situation arises, which may be defined as the *standardization* of context combined with an obscuring of the *direction of experience* to which a technology is inclined.[10] Technologies can thus be radically developed and extended because it is not supposed that they alter the contexts into which they enter, and thereby design experiences and the world, social identities and their environments, to make some constructions possible and to marginalize or destroy others. It needs to be understood and, in some manner, a process of judgment needs to be institutionalized that understands that every development of a technology is ultimately a designing of the world in which we will live and thus also a designing of ourselves such that we can inhabit that world. If such a shift were to take place, the *general legitimation* of technical development by instrumental reason would have been surpassed. Attention would shift from technologies "themselves," to the construction of social identities through which they become practically effective, and we would have to address directly the *evaluation of technologies* in relation to the socio-cultural unity (or, mode of production) and the conceptions of human good which they embody.

The relationship between technology and social relations in the theory of media of communication was not addressed directly by Innis, a fact which has provided some justification for the incorrect tendency by some proponents and critics to regard him as a technological determinist. I will try to fill that gap here. The most common usage of this term suggests that a medium of communication should be understood as a technology that is *applied to* communication, that is to say, to the transfer and dissemination of information. Thus, print, telegraph, television, and film would be technologies of communication and, consequently, "media." One might also include writing and even speech—though the latter is usually excluded because technologies are generally understood as external mechanical contraptions that are distinct from the capacities of the human body. Innis's theory is very interesting in this respect: he regarded orality as a medium of communication and thus did not assume that the separation of a medium from the human body was a defining characteristic. To the contrary, understood in the terms we have suggested above—as a technology-identity relation—there is no difficulty in treating speech as a technology accomplished through the rhetorical arts of memory, invention, and delivery which leads to a determinate complex of human perception, institutions, and cognitive abilities. Similarly, the alphabet is a technology of writing that sets up new cognitive capacities and relations between reader and writer. The common-sense perspective distinguishes technologies applied to communication from technologies applied to other things—such as making shoes, automobiles, or contact lenses. It is based on what is usually known as the transportation model of communication.

Despite the common focus on transportation, the "transportation model of communication" is distinct from Innis's concept of transportation insofar as his theory is a constitutive one concerned not only with transportation *between* different locations but with the constitution of social relationships by traversal, the instituting of a primal scene. The conventional transportation model of communication is distinguished by the presupposition that what characterizes communication is the movement of meaning across space—the *delivery* as opposed to the *formulation* of meaning. In this model, communication is a secondary process presupposing the prior existence of the origin, destination, and content of the message. The technology of communication is thus understood as the *channel* whereby a message, or sign, is transported in space—as the means of this secondary process of delivery. From this common perspective, and again in contrast to Innis, a medium of communication is thus considered to be a particular category of technologies defined by their orientation toward a particular purpose. It can be placed alongside other comparable categories—such as technologies of transportation, oriented to moving people and goods in space, or technologies of agriculture, oriented to producing food. This understanding of communication, though still the most common one, can be criticized by suggesting that this secondary process of delivery is based upon a more primary process, and that this primary process is itself communication, not something other, which has to do with "making common," "being in contact with," "establishing and maintaining participation," and so forth, which are opened in a primal institution. In this understanding, communication is the constitutive process of social relations. A medium of communication persists in space and time through the establishment of connection between its constituent elements. This has two aspects: the construction of a technology with a certain practical goal in mind and the establishment of social identities, or subject-positions, through the formation of constituent relations between them.

With this understanding of communication as a cultural process of constituting technology and social identities, the question of the relation between technology and a medium of communication needs to be posed differently. Media cannot be understood as a certain specific category of technologies, but are the communicative aspect of technologies themselves. Stated generally, the communicative relations of a technology are those social relationships (including their institutional and symbolic forms) which are brought about by the practical functioning of the technology. They are thereby thoroughly imbued with the specific form of the socio-cultural context as a whole. They are ethically, politically, as well as perceptually and cognitively, laden. The technology, then, is the same set of communicative relations looked at from the side of the technical combination—that is, from the side of its *productive capacity*, its ability to accomplish human goals. Technology and communication are thus two sides of the same organization, with technology indicating a focus on the output or consequences of the organization of human abilities, and communication emphasizing the social relations that are required in order to accomplish this output—the construction of social identities in definite relations.

It is for this reason that the explosion of technologies and communications in the contemporary world has thus given rise to a politics of identity-formation. Raymond Williams has noted this qualitative change in the extended, and increasing, development of communication. "The means of communication as means of social production, and in relation to this the production of new means of communication themselves, have taken on a quite new significance, within the generally extended communicative character of modern societies and between modern societies."[11] From this perspective we can understand the complementary character of the social phenomena described within communication as the "information age" and the technological developments that designate this society as an "advanced" or "developed" one in comparison to those described metonymically as the "Third World"—though I want simply to note the relationship between these developments here without endorsing a specific analysis of them, whether they constitute a "revolution," or anything of that sort.

The emergence of a contemporary politics of identity has its roots in the dialectic of modern society that is described in the master-slave dialectic in Hegel's *Phenomenology of Spirit*. I do not want to discuss that dialectic directly here, but rather to explore the primal instituting of a dialectic of mutual recognition in order to clarify the social space within which the contemporary politics of identity operates. The master-slave dialectic is distinguished by its starting-point, which declares that "self-consciousness exists in and for itself when, and by the fact that, it so exists for another; that is, it exists only in being acknowledged."[12] The account of self-identity is thus defined from the outset as *entirely rela-*

tional and the subsequent story consists in showing how the initial inequality of relational identities established in work and war dialectically progress toward a *telos* of mutual recognition between free and equal subjects. It is the ability to inscribe one's desire on the world through work which finally establishes the independence of the slave, or worker, and allows the process of recognition to transcend its anonymity in the world of things. "Work forms and shapes the thing. The negative relation to the object becomes its *form* and something *permanent*, because it is precisely for the worker that the object has independence."[13] Thus, a concept of self that is based on recognition by an other both depends on the material world for the permanence of its expressions (which become signs of relational identities) and transcends the material world in that self-identity is itself nothing material. Charles Taylor has pointed out that this dialectic presumes the collapse of social hierarchies, where previously the process of recognition was hidden behind the unequal honor due to each according to social position.[14] But this presumption accounts only for the beginning of the master-slave dialectic, not its end. The dialectic can begin because the place of each within the social order is no longer automatically determined by the honor due to social position. From here, Hegel's dialectic winds towards a conclusion that is not inevitable from this starting-point: the mutual recognition of free and equal subjects. This *telos* of mutuality is presumed by Hegel due to the fact that his dialectical description includes the possibility of only two reciprocally defined positions. The model of two initially reciprocally defining subjects, subsequently split into master and slave positions, presupposes that there will be a final equality if either one does not drop out by dying (a possibility he does consider) or if no "third" intervenes to stabilize the process by providing recognition for a master who would then not need it from the slave. The master-slave dialectic only works because of this model of duality, or, to put it otherwise, because of the exclusion of a third. Thus, the space of recognition described by Hegel incorporates two assumptions that situate it historically: the previous collapse of hierarchies of status and the internal and deeper assumption of a relational duality of positions.

Contemporary politics of identity are more complex because the assumption of duality that resolves the dialectic in Hegel is no longer possible. Despite the continuity between Marx and Hegel that is normally assumed at this point, it was a key shift when Marx described *relations between workers* as central both to the productive capacity of capitalism and to the possibility that they could change the system by revolution.[15] Because relations between workers are inserted into the dialectic of recognition it becomes possible to imagine doing away with the master(s). This pluralization has gone even further in our own times. Groups based on region, nation, locality, gender, sexual orientation, colonized status—the list is virtually endless—have emerged to define their common identity in relation to the social field as a whole. There is, in principle, no finitude to the pluralization of the politics of identity. It could only be stopped or resolved through the re-establishment of social hierarchy or its simplification into a dualism. Contemporary politics requires the acceptance of this pluralization and the investigation of the relations between identities and the possibilities for social transformation that they propose. While current commentary often tends to omit the material, or world-forming, aspect of identity construction that is clarified through this historical reference to Hegel and Marx, identities and their related material embodiments are both subject to conditions of pluralization. It is this relation between identity-formation and material component in which their relations are expressed which is here described as a technology-identity complex inherent to a medium of communication. My account has attempted to show the connection between the contemporary importance of communication, the proliferation of technologies, and the politics of identity. This connection indicates that these phenomena interact to form a world, through the primal instituting of a historical epoch, whose specificity is indicated by the turn toward discourse and which I have called, perhaps too closely following fashion, postmodern.

CHAPTER 5

Phenomenology of Communication

It was suggested in the previous chapter that the humanist approach to technology evaluation presupposes the externality of ethical evaluation to technological development. This view was criticized and surpassed by conceptualizing the co-constitution of technology and social identities. With the critique of modernity through the concept of instrumental reason in mind, the relation of comparative media theory to phenomenology, at its most basic, concerns the point at which phenomenology might branch off from being mainly a theory of science and critique of scientific civilization toward being a theory of communication and critique of social identities. Considerable work in this area has already been done in phenomenological philosophy and human science, of course. Rather than survey these contributions, I want to describe the precise point at which such an intellectual agenda would diverge from that of Husserl and, later, how the formation of comparative media theory would entail a rejection of Husserl's views concerning communication.

At the outset of the First Investigation of the *Logical Investigations*, Husserl is concerned to conceptually define and delineate the phenomenon of expression because it is the root phenomenon of the knowledge-claims operative in scientific discourse. An expression, as with any sign, fuses a mark with something to which the mark refers—a relation between signifier and signified in semiotic terminology—such that it has a meaning and "in so far as it means something, it relates to what is objective."[1] Thus, Husserl is able to investigate the correlations given in the expression, "the expression itself, its sense and its objective correlate."[2] This lays the foundation for the entirety of the subsequent epistemological inquiry into the theory of logic and science. However, in order to fix his sights on the phenomenon of expression [Ausdruck], Husserl first distinguishes it from the phenomenon of indication [Anzeige].

On the first page of the First Investigation, he points out that not every sign has a meaning that the sign expresses: "signs [Zeichen] in the sense of indications [Anzeichen] (notes, marks, etc.) do not express anything, unless they happen to fulfil a significant [Bedeutungsfunktion] as well as an indicative function [Anzeigens]."[3] Indication thus refers to a state wherein something indicates something to a thinking being. Or, more technically, when "certain objects or states of affairs of whose reality someone has actual knowledge indicate to him the reality of certain other objects or states of affairs, in the sense that his belief in the reality of the one is experienced (though not at all evidently) as motivating a belief or surmise in the reality of the other."[4] In indication, the unity between the two states of affairs is a motivational unity, referring to an association of ideas by a human subject through an empirical unity of judgments, rather than a logical one. By motivation, Husserl means "a descriptive unity among our acts of judgment . . . [in which] the motivational unity of our acts of judgement itself has the character of a unity of judgment. . . . All unity of experience, all empirical unity, whether of a thing and event, or of the order and relation of things, becomes a phenomenal unity through the felt mutual belongingness of the sides and parts that can be made to stand out as units in the apparent object before us."[5] Clearly, the concept of indication is unscientific or, perhaps better, pre-scientific because it is "merely" motivational and not an evident grasping of the reality of certain states of affairs based on the "sense" [Sinn] or "meaning" [Bedeutung] of an expression [Ausdruck].

The motivational unity of an indication may, in some cases, be brought into an empirical-scientific demonstration. In this context, Husserl uses the example of the debate over whether an active volcano indicates that the interior of the earth is molten.[6] But, even if such an indication can, through the resolution of such a debate, take its place in empirical science, the concept of indication itself contains no relation of evident grasping of states of affairs because it does not contain the "meaning" that characterizes expressions. Thus, indications, as a class of judgments without meaning, must be left aside in order to focus on scientific discourse as a logical edifice interwoven through the meaningful content of signs, which is Husserl's thematic in *Logical Investigations*. Even though, as Husserl said, "an expression in living speech also functions as an indication,"[7] the two functions remain distinct and the field of knowledge is accessible only through the relation of expressions to their meanings, and the epistemological goal of bringing such meanings to clarity through evident insight.

By way of contrast, the motivational unity operative in indication refers to the "wider group of facts that fall under the historical rubric of the 'association of ideas'" and occurs by suggesting that "certain things *may* or *must* exist, *since* other things have been given."[8] Plainly, this type of association between ideas is operative throughout ordinary life and culture. As Husserl observes: "We commonly speak of reasoning and inference, not merely in the case of logic, but in a sense connected with empirical indications. This affinity plainly extends more widely: it covers the field of emotional, and, in particular, of volitional phenomena. . . ."[9] Husserl's phenomenology does not exclude investigation of this type of practical reasoning embedded in everyday life, even though he sharply delineates it from "knowledge" (in the strict sense in which he uses the term) which remains the operative *telos* guiding the *Logical Investigations* and, indeed, the whole of Husserl's work.[10]

My interest in primal scenes of communication, however, is precisely in the practical reasoning that includes emotion and volition and, particularly, in the instituting moments that shape and legitimate a specific form of practical reasoning as valid throughout a given space and time, that is to say, which is constitutive of the way of life of a culture. In this sense, my investigations into the primal scenes of communication diverge from, but do not contradict, the intellectual agenda set by Husserl. Indeed, the distinctions that, for Husserl, were preliminary to the theory of knowledge are, in my view, essential to the delimitation of the field of cultural investigation.

The situation addressed by comparative media theory is more than a divergence, however, when we turn to Husserl's theory of communication itself. In Husserl's view, expressions were originally developed to play a communicative function. Indeed, also in the present, "all expressions in *communicative* speech function as *indications*"[11] and what they indicate is the contents of the mind of the speaker. Husserl's special term for such an indication is "intimation" [*Kundgabe*]. In communicative speech, the hearer *intuitively* perceives the speaker as manifesting certain inner experiences. "Mutual understanding demands a certain correlation among mental acts mutually unfolded in intimation and in the receipt of such intimation, but not at all their exact resemblance."[12] His view here is that communication is achieved through the making-known of the thoughts of a speaker to another speaker when the speech functions as a specific class of indication called intimation. The speech thus comprises a "unity of judgment" with the thoughts of the speaker: a unity of two empirical states in which the appearance of the speech motivates the appearance of the speaker's thoughts, though neither "meaningfully" nor "evidently." Thus, it is through the sharing of our minds through intimations of the contents of others' minds as manifested in situationally concrete expressions that society becomes human society, a society of conscious beings who each understand, in some fashion, the conscious lives of others in their world and thus the society in which they live. René Toulemont summarizes the phenomenological account in this way: "Communication opens access to the state of society. For society to exist, it is necessary, in addition, that the unity of subjects be made and developed through the *content* of the communications, and it is necessary that the unity, which is evanescent in communication, aquire a certain permanence."[13] Communication is understood in terms of its content, which is indeed evanescent, and not in terms of the concrete, "material," medium of communication. It is on the basis of communication, so understood, that the "personalities of a higher order" [*Personalitäten höherer Ordnung*], in Husserl's phrase—such as the communities, nations, classes and associations of all kinds that form human society—are constituted.[14]

Communication is thus tied to the transfer of a content (in the speaker's mind) through a medium (the speech, functioning as an intimation) to another location (becoming a content of the hearer's mind). This is clearly a version of the transportation model of communication that I criticize in several places in this book. While it is the most theoretically clarified and sophisticated version of a transportation model of communication that has ever appeared, it still incorporates some of its unfortunate and derivative features.

Husserl's theory asserts a fundamental place for the phenomenon of communication in the constitution of society, but, unfortunately, it assumes that communication should be understood as a function of transferring an already formulated thought, or content, and does not apply to the formulation of thought itself. Consequently, it deals with the foundation of the mutual understanding inherent in culture and society through communicative acts in terms of the classical modern issue of "empathy," which is based upon an inner/outer distinction that suggests that inner meaningful acts are inherently clearer than, and separated from, the outer acts which intimate inner meanings. The theoretical issue that requires a solution when posed in terms of empathy is how a relation between two or more minds can be established such that human society and culture is a field of mutual understanding as well as a material unity. Such mutual understanding, it is assumed, must be built out of the understanding that is supposed pre-existent in individual minds. Thus, the understanding within an individual mind is assumed to be prior to, and essentially different from, mutual understanding. This is why, immediately after the section in *Logical Investigations* that deals with how expressions function in communication, Husserl takes up the issue of how they function in solitary life.

The origin of this posing of the issue is in the main tendency of modern philosophy which conceives society in the form of a social contract between individuals. It also has the consequence of understanding social forms other than individuals on the model of individual person such that "higher-level" social unities are called "personalities of a higher order." This phrasing has two correlative disadvantages: it tends to reify larger social groups by treating them as unified "like," or, in a similar way, as individual persons; also, in an opposite direction, it tends to reduce "higher-level" social unities to accomplishments of individuals, in the manner of social contract theory, and thus to treat individuals as "really" more fundamental than other social unities. Whichever way this reification or reduction goes, it is rooted in the cover-up of important questions concerning the constitution of social unities that are hidden by treating them "like" individuals. A communication theory, in contrast, needs to treat the specificity and uniqueness of the constitution of social unities and consider the specificity of their communicative relations without subsuming them abruptly under the model of "persons."

Even further, the definition of communication through the transfer of a content from one mind to another affects the very definition of an indication itself. Husserl suggests that indications are of two main types, those in which the indication is brought about deliberately—such as memorials, marks, etc.—and those in which there is no intention at work—such as fossils, animal tracks, and so forth.[15] He denies that the latter type should be regarded as signs in the proper sense at all. The utilization of the notion of intention, or deliberate action in inscribing a mark, to delineate two types of signs might be legitimate in some contexts, but to circumscribe the phenomenon of the sign as such through the notion of intention is inadequate, and derives from Husserl's focus on the problem of scientific signification rather than on the general problem of the role of signs in human life that has been raised by the discursive turn—which requires a sense of all perception of the world as significant, i.e., of the world as a complex of signs, and historical epochs as founded on primal institutions. The theory of communication that I am advocating needs to revoke the claim that intention defines a sign in order for communication to be understood as an extension of the expressive capacities of the human body, other bodies, and indeed of the world itself. Culture cannot be founded on intention; it is the always-already-formed background on the basis of which intentions are formulated.

Communication is thus relegated by Husserl to a transfer between minds and stricken from the constitutive process of the formulation of meaning. This is why I chose to begin my theory of the primal scenes of communication from the notion of "original institution" [*Urstiftung*] in Husserl—which is about the origin of a specific form of meaningful tradition that allows communication (in the simple sense of transfer) to occur—rather than Husserl's theory of communication as such. Husserl's view of communication needs to be rejected along with social contract theory, empathy, and the transportation model of communication in order for the theory of communication as primal scenes to address the setting-up, the institution of, socio-cultural forms themselves.

Looking at this conceptual distinction in a wider context, intimations belong to a certain kind of expressions, that Husserl calls "occasional expressions," whose meaning is tied to the here and now of its utterance, and—unlike scientific discourse—are operative in the mutual communication that constitutes society. He says:

> The expressions which name the momentary content of intimation belong to a wider class of expressions whose meaning varies from case to case. . . . [W]e call an expression . . . *essentially occasional* if it belongs to a conceptually unified group of possible meanings, in whose case it is essential to orient actual meaning to the occasion, the speaker and the situation. Only by looking to the actual circumstances of utterance can one definite meaning out of all this mutually connected class be constituted for the hearer.[16]

Scientific, epistemologically validated knowledge—through its other, non-epistemological function as indication—participates in, and intimates, this concrete situation, but never exhausts it, in Husserl's view. In this way the irreducibility of the here and now of a concrete situation is preserved in phenomenology, even though never captured within the sphere of knowledge.

This can perhaps be clarified by comparison to Hegel's conception of language which, by way of contrast, leaves behind the occasional and situational location of indication entirely in order to transform it into the evident and repeatable expressions of science. In the first section of the *Phenomenology of Spirit* on sense-certainty, Hegel considers writing down the truth—of an "essentially occasional expression" in Husserl's terminology—that "Now is Night" and rediscovering the next noon that it has become false. He concludes that "it is just not possible for us ever to say, or express in words, a sensuous being that we *mean*."[17] Knowledge thus leaves sense-certainty behind entirely as ungraspable and unknowable and, eventually, truth is seen to reside only in the whole such that its starting-point becomes irrelevant.

Husserl, in contrast, preserves the element of sensuousness and location that is necessary to any indication, even though it cannot be captured in the content of the expression itself, and thus cannot be transformed into science. It is unknowable, but still graspable in the form of practical reasoning, which includes everyday reasoning, volition, and emotion. It remains the occasional location upon which the objectivating knowledge of science rests, but which can never entirely be brought into the logical structure of science. Expressions are only possible by depending on an occasional location distinct from them and which cannot be carried up into them. This here and now location, rather than being understood through Husserl's deficient model of communication, can be explicated through what I have referred to as the primal scenes of communication that institute society in a determinate given form.

Husserl's phenomenological account of communalization also converges with the Marxist account of language as communicative utterance developed by the Bakhtin Circle. Volosinov makes a similar distinction between an identical ideal content, which he calls "meaning," and the unique and unreproducible "theme," which refers to "the concrete historical situation that engendered the utterance."[18] As dialogic, every utterance has an evaluative accent whereby it expresses the way of life of a social group in a constant tension with its rivals.[19] Thus, by describing the precise point at which a theory of communication diverges from a theory of scientific meaning, it is possible to note a significant convergence between phenomenology and a Marxist critique of a semiotic theory of language. Both are concerned with the function of language in constituting social groupings through intuitive participation and in conflict with other groups. Linguistic communication is understood not as a representation of previously existing social relations, but as constitutive of social unities in its own right. The utterance is not concerned with "internal" meaning, but with the "lateral" construction of social relations through the indication of the content of other minds and the evaluative accent given to a certain way of life.

In this manner, the phenomenological foundation of comparative media theory takes up many of the issues addressed by the phenomenological Marxism of Jean-Paul Sartre and Maurice Merleau-Ponty. However, they thought that turning phenomenology toward concrete history could only be opened up by the rejection of the transcendental turn. In contrast, the phenomenological foundation of comparative media theory here presented articulates the relation between the human sciences and philosophy through the distinction between concrete and transcendental life. It is only through this distinction that historical events can be seen as initiating a historical epoch as the pervasive form of the lifeworld in which events occur. Put another way, comparative media theory intends its own synthesis of the sensuous materialism of Marx with the critique of experience by Husserl.

However, while communication is understood as constitutive, lateral, and agonistic through this synthesis of phenomenology and Marxism, there is not, in either Husserl or Volosinov, a focus on the *medium* of communication and, therefore, no conception of the materiality of expression that has been introduced here as comparative media theory. This focus finds its place in phenomenology in connection to the notion of *institution*, or the instituting of a primal scene, whereby a new formation is brought into being such that it becomes a reference point throughout later developments in a way that constitutes a subsequent tradition. I am suggesting that the instituting of a historical epoch of culture occurs through a given complex of media of communication. This thesis, though it builds on phenomenology in the wider sense, and specifically on the concept of institution, requires a critical departure from Husserl's studies of communication—which are still caught in a distinction between the contents of consciousness and their transmission to another that routes the question of communication toward empathy and a philosophy of consciousness and bars it from addressing communication as the instituting moment of an epoch of culture which the previous chapters of this book have attempted to sustain.

Having thus concluded my outline of comparative media theory in these last four chapters, the next two parts of the book establish the point of origin of this theory in contemporary consumer society and examine the social movements that situate the emergence of reflexivity within it. Since it is both a theory of enunciation and an enunciation, the self-referential constitution of comparative media theory is constitutively paradoxical.

PART II

LOSS OF MEDIATION
IN CONSUMER SOCIETY

CHAPTER 6

From Competitive Capitalism
to Consumer Society

Contemporary social theory and criticism must address the question of whether activities of consumption have become the articulating moment of a form of life that could be called consumerism. In consumerism, acts of buying are not only the appropriation of things for use, but also the selection and use of things as signs of social relationships. Consumer society raises the spectre of a system of signs that has no "outside," in which the appropriation of any sign as a token of social identity tends to confirm the system of signs as an inter-related whole. To the extent that this is the case, consumer society becomes a self-enclosed cultural form in which social identities are confirmed by ritual acts of buying and showing off. Social criticism must investigate this proposed sign-system as a whole to clarify the critical possibility that a social identity defined within the system might become aware of the system as a whole—a possibility which is a necessary precondition for social change. To this extent, the questions of consumerism, social identity, and culture as a form of life with a characteristic style are bound up together in contemporary social criticism.

The term "culture" refers in the first place to the opinions and beliefs imbedded in routine patterns of action which characterize groups and make their members recognizable to each other. In the second place, explicit expressions of these beliefs in historical events and the creative arts bring membership in a cultural group to self-consciousness, which allows a deeper perception of the motives and implications of such beliefs and provides a solider foundation for their persistence in time and space. In this sense, culture is fundamentally about "identity," which can be understood as the self-knowledge of groups recognizable by shared beliefs that is established in self-conscious expressions. Culture is based on the communication of experiences within a group, such that the experiences of others clarify and shape those of the individual. Thus, the medium, or manner, of communication that prevails in a specific context influences the opinions and beliefs which solidify cultural identities, and, especially important, constitutes the *mode of attachment* to such beliefs. Such modes of attachment compose the affective bond which characterizes a given culture.

The first thing to notice about contemporary culture is that it is an *industrially produced culture*. As such, there are two main forces acting externally on cultural change and expression—the economy and the state. A capitalist exchange economy begins by breaking down local hierarchies and traditions and substituting a production-consumption system with an inherent mechanism of accumulation. The apogee of such an expansionist economy is a universal world-system which regulates and replaces all other local and particular sources of cultural identity. The modern state, and the nationalism that created it, was primarily a response to the centralizing features of the exchange economy. But, in some cases, it may be said to have established the *conditions for* such an economy (as a more or less conscious policy) by substituting generalized for local authority and the conception of law as an abstract system of rules over personal, inherited power. Sometimes, also, the state intervenes to *limit and manage* the effects of the economy. The leader, or "center," of the world-system is usually in favor of free trade since the universalizing and centralizing effect of exchange economy favors them. Britain in the nineteenth century and the United States in this century have appreciated this fact. However, the peripheries of the world-system, former colonies and new nations, often need to protect themselves by setting up trade barriers to counter the advantages of size in an exchange economy—to redress the fact that there are no local advantages in a universal world-system. Many countries have erected such trade barriers in the past, though in more recent years they have been largely dismantled in favor of free trade.

Modern society began with the separation of an economic sphere of action from the control of the state. Economic self-interest, which is defined by the private individual, is the sole consideration of value in this sphere. Politics, by contrast, was taken to be the sphere of public deliberation about the good society, where what is good for all is the sole consideration. Thus, we often speak of "conflict of interest" when private, economic self-interest invades the public, political domain. We take the separation of these two institutional spheres for granted and criticize any other society in which this separation has not taken place, or is not regarded as legitimate, as necessarily involving the supression of individual rights. In the first place, we mean here the economic right of the pursuit of individual wealth, but also of rights of individuality in general, such as the defence of a private sphere of action free from state control, participation in democratic self-government, "personal" religious beliefs, and so on. This separation of economics from politics is the liberal core of modern society. Its institutional basis is generally regarded as legitimate by those called "conservatives" and "socialists," as well as those known as "liberals" in a conventional sense.

The American, French, and (more historically drawn out) English revolutions set the stage for this institutional separation. The sphere of economic self-interest, or "capitalism," was taken to be legitimate but not sufficient for the self-governance of society. For clearly a society that was *only* ruled by individual self-interest would constantly tend to be torn apart, or to be taken over by the strongest. Adam Smith's doctrine of the "hidden hand" in economic exchange was important in this context. He argued in *The Wealth of Nations* that a society in which each individual pursues only individual self-interest produces, behind the back of the individuals, without anyone's direct attention, the general good for society as a whole. Variants of this doctrine still abound as defences of a "minimum" of state intervention in the economy. However, even this position requires a minimum state to provide the *preconditions for* a capitalist economy. It must guard against monopoly control of the market and regulate the printing and circulation of money, for example. Moreover, there are several essential functions for capitalism which cannot be made cost-effective for individual enterprise—such as transportation, and, more recently, education. There are still more functions that are required to stabilize society beyond simply providing the preconditions for a capitalist economy (though of course they do serve to stabilize society in its capitalist form), such as combating crime and national defence. These functions have grown much larger as capitalist society has developed. Thus, a minimum wage, regulation of production processes such as the use of chemicals, a certain level of health and welfare for the population at large, as well as subsidies for "culture," have been increasingly guaranteed and developed by the political function of the state. There are considerable differences between countries in the extent to which these functions are taken over by the state, and the United States probably has less commitment in this area than any other advanced capitalist country. Also, in recent years the extent of such social welfare has been cut back in most advanced industrial capitalist societies in the name of "fiscal responsibility." Nevertheless, in all such societies some level of concern with the general good is regarded as the legitimate concern of the state.

In all societies characterized by an institutional separation between economic and political spheres there is a question of how self-interest can be "mediated" such that political life is concerned with the general good and is not just a tool of the most powerful economic interests. How can individual self-interest "pass over" into the public good? In general, it is the function of media of communication to perform such a "mediating" role. In the American Revolution, public meetings, pamphlets such as Tom Paine's *Common Sense*, and newpapers played a key role in articulating individual discontent in such a way that it became a common political issue. This role was ratified in Article 1 of the ten original amendments to the Constitution of the United States of America which came into force on December 15, 1791. It reads as follows: "Congress shall make no law respecting an establishment of religion, or prohibiting the free exercise thereof; or abridging the freedom of speech or of the press; or the right of the people peaceably to assemble and to petition the Government for a redress of grievances." More recently, Article 19 of the United Nations' Universal Declaration of Human Rights (1948) added "through any media and regardless of frontiers" to the phrasing from the U.S. Constitution which had become an international standard. Similarly, the Canadian Constitution Act of 1982 sought to update the reference to freedom of the press by adding "and other media of communication."

It is this article of the Constitution of the United States, and its subsequent interpretations by the courts, that provides the basis for the role of media of communication in mediating private economic self-interest and a public, political conception of the general good. The interpretation of the courts has been that corporations can be considered as "legal persons," and thus their speech has been protected by the same law as the free speech of individuals. This even extends to advertising and other obviously self-interested forms of speech. There are two interwoven issues here. The first pertains to the relative power of "persons" to speak, and to the imbedded economic power of corporate speakers in specific influential media such as television or newspapers. The second has to do with the plurality of media themselves, and the transformation of society by an increasing number of media of communication. These thoughts should be enough to indicate that a mere updating is not sufficient to guarantee free speech in a media-dominated age. A much more radical investigation of the constitutive role of media of communication and their social influence is necessary.

This article of the U.S. Constitution sets alongside each other the three central aspects of the question of mediation—belief, discussion, and action—and implicitly, by its very structure, sets up a relationship among them. First, everyone is free to believe as he or she likes. To say this one must regard "belief" as not having direct social consequences, as an individual rather than a social production. Next, free speech and the press: Public discussion sorts and reformulates the various beliefs that the people hold. In discussion some fall out because they do not stand the test of being universalizable.That is, they remain only private, self-interested, and cannot command general assent. Others are given a universal form and become part of the society's publicly accepted conception of the good life. Finally, the assembly of the people, its private beliefs generalized by free discussion, can act together. Action cannot be directly based on belief, which would lead to a chaos of individual self-interests. But, through the mediation of free communication, action can further the general good.

In a feudal or authoritarian society, where politics is merely the interest of the most powerful, the question of mediation does not arise, but a society that allows individual self-interest must provide a mechanism of mediation in order that it not fall into a chaos of competing beliefs and interests. Once the key role in democracy of free discussion in the essential media of communication is understood in this way, an important contemporary question looms: If there are only three television networks, a few newspaper chains and wireservices, in short, if access to the media of communication is sharply restricted, can the discussion in the media be regarded as really "free"? What are the consequences for democracy if only a few voices, all corporate ones, are heard? It seems that the role assigned to mediation of beliefs by the media is only tenable where there is widespread *access to* the media as well as free expression within them. The model of mediation of beliefs and action by media of communication in liberalism presupposes that economic processes are "prior" to the mediation and that political processes are "subsequent" to it. In other words, it presupposes that the spheres of economy and politics are separate from the process of mediation in communication. Their institutional separation thus entails the presupposition that the necessary mediation is external to them. In consequence, media of communication are considered to be objects of a certain type—such as newspapers, televisions, and so forth—rather than processes inherent in all social life.

The modern liberal institutional separation of economy and politics has been undermined by twentieth-century developments in capitalist society. Concentration of ownership into large monopolies has involved an increasing control of the market and an increased ability to manipulate consumer demand. Moreover, the responsibility for assuring that the profit-driven prerequisites of these monopolies are made acceptable to the public by mitigating their worst disfunctions has become the major function of the political realm. The economy has become a political matter, not in the sense of direct political power by single economic groups, but in the sense that managing or steering the economy as a whole has become a widely accepted task of government. Concomitantly, the political sphere has come increasingly to serve the interests of monopoly capital as a whole. Friedrich Pollock, in a 1941 essay on the then-new concept of state capitalism, phrased this transformation in the following way:

> The hour of state capitalism approaches when the market economy becomes an utterly inadequate instrument for utilizing the available resources. The medium-sized private enterprise and free trade, the basis for the gigantic development of men's productive forces in the 19th century, are being gradually destroyed by the offspring of liberalism, private monopolies and government interference.[1]

This new re-integration of economy and politics has wide consequences. Its tendency is to produce a closed social system in which the economic cycle of production and consumption is validated and steered by the political order—a system in which the needs, desires, and participation of individuals are internalized from the system as a whole. In short, it produces a system in which every individual part confirms the whole structure and in which the whole structure dominates and forms the part such that the capitalist social order becomes not merely an economy with extensive implications, but a form of life with a characteristic style, a unitary cultural form which manifests itself in the economy, in politics, and indeed throughout all dimensions of social life. The predominance and continuation of this cultural form is inherent in the mechanism by which cultural meaning is produced and exchanged—the code of signs. Jean Baudrillard was one of the first to theorize the closed code as constitutive of consumer society. As he put it, "this mutation concerns the passage from the form-commodity to the form-sign, from the abstraction of the exchange of material products under the law of general equivalence to the operationalization of all exchanges under the law of the code. . . . The monopolistic stage signifies less the monopoly of the means of production (which is never total) than the monopoly of the code."[2] The system of production, exchange, and consumption of signs is the cultural cement of the monopoly capitalist form of life. In this system the role of media of communication is expanded from its "mediational" function in liberal society to become the major determinant of this cultural cement.

The cultural code of monopoly capitalism tends to become a unified, closed system in a historical development that consists of two closely related parts. Signs are unhinged from their origin in the life-practice of social subjects. Signs "float" through their circulation in social life without reference to the meaningful practices that produce them. As a consequence of this, signs do not refer to a realm of social practice outside the sphere of signs, but become a "code"—that is to say, a sign is related to a *system of signs*. It is through this double movement—loss of external reference and systematization into a code—that the cultural logic of monopoly capitalism emerges. In this situation the specific character of the sign is arbitrary, or conventional, and its meaning derives from its difference from other signs within the code. Thus, each sign calls forth the code as a whole.

Henri Lefebvre characterized this historical development in the following way:

> a hundred years ago words and sentences in a social context were based on reliable referentials that were linked together, being cohesive if not logically coherent, without however constituting a single system formulated as such. . . . However, around the years 1905–10 the referentials broke down under the influence of various pressures (science, technology, and social changes). . . . In these circumstances it seems that the only basis for social relations is speech, deprived of criteria, veracity and authenticity and even of objectivity. In other words such relations have no foundations, and speech, the form of communication, is now instrument and content as well.[3]

From this perspective, Saussure's insistence on the "arbitrariness of the sign" and its immense influence on subsequent linguistics and social theory takes on more of the character of a historical symptom than an unquestionable first principle of language.[4]

It is in this situation that we encounter the ideology of objectivity in media. As we have seen, early liberal capitalism assigned a key role to media of communication, especially the press, in public discussion. In so doing, media were expected to *form* public opinion, to play the active role of expressing and molding beliefs into statements concerning the general good. This active role of "universalization"—which we can now call the production of consent to the system as a whole, since it is no longer a question of representations but the constitution of a social order—cannot be publicly avowed in monopoly capitalist society precisely because it is so central to the social process. Lack of widespread access to media would be seen to constitute a formidable restriction of democracy if the formative function of such media were acknowledged. Moreover, if the system of signs were recognized as a political formation, the social role of media images would become a source of political contention. The ideology of objectivity serves to keep this destabilizing possibility at bay by asserting that the media simply "represent" what is going on. Only by denying the productive role of media in the legitimizing sign-systems of the logic of monopoly capital can the media play their role. They can only work when veiled. The signs that we circulate through the predominant media of communication are our images of the "good life," which once was the domain of politics.

Thus, a systematic misunderstanding of the role of media of communication is inherent in the contemporary cultural system of meaning. This ideology—which amounts to the occlusion of the opening inherent in the instituting role of a medium understood as a primal scene by the subsequent history of expression thus enabled—is pervasive throughout both popular and academic accounts of media. Its most basic form is the "transportation" model of communication, that is, a model in which the process of communication is simply a transfer of information from one location to another. Consider the following sketch, which is a common presentation of the process of communication.

source → transmitter → signal → receiver → destination

These five aspects of the communication process were distinguished by Shannon and Weaver in *The Mathematical Theory of Communication.* There have, of course, been other influential ways of schematizing the various aspects of communication such as Lasswell's formula "who says what to whom in what channel to what effect," for example, or Roman Jakobson's six factors of addresser, context, message, contact, code, addressee, or David Berlo's source, message, channel, receiver.[5] While these schemes differ from each other in some respects—primarily about where to draw the lines in subdividing the process—they nevertheless contain some basic common assumptions. It is these common assumptions that are significant in characterizing the ideological features of most inquiry into communication. Indeed, it is often the case that an explicit rejection of the transportation model does not serve to adequately displace these assumptions. The basic structure of the transportation model involves a message which is put into acceptable form (encoded) for transmission through a medium of communication, transmitted and received, and retrieved from its altered form (decoded). Communication is understood in this model as simply a transfer of a content from one location to another. The origin and destination of the transfer pre-exist the transference itself and are not altered by it.

We can isolate three main assumptions in this model that have become problematic in a contemporary context. First, there is a separation of channel and content. The message precedes the transfer and exists apart from it at the destination. The contribution of the channel is restricted to "noise," that is, a distortion of the original message. Second, the subjects who communicate are pre-constituted and not really affected by the process of communication. They simply send and receive messages; their identity, or what they "are," is another question entirely. Thus, in this model there arises the intractable question of whether "society affects media" or "media reflect society." It is characteristic of ideology to direct inquiry into such insoluble dead-ends rather than clarifying real social relationships. Third, the effect of communication is understood only as the effect of isolated messages. There is no question of a general social effect and, especially, of a social effect deriving from the medium of communication itself rather than from the messages which it carries.

The liberal ideology of early capitalism, much of which is still effective today, was to pose the relation of individual and society as an opposition. Individual interest was seen as distinct from and opposed to social responsibility, and often a compromise was reached in which private individuals were to pursue their own interests but the state was supposed to pursue the social good. Following Hegel, Marxist political theory projected the *reconciliation* of individual interest and social responsibility through the building of a community in which the distinction was overcome [*Aufgehoben*], though, in practice, this supposed reconciliation led to the submergence of the individual under monolithic state structures in actually existing socialist societies. The "realization" of philosophy seems to take this ironic form, which may be history's revenge for the abstracting and therefore simplifying that is inherent in any theory.

The tendency of the last hundred years in industrial capitalist societies, contrary to Hegel and Marx, has been toward a loss of mediation in social life. The original role of the press in early capitalism was to provide the *reflexive* capacity to mediate private, particular interests with universal, political deliberation. The argument for the freedom of the press was based on its ability to enact precisely such a mediation. The press has been increasingly incapable of fulfilling its function for several reasons. Notably, the concentration of private ownership of the press has tended to make the important media of communication extensions of economic self-interests of particular groups. Also, political action at the level of the nation-state has increasingly been absorbed by the competition between nation-states, diverting it from its universal claims. The mediating role of the free press has thus been largely lost. As a consequence, the politics of media as representation, centered around the idea of a free press, has been supplanted by a politics of media as constitutive, centered around the construction of social identities. Only when speech can be separated from action can the politics of expression revolve around the idea of a free press. Once speech is understood as a form of action, its politics revolves around the effects that are desired by different groups in constituting the social field.

This loss of mediation by key media of communication is symptomatic of a loss of mediation in society at large. Hegel's writing on the English reform law suggested that the central historical reason for the greater freedom of English society was the existence of mediating institutions of a voluntary nature *between* private self-interests, on the one side, and the compulsory and universal character of the state, on the other. He argued that this provided a concrete conception of freedom in distinction from the abstract conception prevailing in France that led to the problems of centralization of authority after the French Revolution.[6] In our current terminology, we may say that the plurality of determinations allowed an identity-formation capable of reflexive awareness of its involvements. By way of contrast, the tendency over the last several hundred years has been to break down mediating institutions such as the church, the parish, the social institutions surrounding the pub, the festival days oriented in local towns, the unions, kinship, and so forth. The consequence has been a loss in reflexivity combined with a greater degree of concentrated organization. This, of course, has not been simply a linear development, but in general, we may say that we have been increasingly confronted with a polarization of power at the level of the nation-state and the trans-national corporation, on the one side, and the isolated individual, on the other. This is why there is such a difficult problem for social change in the bureaucratic, consumer, capitalist system. The polarization of the isolated individual as against the massive organizations of the political economy leaves very little possibility for social change. The problem for social transformation thus becomes the *construction* of new mediating institutions and identities which can steer between isolated, particular self-interest and compulsory, universal corporate interest. The political practice of social movements in the last thirty years has been precisely to begin from and develop such new mediating institutions—community organizations, civil rights pressure groups, environmental protest organizations, women's groups, and so forth.

What is now required is not a *reconciliation* of particular and universal, of individual and society (as classical modern political theory supposed), but rather an expansion of the realm of mediation. We may state this issue of mediation in a threefold manner: as an *environmental* relation between an identity and its context, or world; as a *translation* of its formulation of that environmental relation (understood as an antagonism) into other formulations; and as a new, non-totalizing *reflexivity* over this cultural identity in relation to its environment translating other identities. This new situation is a major index of the historical shift from classical capitalism to what might be called postmodern capitalism.

CHAPTER 7

Reduction of Culture to Information

As a result of the two external factors of economy and state discussed in the previous chapter, the internal development of industrial culture has been through three stages. While these stages tend to overlap and to overlay each other, as in any historical periodization, they nevertheless clarify the development of culture in an industrial setting where there is a continual transformation of culture and, therefore, of group identity. The first stage of industrial culture was a *class culture* which reflected the class character of industrial production. The unequal relationships generated by the sale of labor power in capitalist industry extended throughout the whole of society. The working class and the capitalist class had different opinions and beliefs, different historical and artistic expressions, and inhabited, as it were, two different cultural worlds. The image of the factory crystallizes the first stage of industrial culture.

In the twentieth century, perhaps most clearly in the 1920s, the stage of mass culture began. Since the long-projected and sometimes attempted transformation of capitalist industrial production by social revolution did not occur, the multifarious commodities produced by new production methods began to pervade the entire culture. Stabilization and rationalization of the system of production inaugurated the era of mass consumption, which began with consumer goods but gradually extended to the whole of culture. Mass culture replaced the "two

89

worlds" of class culture with a single self-enclosed world of industrially produced cultural goods. Cultural uniformity was established against the older forms of regional, ethnic, and linguistic differences through the mechanical reproduction of cultural goods. Inequalities in society were then expressed not as different worlds of goods, but as *relative degrees of access* to uniform goods. Cultural uniqueness, such as it was, was expressed as a sum of consumer choices, from a homogeneous set of goods available, in principle, to all. The image of mass culture is the film, the apotheosis of the entertainment industry.

A third stage of industrial culture is now emerging. It has been called the "postmodern condition," the "information society," "post-industrial society," the "society of the image," and so forth. At the outset, it must be emphasized that this is a new and contested field— because of the collapse of mediation, every characterization of it implies a position, a diagnosis, and an evaluation. Nevertheless, within this contested field of competing analyses and interpretations a new configuration of industrial culture is emerging whose image is the computer, or more specifically, the computer-simulated video screen. Jean-François Lyotard, in his report to the Québec government on the current state of knowledge, indicated the new relationship of economy and state that is appearing in this transformation:

> The mercantilization of knowledge is bound to affect the privilege the nation-states have enjoyed, and still enjoy, with respect to the production and distribution of learning. The notion that learning falls within the purview of the State, as the brain or mind of society, will become more and more outdated with the increasing strength of the opposing principle, according to which society exists and progresses only if the messages circulating within it are rich in information and easy to decode. The ideology of communicational "transparency," which goes hand in hand with the commercialization of knowledge, will begin to perceive the State as a factor of opacity and "noise." It is from this point of view that the problem of the relationship between economic and State powers threatens to arise with a new urgency.[1]

In the information society the external forces operating on industrial culture come to *coincide with the content of culture* itself. The economy and state regulation pervade culture, and "information" becomes the content of culture.

The main tendency of contemporary industrial culture is a conver-gence of economic and cultural realms in "information." In the new and contested field of the information society, the self-knowledge on which cultural identity rests is mediated through information-processing. Cul-tural expressions become inputs into the society modeled on the video screen. This might also be called a "knowledge-commodity" insofar as the processing of culture as information colonizes and offers up for *gen-eralized exchange* the opinions, beliefs, and expressions which define the self-knowledge of cultural identities. Information, like the majority of economic goods, is subject to ownership and control by multinational corporations. This is based on the considerable power of the capitalist market economy to determine the development of industrial culture and cannot be expected to disappear as the predominant tendency without a substantial reorientation of the population at large and its representa-tives. Its fundamental notion is that the free play of economic forces yields the most just and uncoerced choices of cultural goods. The part of politics is then primarily to adjust to the mechanism of market rational-ity. All local resistance to the world-system is stigmatized as irrational, retrograde, parochial, and romantic. The reduction of culture to infor-mation not only extends throughout the contemporary world, but also re-processes the past. As Marshall McLuhan has observed of the age that we are now entering,

> In this electric age we see ourselves being translated more and more into the form of information, moving toward the techno-logical extension of consciousness. . . . By putting our physical bodies inside our extended nervous systems, by means of elec-tric media, we set up a dynamic by which all previous tech-nologies that are mere extensions of hands and feet and teeth and bodies, including cities—will be translated into information systems.[2]

In this way, the reduction of culture to information extends to the self-knowledge of all cultural identities in time and space, history and geog-raphy. Information is not merely a new technological development that affects culture, but one of universal significance for the idea of culture itself. The culture of information processes all experience situated in and bounded by history and geography through a universal matrix abstracted from the concrete experience of individuals and groups.

The postmodern age of the knowledge-commodity is the cultural component which corresponds to the dominance of the economy and the state in contemporary life. Several observations can be made about prevailing assumptions concerning these institutions which may encourage a receptivity to another, more critical, characterization: The economy is usually taken to embody "free and equal" exchanges and thereby to promote the liberal values of freedom and equality throughout society—freedom because no one is compelled to exchange and equality because commodities of equal value (or prices) are exchanged for each other—but the concentration of economic power in multinational corporations severely circumscribes the possibility of exchanges between uncoerced individuals. Resources must be sold to someone who has the industrial organization to use them, and if most of such corporations involve huge concentrations of power and often a monopolized sector of the market, these transactions can hardly be called "equal." Such an economy has nothing to do with "free enterprise" in the sense of individual initiative. Moreover, the "freedom" inherent in market exchanges has, for the majority of the population, been narrowed down to consumer choices between commodities offered on the market. This is a freedom only to choose from what is handed out, not to determine or change the conditions of one's life. Similarly, with respect to the state in which the "national identity" is determined by citizens and their representatives (rather than partial groups), the claims of freedom and equality do not apply across the board. There are internal centers and peripheries and an unequal economy dominated by the leading commercial interests.

These two main social institutions of economy and state give rise to corresponding institutionalist positions on the proper role of communications in society. The market-oriented perspective suggests that communication is simply a commodity like any other that is best organized through the free trade. State-oriented perspectives tend to argue that at least a modicum of government regulation is necessary to avoid the excesses of an exclusively market-oriented approach. Public discussion of communication systems tends to be confined within these two perspectives; the choice seems to be limited to either state regulation or the unregulated market. However, this choice is severely circumscribed and tends to obscure the relations of power stemming from both the market and the state which strongly influence the development of contemporary communications systems.

I want to argue that the inadequacy of these two institutionalist perspectives on culture becomes particularly evident with the contemporary coincidence of culture and economy in the information society. Through an analysis of the present reduction of culture to information a third position can be justified. Rooted in a critique of institutions—especially economy and state—this position centers on the *inherently local* source of culture in oral encounters, and seeks to articulate the silences that have fallen on "localities" in the shadow of these dominant institutions.

Consider this typical description of the "information revolution" taken from a Canadian government report: "The extraordinary evolution and diffusion of information technology since the Second World War is the second major manifestation of the information revolution. Such technology is the product of a melding between computer and communications technologies—a convergence which has created powerful systems with vast capabilities for computation, analysis and access to enormous amounts of information."[3] This and other reports typically mention concerns of national sovereignty, privacy, and freedom versus ownership of information, and, more generally, often refer to the potential effect of new information technologies in increasing the already widespread sense of alienation and powerlessness. Despite these warnings, it is also typical to suggest that these dangers posed by the information revolution can be managed so as to provide virtually unmitigated benefits and, lest we remain unconvinced, they hasten to assure us that the present transition is, in any case, inevitable.[4] Such reports provide a convenient example of the confining of public discussion to the two main institutional perspectives. Their argument is a vacillation between the relative merits of unimpeded market forces and state intervention through public policy. It is usually assumed that these two institutional forces can be harmonized to produce a beneficial effect, but, most importantly in the present context, it is an unquestioned presupposition that the institutions of state and economy set the parameters within which discussion of "benefits and dangers" must take place. This presupposed ideological limitation of discussion results from the almost unquestioned power of market and state institutions and results in an impressionistic and unclarified notion of "information" that is at work in public discussions. It is common in this government policy milieu to describe information simply as the convergence of computer and communications technologies.

If, however, one is to go beyond these two institutionalist positions on postmodern culture, the notion of information has to be understood not only as a convergence of technology and communication, but as the specific configuration of cultural life corresponding to the contemporary world-system. Moreover, this is a configuration which involves the reduction of all present and past culture to information and thereby involves a unique endangerment of cultural identities. For a critical social theory, the notion of information itself must be clarified and criticized.

The basic bit of information from which the massive computerized information-processing systems are built up is a binary option—a yes/no or on/off choice. All culture that can be coded in this form is a multiplication of such minute choices to complex arrangements, or patterns, which *represent* the cultural content that has been thus coded. This content can then be trotted out whenever those in control of the information think it appropriate. Such binary coding is the microcosmic analogue of consumer choice, which is a choice between goods arrayed in front of an individual subject. There are two main aspects of such a choice: First, the choice *between* finished goods excludes the consumer from the process of making goods and deciding what goods will be made. Second, the consumer-subject is not required to *justify* his or her choice; it is arbitrary in the precise sense that it is not necessarily subject to discussion of its presuppositions or influence on the *context* of other consumer choices—whether by the same or another subject. Thus, the cumulative effect of these choices on the individual and on society is outside consideration, as is the making process itself. It would require an overarching sense of cultural identity to situate such choices within a historically and geographically specific identity-formation, but the reduction of culture to information excludes such an overarching sense of culture and leaves the cumulative effect of consumer choices and the process of making culturally unassimilated. Culture as information excludes the *designing* of alternatives by *self-forming identities*, whether of individuals and groups. Information is both the contemporary state of culture and the reduction of culture, since culture in the genuine sense requires not only isolated choices but the *formation* of individuals and groups through *expressions* which communicate specific experiences and their interpretations which are interwoven with daily praxis.

Computer processing is based on binary coding, or digitalization, but binarism isn't the central cultural characteristic of information. The above critique, which centers on the connection between binarism and consumerism, is valid only for those who are "inside" the information systems enough for their cultural understanding to be formed by binarism. While this is by no means a negligible effect, the reduction of culture to information affects the rest of us in a more complicated and pervasive fashion. Though binarism is key for the internal functioning of computers, the functioning of computers as a medium of communication mediating human experience is actually more influenced by manifest characteristics such as the video screen, keyboard, and so forth. First of all, one should note that computer processing is not the first sophisticated binary system of communication and therefore its cultural effect is not limited to contemporary societies. The recoding of culture as information is actually a deep-rooted possibility inherent in the reflexive capacity of culture itself. To take one example, Walter Ong has described the binarism of African drums which operated among and between hundreds of different cultures in sub-Saharan Africa.[5] There were elaborate systems of relays set up from village to village that allowed messages to be carried for extremely large distances. The talking drums were based on a tonal language of two tones, a binarism. Any drum will provide at least two basic tones—when struck in the middle as opposed to being struck on the edge. A more sophisticated method involves two drums, which were normally referred to as male and female.

In this medium of communication, a word is translated into a binary code. That binary code has a couple of problems. First of all, the word is easy to miss. If you miss hearing the first part, it becomes something else. So it must be repeated. Second, the words themselves are not sufficiently complex structures, so rather than using a single word one uses a stock phrase, which is characteristic of orality. Instead of banging out "tree" one bangs out a much more complicated and lengthy stock phrase such as "the heavy oak tree down by the river" whose pattern will be recognizable even if it is not caught in its entirety. This is a characteristic that is similar to computers. When something is translated into a binarism, it becomes much longer. The very long phrases on the talking drums allow the communication to issue in a continuous drumming. The length and the repetition "disambiguate," in Ong's phrase, the sounds which might be misunderstood if only a short phrasing were heard. While one may think of language as composed of simple phrases and as becoming more complicated with the addition of more phrases, Ong describes a system of communication which is initially ambiguous but adds to itself to achieve clarity. Ong finds the characteristics of the talking drums to be characteristic of orality in general. If effort has regularly to be put into disambiguating meaning, innovative use of different stock phrases or different forms of phrasing is just a lot of noise. It will interfere with and retard the whole process; so there is a conservatism built into this medium of communication.

The point of this example of oral binarism is that binarism is not confined to the binarism of computers. This system doesn't share many of the characteristics of computers, but it is indeed a binarism, from which we may conclude that binarism as such is neither a specific nor thorough description of the electronic or computer world. In comparing the talking drums with computers, Ong points out that the drums do not *store* information, but simply transmit it.[6] It is the initial process of storing that is the key to the four main parts of the electronic medium: (encoding and) storage, processing, transmission, and retrieval (and decoding). Since one can't store either writing or speech directly into the computer, it has to be encoded to be stored. Similarly, with retrieval, there has to be decoding. Somebody receiving a computer disk on which information is stored does not really adequately retrieve. It has to be retrieved in a form like language or speech. Encoding and decoding are intrinsic to storage and retrieval.

From these four parts one can schematize the political concerns that arise in connection with information. The question of *access to* information arises at the point of retrieval. Once it's stored, who can get it out? There is also a politics of storage, though often its distinctness from the problem of access is not noticed. Here the question is who can collect information about whom, or who can *put information in*. In some union agreements, for example, one has the right to put something into one's personnel file, even though one can't take out any information. There is a politics of both retrieval and storage. Third, there is also a politics of transmission. The most clear-cut and debated example of this is transborder data flows. Can information that is collected in one place be used in another place? One example of this is the collecting of information on mineral deposits from satellites, which can then be used for buying of rights on land. Often this information is not known to the people who are selling the land or making the decisions about the land. All the information involved in transborder data flows involves the question of access, but it is also a question of moving information over a border and into another jurisdiction. Is there, to turn to the fourth aspect, a politics with regard to processing? Once information has been stored, is there a politics about how it can be processed? If there isn't, there will be soon enough. For example, as lectures get increasingly recorded, lecturers become increasingly unnecessary—especially if the lectures are made in one context, say for a small class of thirty people, and reused in a much larger context, for example broadcast over television. Who owns the recording? Will there be royalties? Could the lecturer stop publication? Similarly, writers' associations in Europe and Canada are pressing their governments and international regulatory bodies to extend writers' rights to electronic copying. Such a politics of processing will become increasingly important in the next few years. The concept of information involves four aspects—encoding/storage, processing, transmission, and retrieval/decoding. There are important political issues at each of these four points already being contested in the information society.

To come to an even more fundamental point, the four parts of information presuppose something prior that is encoded and stored. Reprocessing of previous cultural productions, the processing of culture turned into information, is substituted for production of culture. Indeed, the very idea of originality comes into disrepute. There are two implications of this. First, there is a "crowding out" phenomenon. As culture is reprocessed, transmitted over large areas, and retrieved by increasing numbers of people, less originality is needed. One doesn't need sixteen zillion rock groups—about fifteen will do it for the whole world. The loss of the importance of local musicians is very important; it is in the first place primarily a problem of economics. If people cannot make their living from being musicians unless they are as good as what can be heard on some recorded facility, there will be fewer musicians in all. A further aspect of this is the general loss of amateurism. It is not necessary for everyone to be able to play an instrument, as was the case, for example, in my mother's Cockney family only one generation ago. Then, everybody wasn't expected to be good; they were just expected to be able to play, so that when Saturday night came around people wouldn't be bored out of their brains. They could always say, "Give us a song." The loss of amateurism is really a fundamental feature of our contemporary society and it's a great tragedy. A second consequence is the proliferation of reproductions. Culture tends towards more and more recyclings of stuff that's already there, rather than productions. This is part of what is at issue in contemporary discussions of postmodernism and popular culture. We seem to be losing the idea of originality itself, the idea that one can articulate a genuine statement about the world in which one lives. One can speak of this contemporary situation as a "reduction" of culture since information-processing does not *generate* culture in the genuine sense of a primal scene but *presupposes* its historical and geographical formation and expression. The processing of cultural heritages is a parasitical recording of their content within a form which blocks their assimilation. All culture can be coded, but codes do not exhaust culture.

While previous expressions of cultural experience can be reprocessed as information, the character of information-culture is most apparent when it codes the world directly. Since the origin of industrial culture in the photograph, its tendency has been to process the world without the intervention of the *interpretations* that prior cultural expressions required. To be sure, someone holds the camera and presses the switch, but such activities do not require mediation by a process of assimiliation and interpretation such as that required by a novel, a poem, or even—though in reduced form—contemporary journalism. This unmediated character of iconic images accounts for their force, as well as their tendency to repel reflection. An iconic, or directly representational, image is an ensemble of binary bits of information whereby the worldly event is duplicated as culture. The binary translation and mechanical reproduction of a direct imprint from the world produces an image that resembles the chosen segment of the world. In such images, society confirms itself; and confirms itself, confirming itself; and so on. Images replace the critical transcendent element in traditional cultural expressions, which include interpretations and thus demand to be reinterpreted, with a process of continual iteration of images that tends towards a self-enclosed system of signs. The image is bounded and abstracted in space and time. While it derives from worldly experience, image-making consists in cutting off the continuousness of the world in both space and time. An event in the world is *preceded and followed* by other events in a continuous flow which provides the experiential basis and motivation for understanding the event. Similarly, an event occurs in a *particular place* surrounded by others which puts it "on the map" of a wider experience of the world. This twofold continuity is shattered by the image due to the technological process which imprints and reproduces it. The image is a coincidence of technology and communication in an abstracting and duplicating procedure which achieves a direct coding of the world as information.

The reduction of culture to information in a planetary culture poses the danger of losing the very origination of culture itself. There are the emergent four politics within information society, but there is also a more fundamental politics about the meaning of this age itself. We may forget what culture is and create it only by accident and only occasionally. It seems unlikely that humans can live without creating culture at all, but we may be in the unhappy position of experimenting to find out. Thus, the fundamental question posed by the information culture is not this *versus* that identity—a question posed as a consumer choice or as an enlargement of the range of commodities available to consumer choice. It is the question of "identity" as "loss of identity," of a culture of anonymity, the production of *silences*. It is not basically an issue of "access to" information, or even "production of" information, but of information as the loss of the historical and geographic *fundament* of cultural experience inherent in primal scenes. The continuousness of worldly experience in space and time requires expressions to incorporate interpretations, which then call forth further interpretations and generate a contextually specific dialogue that reflexively constitutes cultural identities in an ongoing tradition. This fundament of expression is uniquely endangered in the planetary information age. Consequently, such local expressions have an important critical function as the undoing of a universality that denies particularity and issues in dispossession and silences. Moreover, without one's own particular culture, one is not able to move into a genuine dialogue with other cultures, but is *dispossessed*, cut off at the root, which allows the information culture to expand unimpeded.

CHAPTER 8

Representation versus Constitution

The erosion of the institutional separation of economics and politics during the twentieth century requires a conception of the cultural logic at the center of the whole process of social reproduction. Instead, communication is generally understood as a certain set of objects whose function is social representation—television, newspapers, and the like. The ideology of objectivity attributed to the functioning of this set of objects denies the productive role of media in the prevailing cultural logic and thereby serves to keep it disguised and depoliticized. The most basic claim in such an ideology of objectivity is that media are purely and simply representational, in other words, *media simply represent* events previously existing in the world. At present, we need to go beyond representation to the recognition that *media constitute reality*, that media are constituents of the social world. Whereas the representational function of media derives from its position in modern society, the constitutive function of media can be called postmodern.

From this perspective, Marshall McLuhan's media theory is an important point of departure. He viewed media of communication as technologies that extend and develop the capacities of the human body. Thus, the bodily capacity for movement by walking is externalized in technologies of transportation such as bicycles, automobiles, airplanes, and so forth. As we externalize our capacities, we remove them from the exercise of our

101

own bodies; McLuhan called this an auto-amputation. The development of media technologies is thus a continuous process of altering the environment by amputating our human capacities and delegating them to media. The characteristics of these media are the significant elements in cultural change. Whatever their content, the media are potent constituents of culture. For example, McLuhan is not interested in what is on television (why these programs rather than those programs?), but in the significance of television as a medium of communication in defining the cultural environment and thereby the perception of individuals. This is the meaning of the slogan "the medium is the message." Media do not have a definite content for McLuhan, rather they define and convey the perceptual patterns crystallized in previous media. The "content" of TV is the play, the public announcement, and the con artist. What is new about TV is its form, the technological alteration of perceptual experience, and its influence on the whole media environment—which includes also other media such as film, speech, computers, and so on. This starting-point recognizes the significance of media in constituting social reality (not merely representing it), a recognition that is particularly important in our media-saturated era, though it is not confined to it.

In the critique of Marshall McLuhan's media theory by Raymond Williams there is an instructive confrontation between a postmodern theory of media and a Marxist theory that recognizes the constitutive power of communication. McLuhan's approach to media can be called postmodern because it does not situate media within any larger totality but uses the plurality of media itself as the basis for an investigation of culture. Communication is the figuration of culture. For Williams, on the other hand, media of communication are a force of production. He regarded it as a major failure of traditional Marxism that it has relegated issues concerning communication to the superstructure and, consequently, a second-order process, thereby missing "the inherent role of means of communication in every form of production, including the production of objects."[1] Analysis of this role of media of communication must therefore be undertaken with a view to the larger totality of the capitalist mode of production.

In this debate I want to focus on two main issues. First, the charge by Williams that McLuhan is a technological determinist; second, the notion of continuous, planned flow that Williams sees as characteristic of video experience. Williams claims that social institutions provide the limits and pressures within which a technology of communication develops and therefore determine the content of the medium, the uses to which it is put, and its effects.[2] Consequently, he charges McLuhan with technological determinism, that is, with leaving out of consideration these social institutions to make it appear as if the technology itself were the cause of its uses and effects.[3] Williams notes, for example, that the development of radio technology was first as a person-to-person transmission. This sending of private messages from one source to one receiver and back is characteristic of private media now in use, such as the telephone. This use is identical to the transmission model discussed above, with the single exception that the destination by turns becomes the source, thereby constituting a continuous circuit. Radio technology, however, was easily adapted to the model of broadcasting. Broadcasting is a medium of communication coming from one centralized source, dispersed widely in a society, and received by a number of widely dispersed, private receivers which do not rebroadcast back to the source. It can be diagrammed this way:

$$\text{source} \rightarrow \text{transmitter} \rightarrow \text{signal} \rightarrow \text{receiver} \rightarrow \text{destination}$$
$$\text{receiver} \rightarrow \text{destination}$$
$$\text{receiver} \rightarrow \text{destination}$$
$$\text{receiver} \rightarrow \text{destination}$$
$$\text{etc.}$$

This model of broadcasting is of course the dominant, though not the only, model of communication in contemporary society. Williams points out that since the technology in both cases is the same, the shift from the model of person-to-person private transmission to a broadcasting model has to be explained in terms other than technological ones.[4] He argues that it is the influence of social institutions that has made the broadcasting model prevail in radio and, by extension, has made television be used on a broadcasting model. A similar point could be made with regard to new business uses of the telephone. Aside from referring to capitalist society in general, Williams gives more specificity to the form of social practice in the post-war period through the notion of "mobile privatization."[5] Mobile privatization describes a society of capitalist, industrial production co-existing with a private mode of consumption— primarily, within the family. The combination between highly organized and developed capitalist production and highly isolated and dispersed familial consumption requires bridging the potential tensions inherent in this relationship. These tensions are bridged, according to Williams, by media of communication in the form of broadcasting, primarily television. Broadcasting is thus a condensation of general social structures and practices, but also a response to tensions in those practices that smooths them over.

There are three problems with technological determinism, according to Williams. The first and most general, noted above, is that there is no notion of "real social practices" or the influence of social institutions on the development of a technology. Second, because of this lack of a notion of social institutions, there is no notion of "intention." It is individuals and social institutions that have intentions, and that design technologies for certain purposes.[6] Third, because there is no notion of intention, there is no analysis of media content by McLuhan. A technological determinist sees society as simply an abstract totality, not as a concrete totality. Society seems to act rather than certain groups within society whose intentions and interests are at variance with those of other groups. This emphasis on the opposed interests of groups with different intentions is, of course, the Marxist component of Williams's theory.

In order to assess Williams's critique, we might ask whether he presents an adequate view of McLuhan's theory. The short answer is no. There is a notion of intention in McLuhan. The first use of a technology is always the result of a social group pursuing a defined purpose that has become thematic in cultural life, but McLuhan goes on to claim that a medium of communication has two cultural effects, a first effect and a later one that is a reversal of the first. The first effect is due to the fact that a technology is introduced by specific social groups in order to fulfil intentions that they already have. The new medium is thus filled up with a previously defined content which it presents in a new fashion. This function of a medium may be called "representation" insofar as its function is limited to a new manner of presenting a prior cultural content. McLuhan is not very interested in this first effect, while Williams certainly is—though it is interesting that he noticed that "in the earliest stages there was the familiar parasitism on existing events."[7] Williams and McLuhan thus seem to agree that the first use of television is carried over from previous media of communication. For Williams a decisive move occurred when television shifted from broadcasting discrete works, characteristic of previous media such as cinema or theatre, to offering a "whole social intake"[8] which seems clearly dependent on its use in the private home. It is at this point that it becomes important to analyze exactly what the distinctiveness of video experience is, what we might call the phenomenology of watching television. This is the second topic of the debate: Williams's notion of video experience as a continuous, planned flow.[9]

To describe video experience Williams appeals to what he calls our "normal experience" of television. We tend not to watch one separate show but rather to "watch television." Our way of speaking about the activity indicates that it is in relation to the medium, not in relationship to various sorts of content on the medium. Also, television, once it is on, is hard to switch off. In order to explain this, he makes a general contrast between previous media of communication and television. Previous media dealt with separated, isolated events. One might go to a sports game, a theatre, a film, a public speech, and so forth, in which there was a distinct beginning, duration, and end of the event. Usually, one had to leave one's home, partake of the event, and return to one's home. Even in the case of a novel, the separate sequences in which one is reading are imaginatively put together and separated from the normal activities of life. Different occasions such as these in which one attends a specific event involve specific and characteristic distinct forms of attention on the part of the viewers. Also, the social relations set up by the medium are specific and temporary. These are discrete events, bounded and separated from the general flow of experience in everyday life. In contrast, television experience is a flow assembled from separate pieces. There are a number of factors that have led to this development. In the early days of television there tended to be more clearly marked transitions between the different parts of the broadcast. There were station breaks and even dead time. Now the transitions between the different segments of a television broadcast are continuous and unmarked. The flow of any particular event, or content, is continuously broken up by advertisements, announcements of future shows, etc. The actual sequence on television is thus a new kind of unity constructed from the juxtaposition of diverse contents. Thus, the experience of watching television is constructed from the resonation of messages from different "contents" with each other such that the real messages on TV have to be interpreted from the resonances rather from specific shows or announcements. For example, Williams says that the messages about drugs that are presented in the anti-drug commercials resonate with the messages about drugs in dramatizations and in advertisements for drugs and so forth. Consequently, the message that television actually makes is not an anti-drug statement; it is a statement against illegal drugs but very much in favor of legal drugs. Similarly, the dominant message is against non-legitimate violence, but not against violence as such.

The new form of unity characteristic of the television viewing experience makes television hard to shut off and the new unification of discrete, isolated events makes it difficult to interpret the flow as a whole. There is a tendency to be pulled into the flow, which discourages the critical distance that would allow one to analyze the flow as a whole which consists of a rapid succession of images. There is a new relation between whole and part in video experience. The smallest unit is the image, not the program, and images are combined across programs. The largest unity is, of course, the continuous planned flow as a whole. This leads to a general gullibility with regards to issues pertaining to the totality of experience as a whole and a focus of intention purely within a given flow, rather than to the characteristics of the flow itself. We may say then, if the planned flow realizes the possibilities inherent in video as a medium, then the extent to which programming is replaced by a succession of images is an index of the degree of development or realization of television as a medium of communication.

This focus on the phenomenology of viewing, which allows Williams to characterize the continuous, planned flow of television, provides the closest convergence between Williams and McLuhan. It is the second effect in McLuhan's sense, the one most characteristic of video itself. But while Williams traces this back to social decisions to produce a unified intake and the domestic setting of television viewing, for McLuhan it is a consequence of the reversal effect of the technology. As a medium is developed the technology improves, and the perceptual and sensual auto-amputation that it achieves is progressively more successful, requiring less and less active participation from the viewer. In McLuhan's terminology a medium "heats up" over time and accelerates the externalization of human capacities. Moreover, the technology becomes more widespread and affects more pervasively the whole cultural environment. It no longer simply represents a previous content, but becomes a significant new form of experience itself. In short, it becomes a constituent of a changed cultural order. This constituent role is not simply different from the first—a more limited effect—but *reverses* it. This reversed use is not predictable and is not traceable back to the intention of those who designed the technology. For example, the road was initially a means of transport between cities, but has now come to define the inner organization of cities themselves. War was initially a conflict on the edge of communities, but has come to define the inner structure of societies themselves through a constant military preparedness in the name of national security.[10]

McLuhan's notion of a second, reversed effect of a medium of communication is an example *avant la lettre* of Jacques Derrida's notion of a supplement, which was developed through a reading of Rousseau on writing. The first, representational use of a medium needs the second in order to be completed in the sense that television has not come into its own if it broadcasts on the model of a sporting event. In a similar fashion, a supplement is needed to complete an original in Derrida's description. Thus, the original contains a lack, is not fully itself, and comes into itself only with the addition of a supplement that is outside itself. As Derrida says, the logic of supplementarity is that "the outside be inside," "that what adds itself to something takes the place of a default in the thing," and that the default "should be already within the inside."[11] For investigation of a medium of communication, it is the default that is more interesting than the supposed defined characteristics of a medium. Why is it that a medium's use continually changes in a manner that takes it closer to itself, not further, but has no teleology (the earlier is not improved by the later form)? The supplement unsettles the presumption of a self-sufficient inside, or origin, that is characteristic of metaphysics. "One wishes to go back from the supplement to the source: one must recognize that there is a supplement at the source."[12] Neither origin nor goal can be normative, only the process of alteration. This logic, be it called supplementarity or heating up, emerges whenever one thematizes a medium within a context that is not assumed as determinate, but is constituted by other media. It contains three terms—content, medium, context—in which the investigation of each term returns one to the others, i.e., a relational definition: Content is a previous medium; a medium is the totality of its effects on the context; the context is a media environment defined through the interaction of a plurality of media.

As a technology improves and increasingly comes to pervade the environment, it reaches what McLuhan calls a "break boundary" in which the initial effect is reversed and the medium plays a constituent role in defining a new mode of perception and social relationship. Not only does this occur with each medium of communication, it also occurs to the whole process of communication itself when this process reaches a break boundary. The externalization of human capacities in media technologies comes to a break boundary when the most basic capacity of the body is externalized. The nervous system, the means of coordination of capacities in the human body, is externalized in the electric age. Not only capacities, but what coordinates them into a functioning whole, is externalized. The patterning and coordinating function of the nervous system is auto-amputated and externalized into the global system of automation. At this point the extension of human capacities through technologies comes to a break boundary. Having expanded, or "exploded," to its farthest limit, the process reverses. Media technologies now "implode" to define the innermost capacities of the human individual, uniting each one in a coordinated global village.

The stepping up of speed from the mechanical to the instant electric form reverses explosion into implosion. In our present electric age the imploding or contracting energies of our world now clash with the old expansionist and traditional patterns of organization. . . . Obsession with the older patterns of mechanical, one-way expansion from centers to margins is no longer relevant to our electric world. Electricity does not centralize, but decentralizes.[13]

McLuhan's global village of unimpeded, multi-directional information flow is his utopian projection of the tendency of media of communication in the electric age. It has often, quite correctly, been criticized for ignoring the political and economic constraints under which this global system develops—though it has been less often pointed out that this central utopian theme is a specific polemical denial of the center-margin dependency theory from which Harold Innis developed his communication theory and which was very influential in the development of McLuhan's work. Nevertheless, he quite clearly saw that this state was not yet achieved and that the present era is as much defined by anxiety, unconsciousness, and apathy as by integral connection. Where global connection rules, the opposite tendency is toward total drop-out, a depth anxiety from which there is no escape. "Such amplification is bearable by the nervous system only through numbness or blocking of perception."[14] It is this tension between a total, free-flowing integration through information and a numbing anxiety of disconnection that is McLuhan's diagnosis of our present state as we enter the information age.

The difference between these two theories of communication can be characterized this way. McLuhan's model is that of an organism whose relation to its environment is mediated by technology. The history and interaction of technological mediations is thus the development of culture out of its source in the human body and toward reunification outside it. Williams focuses on the organization of social relations, or institutions, and argues that this is what is specific to one medium, or model, of communication over another. Beginning from the dominant broadcast model of a centralized transmitter and widespread availability of the message received privately by individual sets which do not return the signal (as described by Williams), it can be clearly defined what an alternative model of communication would be: the message would be sent from many different sources and the receiver would also be a sender. One would have a plurality of circuits. (It might also be that the message would not be designed to be received by everyone but by more specifically defined interest groups, though I think that this is a less central consideration.) At this point Williams argues that such possibilities are important possible alternative uses of video that are not determined by the technology.[15] His emphasis on social relations and power leads to a concern with the institutions within which media of communication develop and their influence on the content that is broadcast. However, when he comes to what is most unique about television, the emphasis on content decreases in favor of the rolling up of contents within a new experiential form. Social relations provide only the precondition for his phenomenological examination of the viewing experience, which seems entirely consistent with both McLuhan's approach and his theory. McLuhan's emphasis on the relation between organism and environment places great importance on technological mediations and their influence on the changing sense ratios of human perception that characterize the planned, continuous flow. However, McLuhan claims these characteristics for video outright and completely ignores the issue of other social forms within which this technology can be utilized—some of which are already apparent since the development of cheap video cameras.

Thus, with regards to the notion of social practices and institutions, it is clear that McLuhan does not investigate these in the manner that Williams or any Marxist would. Nevertheless, if we ask the question of what constitutes a given state of society, McLuhan does have an answer. The given state of society is produced by the current state of the translations between a given plurality of media of communication. That is, unlike a Marxist view which would see society as constituted by the mode of production, for McLuhan society is organized through the means of communication. It is not a technological determinism, as Williams claims, because the reversal of a medium's effect is not an internal consequence of the technology, but a consequence of the relation of the technology to the cultural environment as a whole (constituted by translations between a plurality of media). Williams makes a clear distinction between broadcasting and private reciprocal transmission use as different media of communication because they incorporate different social relations within their structure. Nevertheless, he would say that both uses of radio or television involve the same technology.

Technology, as understood by Williams, is restricted to hardware and in this sense is contrasted to communication which involves social relations. It is this understanding of technology in a popular sense as simply hardware that can, of course, contrast the same hardware being used in different ways. On this point, Williams seriously misunderstands and misinterprets McLuhan, whose understanding of technology is far wider and deeper than this, since it developed from the communication literature which focuses on the concept of medium from which I have developed the notion of a "primal scene." For McLuhan, a technology is not simply hardware, it is the explicit purpose thematized against the background of culture. But there is no distinction between a medium of communication and a technology in McLuhan, as there was not in Innis. Thus, the social relations involved in a medium are attributed to the technology itself and the possibility of alternative models of communication is obscured. While it is necessary to remain attentive to this component of Williams's critique of McLuhan, exploration of the contemporary media environment and its tranformations of experience has a better starting-point in McLuhan's postmodern theory.

The media environment is comprised of a plurality of media which together constitute the contemporary cultural order. Media are not isolated from each other but refer to each other continuously. For example, there is a sense in which an event seen on television, read about in a newspaper, and told about by an eyewitness, is the same event. If we consider media representationally, this is simply because all the media *refer to the same event* that exists in the world outside media representations; but when we consider media as constitutive of cultural order, this comparison of media representations to "real" events is not possible. The identity of the event in this case is not based on its "reality" prior to representations, and one may doubt whether there is any longer such a single, unified event behind its appearance in many media constitutions. However, on reflection, a certain unity of the event is established by the mutual "translation" of various media versions. Media continuously translate each other; thus, they constitute an *environment*, rather than a simple plurality.

Postmodern society is constituted by a media environment characterized by the continuous circulation of signs and messages. Postmodernity is the emergence of a continuous, non-hierarchical, flow of experience whose meaning does not seem to be self-generating and whose totality is virtually impossible to conceptualize. Its politics reside more in the conflict between the planning, or staging, of this experience by powerful social institutions versus the possibility of its self-organization, than in a global acceptance or rejection of this emergent experiential flow itself.[16] The distinctions between reality and a model, or a map and the territory, which are representational distinctions, become insufficient to grasp the "simulation" of signs by the media. They are not copies of "real" events, but the simulation of media events that produce real social relationships—the simulations have become a constitutive primal scene. Even material objects such as commodities are drawn into simulation through the mediascape. They function through their sign-value, which is the translation of every medium of communication into information.

Information can therefore be described as the universal translation of communication which proposes a new stage of human culture. In this vein McLuhan said that "previous technologies were partial and fragmentary, and the electric is total and inclusive. An external consensus or conscience is now as necessary as private consciousness. With the new media, however, it is also possible to store and to translate everything; and, as for speed, that is no problem."[17] Information is thus the reprocessing of all the previous content of culture and situating it within a mediascape of simulation. Whereas McLuhan sees a new utopian possibility for communication here because of its unprecedented universal scope, on closer examination a far more ominous situation is emerging. Indeed, everyone is potentially included in the new coding of culture, but the form of this inclusion is determined by the specific character of its universal translation. Far from allowing "participation," the responses demanded by contemporary media systems are provoked by previously defined questions. In Jean Baudrillard's words,

> no contemplation is possible. The images fragment perception into successive sequences, into stimuli toward which there can be only instantaneous response, yes or no—the limit of an abbreviated reaction. Film no longer allows you to question. It questions you, and directly. Montage and codification demand, in effect, that the receiver construe and decode by observing the same procedure whereby the work was assembled. The reading of the message is then only a perpetual examination of the code.[18]

In short, the production, reprocessing, and exchange of the coded messages serves to introject the code into the receiver. The code has been severed from the life-practices which produce meaning and closed into a self-referring system. In order to close the system it requires the turning of switches that complete the circuit. The code interrogates the receiver and returns the minimal yes/no messages, recoded as inputs, into the simulation system.

The role of this interrogation-function in information as constitutive of social relationships is to form all social groupings increasingly on the model of "masses." Masses have no direct relationship to each other;

they are connected only by their role in being interrogated. They are a series, rather than a group, in Sartre's terminology. Yes/no inputs are their life-line to social life. Their compulsory participation completes and closes the code. For Baudrillard, the "implosion" of the media destroys all distance between social subjects, the "one" and the "other," which is necessary for them to initiate communication and thereby constitute culture. The mass is the indistinct plurality of points of input, who have no relation between themselves, whose relation is only simulated as a side-effect of the media system. "There is no longer any polarity between the one and the other in the mass. This is what causes that vacuum and inwardly collapsing effect in all those systems which survive on the separation and distinction of poles (two, or many in more complex systems). This is what makes the circulation of meaning within the mass impossible: it is instantaneously dispersed, like atoms in a void."[19] The implosion of universal translation and simulation destroys locations from which there could be social relationships and the give and take that produces meaning. Implosion shatters relationship and thereby meaning. The most basic feature of culture is eradicated when sign-systems circulate divorced from any meaning for those within the system. It seems that one no longer uses media of communication to say what one means, but rather one becomes a simulated effect of a system that itself produces its own inputs.

The tendency of postmodern culture is to simulate society by shattering meaning in the reprocessing of cultural remnants. It is like a genetic code, in which there is no distinction between the code and the "real" effect of the code. The map simulates the territory in the hyperreal geography of effects that produce their causes. What comes first is the code, which spurts forth its effects; content is irrelevant; in every case it is the code that is its own message, produces its own audiences, and simulates social relationships that howl for another fix of the code. Information is the interrogation of the masses by the code which simulates hyper-reality.

The transportation model of communication, including information theory and cybernetics, becomes ideological by treating communication merely in its representative dimension and disregarding its simultaneous (and at present more important) constitutive dimension. While media can be analyzed as *referring* to social life, as mirroring it well or badly, they also *produce* social relationships. Any communication has both of these dimensions—representation and constitution. Moreover, these are not merely separate dimensions that could be properly understood in isolation from each other. Every representation is simultaneously a constitution. Media as constitutive of the cultural code posit a representation that refers outside itself to an original that supposedly precedes simulation. Understanding media beyond representation requires acknowledging the constitutive role of primal scenes of communication media, but also that the representative role is produced in constitution.

CHAPTER 9

Consumer Identities

The implosion of media toward the construction of identities through the code of consumption has historical preconditions. The destruction of traditional forms of identity-formation and social solidarity is necessary for these processes to devolve upon the consumer code. As Marx and Engels pointed out in *The Communist Manifesto*, the capitalist mode of production and exchange requires a continuous revolutionizing of the mode of life. "All fixed, fast-frozen relations, with their train of ancient and venerable prejudices and opinions, are swept away, all new-formed ones become antiquated before they can ossify."[1] On this basis, traditional forms of identity-formation can be passed over to other, newer processes: first, to the site of production, upon which the Marxist political project was articulated, and then, to the process of consumption. Thus, while the *figure* of consumer society is the simulation of identities, its *ground* is the dissolution of all previous and stable identities. The simulation begins from lack, though it produces excess. Modernity can be defined as the domination of nature to produce a wealth of commodities intended to sustain a community of mutually recognizing free and equal subjects. Postmodern culture consists, not in discarding this project, but in its infinite delay. The apogee of the modern project in the simulation of identities in consumer society short-circuits the mutual recognition of autonomous subjects. The accumulation of greater and greater "means" to the modern goal of wealth and mutual recognition permanently delays arrival at the end. The end remains as the motive for perpetuation of the means, which in turn delays the end—a vicious dialectic without hope of resolution.

Walter Benjamin's essay "The Work of Art in the Age of Mechanical Reproduction" (originally published in 1936) has become an essential reference point for subsequent discussions of mass culture and the industrial production of identity. He described the specific difference between traditional artworks and mechanically reproduced cultural products as the loss of an "aura" that attaches to originals and unifies the historical process of reception. Originals radiate an authenticity, an aura, stemming from the origin of art in mythic cult. Aura is a "unique phenomenon of a distance, however close it may be" which is the basis for the empathy of the traditional aesthetic subject with the artwork. The mechanically reproduced artwork puts "the public in the place of the critic." Nevertheless, this position is "absent-minded" and requires no attention; it is "consummated by a collectivity in a state of distraction." In contrast to traditional aesthetics, which is focused on the artworks themselves, mechanical reproduction shifts the emphasis to reception—which dovetails with the Marxist stress on the historical and class formation of the audience. With this convergence of the social and aesthetic dimensions of the artwork we have the beginning of cultural criticism as the analysis of the formation of (social and individual) subjectivity through the production of meaningful objects. Loss of aura due to mechanization accounted, for Benjamin, for the democratic potential of contemporary politicized art to reverse the entire historical division of labor originating in the mythological power of the shaman. This potential is in tension with the other main tendency of mechanical culture—the aesthetization of politics, regarding politics as a spectator sport for the viewer's pleasure which leads to war and the fascist manipulation of masses. The cultural object has lost its distance from the viewer and functions directly as a constituent of identity.[2]

For Theodor Adorno, Benjamin erred in describing this momentous cultural shift solely in the mechanical apparatus. Rather, it was the development of the apparatus under the conditions of commodity production that gave rise to the contemporary tension. Aura has not been replaced, but rather shifted to a new mythology produced by the capitalist commodification of culture. Thus, the diagnosis of mass culture was extended from direct fascist manipulation to the generalized and anonymous subjugation of individuals by the cultural apparatus of industrial production for exchange.

Hence the style of the culture industry, which no longer has to test itself against any refractory material, is also the negation of style. The reconciliation of the general and the particular, of the rule and the specific demands of the subject matter, the achievement of which alone gives essential, meaningful content to style, is futile because there has ceased to be the slightest tension between opposite poles: these concordant extremes are dismally identical; the general can replace the particular, and vice versa.[3]

Industrial homogenization of culture reduces the transcendent experiences of traditional art within a totalizing framework that traps the audience into a repetition of experiences and thereby blocks their assimilation and criticism. Adorno proposes a modernist defence of avant-garde art as the marginalized site of individual opposition to mass culture. Through its individual style the avant-garde artwork generates a tension between particular and universal. The methods of transgression and shock transfer this tension to the viewer who can then experience the lack of fit between his or her individual needs and experiences and the total structure of society. Thus the possibility of social criticism is retained. Film is the litmus test of mass culture, where the total externalization of culture is an index of one's response to the interplay of technology and commodity production. For Adorno film simply repeats psychological mechanisms without leaving any room for distance and critique.

Benjamin saw a tension between the politicizing and aestheticizing tendencies of each medium, due to his emphasis on the technological component of this cultural shift, but Adorno situated these tendencies within the commodity-structure of the society as a whole, and thereby circumscribed the possibilities of identity-formation with the polarity of mass culture and the avant-garde. The debate here revolved around the relationship between technology and the commodity-form. Benjamin regarded the technology of mechanical reproduction as tending toward "critical collective abstractedness," though it could be offset by direct fascist manipulation of technology and the masses. For Adorno, the issue is not direct manipulation but production of cultural goods for exchange, which issues in indirect manipulation through the elimination of style. The tendency of technique (if it could be liberated from the commodity form), on the other hand, is toward the expression of the state of freedom in art; but this requires a sophisticated audience for avant-garde works; one which perceives the *structure* of the works, and is not just affected by them. What is fundamentally at issue between

Benjamin and Adorno is the extent to which the new possibilities brought forth by mechanical reproduction tend to become democratized through the mass audience, as Benjamin suggested, or whether they are marginalized by capitalist production processes which also create a regression in the perception of the audience.[4] For both it is the "loss of distance" that constitutes mass culture, though the potential of this for a critical audience is analyzed differently.

From the present perspective it is more enlightening, rather than entering this debate directly, to take note of the axes around which it is conducted in order to characterize the present situation, which has passed beyond the initial stage of mass culture analyzed by Benjamin and Adorno. The following discussion makes two observations—the first concerning technology and the second with respect to commodity production—that suggest that this debate must be reformulated to account for a new postmodern stage that has replaced mass culture.

While the Benjamin/Adorno formulation applies to the *decline* of aura due to the homogenizing effect of introducing industrial produc- tion methods into culture, it does not adequately capture the *simulation* of authenticity in fully industrialized cultural production. It is notable that Benjamin did not distinguish clearly between the mechanical repro- duction of previous artworks, such as the Mona Lisa, and the industrial production of cultural objects itself—which began with photography and now extends through electronic media of communication to perme- ate the whole of contemporary consciousness and identity-formation. But mechanical *reproduction* is not the same as technical *production*. Where he does note this distinction, it is in order to suggest it is a ques- tion of "greater degree," rather than a qualitative difference.

> To an ever greater degree the work of art reproduced becomes the work of art designed for reproducibility. From a photo- graphic negative, for example, one can make any number of prints; to ask for the "authentic" print makes no sense. But from the instant the criterion of authenticity ceases to be applic- able to artistic production, the total function of art is reversed. Instead of being based on ritual, it begins to be based on another practice—politics.[5]

The primacy of politics indicates that the audience's relation to the art- work has become fully conscious and rational. However, when the cul- tural world is completely pervaded by "copies" without "originals," it is impossible to regard them as "copies" any longer. We are faced simply with a plurality of images that are not simply identical but refer to each other. The many images of Mickey Mouse refer to each other, but we will not find the original at Disneyland, or at Disneyworld either. Even in the case of a supposed "original," the self-referring set of images precedes it. We recognize the Statue of Liberty because many images of it already pervade our cultural world. The experience of "originality" here has not declined, as Benjamin suggested, but is *simulated*.

We can describe this new postmodern experience of culture as follows: Circulation of a self-referring set of images constructs a cultural meaning, such as "liberty" or "Mickey Mouse-ness." We recognize and express our subjectivity as individuals and as groups through our relations to these image-sets. Of course, there are a lot of these. Especially in a consumer-oriented capitalist society, there are new image-sets continually becoming available. Thus, social differentiation within postmodern culture consists in different relations to this plurality of available image-sets. Each such image-set *postulates* an original, an authentic experience, that is not within the image-set itself but is created by it. Thus, the Statue of Liberty is immediately recognized by tourists who see it on the basis of a prior circulation of images. In this moment they confront an original and have an authentic experience of "liberty"— "authentic" in the sense that it is the image inherent in the image-set by which it is constructed. It works the same way with Mickey Mouse. In this sense at *both* Disneyland and Disneyworld one can experience the "real" Mickey Mouse. The singleness of the "original" is no longer important for the experience of authenticity, if it ever was. Authenticity requires "distance," that is, an experience of a cultural object which stands over against the viewer as a *source* of meaning, as not being at the audience's whim. Now, the subject is previously formed by the image-sets and is thereby confirmed in his or her cultural being by touristic pilgrimages to view originals. The closeness of the image-sets constructs the distance of the original; viewing the original confirms the relation to image-sets. It has become a closed and self-confirming cycle that reproduces the code.

In short, mechanical reproduction does not simply copy, which would be merely an acceleration of ancient mimesis and ritual repetition. As Benjamin noted, "in principle a work of art has always been reproducible."[6] Reproduction produces a "second"—another whose likeness to the first is not perfect. Only after the second can there be an issue of determining the "original." This characterization of postmodern experience here is consistent with Jacques Derrida's critique of metaphysics, in which a centered structure is only possible through the effacement of a play of differences. Only the "second" promotes the anxiety to *establish* an origin, a "first."[7] The first major diagnosis of mass culture rests on a loss of "authenticity" because industrial reproduction is still seen as mimicking an original—as the Mona Lisa in the subway ad hearks back to a Renaissance smile. But now there is no need to reproduce original artworks. Photography, film, all electronic media simply simulate the world. There is no copy, no original, neither firsts nor seconds. Authenticity is not lost, but *staged*.

The second observation that I want to make in this connection is concerned with commodity production and therefore applies more directly to Adorno's position. He argued that industrial production and exchange of commodities produces a homogenized mass of consumers of culture. "Now any person signifies only those attributes which he can replace everybody else: he is interchangeable, a copy. As an individual he is completely expendable and utterly insignificant."[8] More recently, however, subjection of the individual has given way to the stimulation of consumer choice from a bewildering array of cultural goods. Subjection has not been entirely replaced, but it has been overlaid by a simulation of the individual through uncoerced and unrelated choices from a plethora of industrially produced commodities. It is not so much goods that are for sale nowadays as lifestyles and here, it may well be, the inner logic of industrialism reaches its apogee: not goods *for* individuals, but "individuals" produced *through* the staging of goods. Cultural identities are produced industrially and exchanged at will. The earlier cultural homogeneity due to the uniformity of *production methods* has been displaced by a diversity of cultural identities focused on *consumer choice*.

If we put together these two observations, it may be suggested that the new postmodern era of mass culture be called "staged difference." The plurality of image-sets sets the stage for "authentic" experiences; commodities are produced for "individuals" who define themselves through their difference from other consumption groups. It is not so much the loss of distance from the object as the simulation of a distance within the self, of the self as other. The overlaying of the homogenization of mass culture by the staged difference of postmodern culture requires that the strategy of the avant-garde be similarly displaced; the historical avant-garde has become a consumer choice within a fractionated market. The total externalization of cultural and perceptual qualities in film is not simply introjected as a uniformity that can be subverted by the avant-garde, but as the self-recognition of an audience that identifies with this film, and more significantly this genre, *as opposed to* others known to be available. Similarly, the methods of shock and transgression only work if there is a bedrock of cultural identity to be roused to reflection and action. Without such a bedrock, they only reinforce cynicism, which is merely one stage in the cycle of postmodern culture. The general availability and uniformity of production for exchange has been displaced by the reproduction of individuals through simulated identities; the reproduction of the labor force through their time outside it, in the specific form of differentiated and mutable identities. This is a labor force suited to perform multifarious roles, including marginalization and unemployment, in a constantly shifting division of labor, but which does not aspire, in Marx's terms, to become the *subject* of production, or of culture either.

Beyond the first stage of mass culture, postmodern industrial culture is not a *repression* but a *simulation* of identity. There is no "alienation" from an original identity to which one can authentically "return." It is possible to interpret this development as a utopian surpassing of industrial specialization. However, against the ecstacies of McLuhan, electronic simulations do not "recombine" individuals separated by the division of labor and "mediate" a new face-to-face global village. Identities are no more coherent than a stacked deck of cards; technology and commodity production serve to define the rules by which we shuffle the deck. The dissatisfaction and anxiety produced by seeing one's identity available and increasingly adopted by many fuels attachment to renewed tokens of difference. In postmodern culture pleasure ensues from the release of anxiety in which identity is signaled by the consumption of differences. We desire our tokens of identity; they are not forced on us by industrial uniformity; we find ourselves in our simulated difference from others.

This cyclical character of postmodern consumer society can be illustrated through the present articulation of sports, masculinity, and militarism on television in the United States. Commercials broadcast during basketball and football games show images of men identified as army personnel performing athletic-type feats with good cheer. "Be the best you can be in the army," the jingle goes, as it associates sports stars with army recruits. The selection and combination of these images into a set produces a cultural meaning—a fantasy of masculine control, strength, and success—from whose circulation identities are formed. These identities are constructed through the association of sports and military service. Though such image-sets are not all-powerful and some may react against this identity, the constructed meaning is the basis from which they react. This association postulates an original masculinity "beneath" its expressions, which is supposed to transmit meaning to the expressions. Moreover, this postulated original seems to be available for "authentification" through confirming experiences apparently outside the image-set, but whose cultural meaning is actually constructed by it. For example, hunting, fishing, drinking, and so forth seem to be true expressions of the same masculinity that occur "outside" the media system. Thus, the media system *appears* to be confirming prior authentic experiences that it simply represents. This is, as demonstrated by the present analysis, merely apparent. The postulation of originals is accomplished by the image-set; therefore, the media system provides—or at least calls forth—its own confirming instances.

This account differs from that of Jean Baudrillard and other critics who focus on the construction of images insofar as the hermeneutic component of authenticating originals is not regarded as exploded or eliminated in the account that I have presented, but as itself constructed by the media system as a merely apparently outside. Therefore the ideology of media as realistic, as "merely reflecting a prior reality," is seen as essential to its present functioning and, most importantly, as imbedded in the concrete practices of both the media system and of individuals in their "own" activites. Many contemporary cultural critics lay emphasis, in polemical relation to traditional Marxism, on the contingency of the association of these images into sets. This seems overstated. One can imagine the difficulty of articulating together sports with cooking or ballet. The "solidity" of the historical accretions of culture that constrain associations needs a better account at this point. This presentation, through the account of postulation of originals, provides the basis for understanding this solidity based in the theory of media of communication.

No sooner does an event occur in advanced industrial culture than it is reproduced, simulated, commodified as an image, and devoured. Reproductions attract afficionados whose identity is invested in pleasure directed to simulated events. Through industrial duplication we become fractionated audiences of ourselves, contemplating our own identity as we search for a new original to authenticate our choices from the promiscuity of simulations. Thereby we open a distance within the self, regard the self as an "other" to be searched for and authenticated. Postmodern culture thrives on its own uncertainty. Availability reduces identity, fuels the postulation of originals, and allows us to recognize ourselves by bringing them closer, setting the stage for renewed dissatisfaction. The industrial production of identity is a cycle of pleasurable recognition and cynical dissatisfaction, reduplicated oscillations of novelty and boredom.

The system of internal differences in industrial society staged by the world of consumer goods is matched by an external difference from non-consumer industrial society. Encircling the system of simulated internal differences, in which the badge of our freedom is a glut of commodities, is the face of the other—the other whose opposition to the consumer society insinuates an insecurity in postmodern identities. Non-consumer identities are often treated as enemies because of this anxiety. Fear of the enemy outsider exerts a control on the internal system of differences. Postmodern culture is circumscribed by this unstable synthesis of consumption and otherness, pleasure and coercion. As the self becomes other through staged difference, the other becomes enemy. In the new social movements such as ecology, feminism, sexual minority movements, and local, regional and national liberation movements, we have the possibility of encountering the "other" beyond the destructive immobility of fear. It is in these movements that there is to be found the internal critique of consumer society.

Modernity is defined by two central affirmations: That nature is to be dominated as a means to human ends, and that human ends can be reconciled with each other through mutual recognition of free and equal subjects. If the two affirmations of modernity are questioned radically in the light of twentieth-century experience, the ground for their common articulation is eroded. The domination of nature has led to a profusion of commodities that cannot "fulfil human needs" because it has come to simulate identities. "Needs" simply ask for the system to be extended further. This internal dimension of consumer society is matched by an external one: Scientific-technical domination of nature is entwined with the eradication of all identities which are not simulated in consumption. Thus, the modern hope that the domination of nature would produce a society of autonomous and mutually recognizing subjects is no longer possible. While the central beliefs of modernity serve to extend and develop the system, instead of reaching its avowed goal they fuel the cycle of simulation and destruction of alternatives. New departures are required. Postmodern culture is this self-reproducing end-circuit of modernity. It consists of *staged difference*: The self becomes an other as a token authenticated by experiences postulated by image-sets. It demonstrates the failure of the modern search for free and equal autonomous subjects and requires a radical investigation of the formation of identity as relations of dependence between self and other. The metaphysical assumptions of the modern concept of the self can be discerned in two dimensions: Modernity is displacement, from which we project authentic origin—and, thereby, the goal of *reappropriation* of this origin; also, authentic self as against the difference of the other—and, thereby, the goal of *reconciliation* with this difference. Authenticity attempts to close the pain of displacement within a story of alienation which returns us to our origins and to others. The overcoming of alienation is a progress guaranteed by the domination of nature which produces a wealth of commodities. The future path of critical thought is anything but secure, but this option is now closed to us. Through this circumscription of postmodern consumer capitalist culture, we may begin to determine the contours of another path as expressed by the social movements which contest consumer identities.

Part III

SOCIAL MOVEMENTS

CHAPTER 10

Three Strategies of Resistance

The politics of media of communication as representative of events in the world centers on the question of access. Traditionally, political power undermined resistance by repression, by denying the power of expression. Power attempted to silence opposition, and criticism responded by demanding access. This form of repression still exists, surely enough, but it is not the main form of silencing of opposition in Western capitalist democracies. How is this silencing now produced through the simulations of consumer society? Opposition is not so much repressed as drowned out by the noise of mainstream media, understanding "media" to refer to the entire constitutive process of social communication through the primal scenes integrated in the production, transmission, and reproduction process of consumer society.

Monopolization of the media as the code of consumer society has undermined the crucial mediating role delegated to media of communication by liberalism. The question of access to media representations is by no means unimportant, but it remains insufficient unless it is based on a politics of media as constitutive of social identities in consumer society, and, thus, on an alternative form of identity-construction in the movements that are critical of consumer society. The construction of new anti-consumer identities in social movements is a part of their introduction of new primal scenes into the consumer code. How does this

127

politics of identity work such that social movements can articulate their criticism of consumer society?

We can broach this question by focusing on a central element in the transportation model of communication by which its general ideological nature becomes concretely political. I will argue that in regarding the production of "noise" as extrinsic to the content of a medium, the transportation model conceals its politics. Let us look at the Shannon and Weaver model again, this time with the component of noise included.

$$\text{source} \to \text{transmitter} \to \text{signal} \to \text{receiver} \to \text{destination}$$
$$\uparrow$$
$$\text{noise}$$

Noise is introduced into the signal during transmission. The amount of noise introduced is considered an index of the efficiency of the channel. Since noise increases the unpredictability of the message, by definition it increases available information, due to the increased freedom of choice in decoding a message. Thus, there is a contradiction inherent in the transmission model such that the introduction of extrinsic noise appears as equivalent to the production of new information. In a manner characteristic of ideological thought, this contradiction is neither addressed or resolved within the transmission model, but is simply arbitrarily and stipulatively removed. Weaver commented that "It is clear where the joker is in saying that the received signal has more information. Some of this information is spurious and undesirable and has been introduced via the noise. To get the useful information in the received signal we must subtract out this spurious portion."[1] But who decides what is spurious? Even more important, what is the function of noise? Not only Shannon and Weaver, but mainstream communication theory as a whole has no answer to this question. Indeed, it never even formulates the question clearly.

One of the main ways ideology operates is by treating a necessary aspect of a system as merely a contingent, extrinsic factor. A critical theory of contemporary media must reverse this ideological view and focus on the political dimension of noise. Production of noise is a central and necessary political function of contemporary media, especially insofar as a general translatability is constitutive of social relations. Opposition to noise is the common denominator of the three strategies of resistance by social movements within consumer society.

One strategy has been observed by Jean Baudrillard. Insofar as the media interrogate the masses to force their completion of the circuit of the cultural code, the masses respond with silence; they refuse to throw the switch of their yes/no inputs.

> Thus, in the case of the media, traditional resistance consists of reinterpreting messages according to the group's own code and for its own ends. The masses, on the contrary, accept everything *en bloc* into the spectacular, without requiring any other code, without requiring any meaning, ultimately without resistance, but making everything slide into an indeterminate sphere which is not even that of non-sense, but that of overall manipulation/satisfaction.[2]

The masses reject the manipulation of meaning by rejecting meaning. The proliferation of simulations which hopes to confine the masses to switches in the circuit may be undermined by the withdrawal from simulations of their necessary input, with a silence that is a strategy of objectivity, like a recalcitrant child.

Sheldon Wolin has proposed a similar analysis. He uses the term "rejectionism" to describe a pervasive "gesture of defiance in the face of a system that is immovable and so interconnected as to be unreformable as a totality."[3] While I do not want to contest the tight interconnection of the social system such that it can be called a code, it seems to me a considerable over-interpretation to regard all defiant withdrawals of complicity as equivalent to strategies for social change. Wolin argues that genuine change can occur only if "citizens withdraw and direct their energies and civic commitments to finding new life forms."[4] Such a withdrawal is indeed characteristic of the attempts at social change in the new social movements. However, there is a crucial mediating link between rejectionism and the proposal of new life forms that is ignored in the analyses of Baudrillard and Wolin. This mediation is to be found in the role of social movements, which form the identities of their participants through their activities in a manner that transforms a drop-out rejection into a political project demanding social change. In Marxist terminology, this was called the problem of the transition from a class in-itself to a class for-itself. Despite the fact that our present analysis problematizes the central role of the working class in social change as it is understood in Marxist theory, this problem of transition remains fundamental. Its possibility was pinpointed in Marx by defining the working class as both particular and universal, as "in but not of" civil society, but there is no direct passage from recalcitrance to creative institution.

It is precisely the formation of this passage that is the key invention of the new social movements. A space for the passage has been opened up that is at once less decisive, or predetermined, than in Marxist theory—while simultaneously more plural, creative and richly articulated. The rejectionist strategy does follow from a telling analysis of the contemporary role of the communication process as defining the social system through a constricted feedback loop, but it is nevertheless unsatisfying as it undermines any attention to the formation of political direction in the name of a generalized obstinacy. It is less a strategy of change than a resignation of the possibility of change for a petulant pout, and this is indeed widespread nowadays.

The response to the question of noise by Gregory Bateson is somewhat better, but is still caught in a mirror-like resemblance to that of Baudrillard and Wolin. Bateson argues that noise introduces the unexpected and the new in a communication and, for that reason, is more interesting than the duplication of the signal since it contains the possibility of change.[5] In this way, Bateson grabs the other end of the stick from Weaver, as it were. While Weaver wants to cling to the replication of identical information, Bateson focuses on what is new and unpredictable. The problem is that it is not only new and unpredictable, as communication and social change must indeed be, it is *entirely random*. Noise enters from outside the communication process under consideration and, therefore, it is simply an extrinsic and unpredictable element. Bateson thus reduces the problem of change to that of random variation, which he then connects to a biological model, and he does this by virtue of holding on to the same notion of communication as transmission of a signal that Shannon and Weaver use. Though the inflection is different, the theoretical status of noise is the same.

Batesonians, when confronted with this point, tend to argue against a position (often described as Marxist) that the consequences of change can be predicted and planned—thereby reducing change to technocratic manipulation. While they are right enough to reject this as an insufficient account of the novelty involved in communicational and social change, it is not the case that change must be thought of as random mutation in order to avoid this implication. Social change can be deliberate and intended, even though it brings into motion a process that cannot be controlled. It is hard to imagine a process of social change in which the actors strive for change without preferring some type of change over another. The dynamic of social change cannot be captured in a caricature that reduces it either to planning or random variation. For this reason, I regard a Baudrillardian refusal of participation and a Batesonian embracing of random change as mirror-images of each other, both rooted in a traditional concept of communication as meaning-transfer. Neither of these responses can properly be called a "strategy of resistance" for this reason, since they remain within the established circuit of communication.

Perhaps these reflections can motivate us to take another look at Baudrillard's rejection of traditional strategies of resistance which he described as consisting in reinterpreting messages according to the group's own code. Baudrillard rejects this possibility as merely traditional and insufficient because he regards the social distance characteristic of modernity as having imploded such that the audience simply becomes a completion of the code, a switching that is reduced to a yes/no. Identities are thus entirely simulated and can only be accepted or rejected in their entirety. This analysis was discussed in the previous part of this book. Through various criticisms I finally argued in favor of an account of the consumer simulation of identities through staged difference and the postulation of a supposedly authentic experience outside the media system. This analysis opens up the basis for an experiential encounter that does not, or not entirely, fit within the simulations. It is not, of course, as if simulated identity and "authentic" identity could be independently available for comparison. This would be a return to a modernist concept of authenticity and a conception of theory as objective representation criticized above. Nonetheless, it does mean that simulated identities do not cover the entirety of experience. Experience is not available independently of simulated identities, but it is possible to undergo a crisis in which the available identity is experienced as inadequate, as not sufficient in some way. Such crisis-situations motivate the search for a new identity.

No project of social change is possible without some such conception of "lack of fit." The elements of experience that are not included in the consumer circuit are normally *discounted* in the simulation of identities. Such identities are haunted by an indeterminate ghost suggesting their incompletion. In order for consumer identities to transform themselves into critical identities engaged with social movements, this discounting process must be undone. The origin of social resistance is thus a process of *un-discounting* whereby the indeterminate dissatisfaction becomes an analysis of consumer society and a project of social change. Consumer society cannot do away with this dissatisfaction because it is generated by the simulation of identities through consumption of objects. Each object reveals itself as insufficient to the constructed identity because it is routed through the entire consumer code and is thereby unsettled by any change in the system. Of course, the consumer code requires change to stimulate new purchases. Thus, the identities it constructs are instable and always haunted by that which is discounted. Consumer society, despite its simulation circuit, also short-circuits and opens the indeterminate possibility of new identities opposed to the consumer model. Social movements begin from this indeterminacy and render it determinate through contesting given definitions of the social order and proposing their own. They thus introduce new mediations into consumer society that open the possibilities of transition to another social form.

This is not a modernist account insofar as it is not possible to reach beneath the identity-in-crisis to an unspoiled authenticity. All such apparently unspoiled authenticities are themselves simulated by prior media of communication. Thus, the lack of fit is a genuine crisis, and can only be "solved" by a process engendering social change. Social movements are thus movements for the construction of new identities, and it is the purpose of this part of the book to explore some of the strategies of this self-constructive process. With these reflections in mind, it is possible to see that Baudrillard's characterization of a traditional strategy as an interpretation of messages according to the group's own code is not an adequate account of what happens in new social movements. Because the interpretations are generated in a process of self-construction, the "group's own code" itself becomes internal to a process of self-discovery and not a presupposed starting-point for interpretation. The interpretations are thus also self-interpretations and the self-identity of the group is continuously defined and redefined. This cannot be called a traditional strategy in Baudrillard's sense since it occurs entirely as a distention of the circuit of reproduction of consumer society. In short, his rejection of a role for the interpretations of social movements is a consequence of his notion that authenticity is erased, rather than simulated, in postmodernity. My present account uses the notion of simulated authenticity to propose the possibility of a "lack of fit," an experiential dimension that is nevertheless not conceptualized along modernist lines. It is a main theme throughout this book, which accounts for my appropriation of phenomenological themes and concepts pertaining to the experience of social actors, without which it seems to me the project of social change must come to naught.

A second reflection may also be helpful here. I once attended a conference in which Baudrillard's account of the "disappearance of the social" was carefully explicated, compared to the current state of society, and finally judged wanting because "society isn't really like that." It was a charmingly naive paper, but I was amazed to find later that there are many people who think that they can read Baudrillard in this way. If Baudrillard is right, there is no access to what society really is (as it were) outside of the simulations, and the possibility of representational social knowledge has evaporated with the distance between subjects charateristic of modernity. In other words, this isn't a "reading" of Baudrillard at all; it begins from a standpoint which is bound to reject Baudrillard's "theory" since its very presuppositions are anti-Baudrillardian. This doesn't mean that Baudrillard is necessarily "right," or that "anything goes"—as many people seem to think about postmodernism. What it means is that the status of the Baudrillardian discourse has to be taken into account in its reading, if the result of the reading is not to be foreordained.

Baudrillard writes, it seems to me, in a prophetically apocalyptic vein. He shows us the image of the society that is, or may be, coming. Why? I suppose, at least from my own reaction, because such a society is to be avoided at all costs. It is a nightmare of the future dreamed in the present. For this reason, it works upon the reader in much the same way as science fiction. Does it "exactly fit" the present condition? Of course not, but that's hardly the point. That's why, in my use and development of Baudrillard's analysis in the previous chapter, I attempted to push it to its conclusions, and begin my own analysis from its conclusions, rather than retreating into a supposedly scientific posture.

The upshot of this reflection is that postmodernist writing, including this book, is much more concerned with the process by which a communication produces certain determinate effects than about producing a "correct" analysis, more with rhetoric—in this case, media rhetoric—than with science. This project has its logic, which is quite demanding in its own way, but it does not terminate in a plan or technique. It is, rather, thinking situated at the point of action and does not consider social action as a mere derivation from either a theory or a social structure. Such a theory situated within social action is a meditation upon the "lack of fit" mentioned above, but terminates neither in a scientific knowledge nor a dispelling of the mystery. There is a mysterious component in this lack of fit; it is the mystery of freedom itself—about which one can speak, which one can open up to examination, and which provides the germ of thought—but which one can neither finally explain nor dispel. In short, unlike the analysis presented by Baudrillard, I do not regard the reinterpretations of social reality proposed in social movements as merely traditional strategies because the identities of the interpreters are wholly at issue in the reinterpretations; there is no pre-defined identity which would remain unsettled by the consumer code. Consequently, it is worthwhile discussing the language strategies of the social movements in some detail, which is the purpose of the next chapter.

A second strategy of criticism by social movements can also be discerned which focuses on the widespread production of simulations. This is not a strategy of refusing inputs as suggested by Baudrillard, but is concerned rather with the *proliferation of simulations*, an overburdening of the cultural code by excess, that may undermine the self-confirming character of the code that is required by monopoly capital. Armed with video cameras, cultural guerrillas may multiply simulations beyond any possibility of control by a code. While this may degenerate into a proliferation of random variations as discussed above, when properly used it involves a reflexive bending of the dominant code that requires a careful analysis and deliberate activity of transformation directed toward selected key conjunctures. This strategy is a redesigned activity of the artistic avant-garde and I do not see any reason to regard it as entirely exhausted. However, it is less central to the activities of social movements and I will not discuss it any further here.

There is also a third strategy which is not merely traditional, as Baudrillard might think. Since information is a universal reprocessing of culture, it undermines the core of activity that produces meaning. There is a loss of the fundament of culture in the embodied and local enactments of speaking subjects. A recovery of this fundament of the production of meaning is not merely a traditional strategy in the sense of a "reinterpretation according to the group's own code," since it refers to the conditions for producing any sort of cultural meaning, not merely to the assertion of a given meaning. It is a radicalization of the traditional strategy that responds to the endangerment of the fundament of culture in the conditions of universal reprocessing and translatability of its reduction to information.

The primal scene of consumer society and information culture operates through the imposition of *silences* on the diverse sources of culture. The critical concept of particular oral traditions incorporates a lament for a way of life that has passed. Thus, we may well tend to idealize it in the same moment that it is characterized *from outside*—in the very terms that have replaced living oral tradition with industrial culture. But in our time, this lament can also become the source of a protest. Then we are faced with an opposite movement of thought of characterizing what may appear in the future in terms of the present. In neither case is it a question of the literal past or future, but of their characterization on the basis of a perceived degeneration of culture in the present. If oral tradition contains the germ of a critical possibility, it can be discerned in this tension between lament and utopia in the present: the primal scenes of oral tradition re-figured as resistance to consumer-information society.

Postmodern culture reprocesses images that enforce silences on particular traditions. On the basis of this present reduction of culture, we are motivated to discover the generation of articulations from which culture emerges. This meaning-fundament from which culture emerges is the *event*—the enactment of oral encounters in embodied presence. Beginning from the event, we avoid the intractable oppositions of rule-obeying *or* original actions, individual *or* social creations, with a focus on the embodied encounters in the *here and now* that are the source of cultural expressions. Rooting culture in oral encounters implies that cultures are essentially diverse and internally articulated in spatial and temporal dimensions. The pluralities of food, language, and music are necessary to the *source* of human culture; recovery of these pluralities in the present resists the undoing of culture by industrially produced uniformity.

Oral encounters articulate a localized display in which the coordinated senses of all present are embodied in an event. Such an event is an *inscription* of meaning in the here and now. Its only mode of transmission to other encounters (there/then) is through the participants who witness the event. The transmitted expression *evokes* meaning in the participants in another context. Oral tradition is the mode of communication that connects inscription and evocation of meaning *solely* through the continuity of participants in a succession of encounters. The continuity of cultural expressions sustaining a localized identity is inseparable from the social assembly that witnesses events. The social assembly can be divided into two groups whom it would be tempting but inaccurate to term "performers" and "audience." In oral encounters all are enactors to some degree, even if only to the minimum involved in nods of assent at the end of verses or exclamations during a jazz solo. The minimum degree of co-enactment is that the structure and meaning of the traditional material is known to the coactor apart from the present event. They are not *initiated* into the material by this performance as are most modern audiences; rather, their *belonging* to the social assembly is *confirmed* by their presence at this event. The degree of participation by co-enactors is usually considerably larger than this minimum: consider the singing along on choruses in traditional folk songs, for example. Similarly, the song does not belong to the performer; it is only borrowed from the social assembly for the duration of this event. He or she is, for example, "one who is singing," an amateur, not a "singer"—a specialist in the current division of labor. A single enactment gathers together a relationship between past and present, between repertoire and performance, that establishes the continuing perdurance of the social assembly from the past into the here and now. Songs and stories of home, clearances, and emigration establish the continuity of the assembly in space to match that in time.

Enactment establishes not only the *fact* of continuous cultural experience but also its *validity* in the present. The compactness of fact and justification in oral encounters enacts the identity of the social assembly as a *display* of uniqueness which confirms the *value* of this uniqueness. Such an essentially diverse fundament of culture is the ground for a recovery and renewal of self-expression and cultural identity. The source of culture is to be found in the articulation of experience in a wager that particular encounters can give rise to *unique value*. Such a wager rescues and defends precisely what is marginalized and silenced in the information culture—the geographical and historical extensions required for the formation of cultural identity. The present state of culture requires the preservation and justification of the pre-industrial *fundament* of cultural experience in oral expressions rooted in the interplay of the human senses in bodily presence. Bodily enactment is an engagement of the whole person in a social assembly. The event is the common source of belonging and justification. This common source is bifurcated in the reprocessing of culture as information—knowing is separated from doing, interpretation from belonging. The source of culture is in community, in the gathering-and-belonging together in which expression gives rise to the diversity of cultural forms. Only by rediscovering and extending the oral and particular *source* of culture can we find strength and hope in the present for resistance. New social movements engage in this rediscovery of the fundament of culture to the extent that they turn away from postmodern consumer culture toward the reinvention of culture in community.

These three strategies all resist the noise produced by contemporary media—either by reinterpretation as a process of identity-construction, by the increase of noise beyond control, or by recovery of the local and embodied conditions for speech. None are simply traditional strategies directed primarily to the representative dimension of media insofar as all three address the universalization of political strategy to questions of identity provoked by the constitutive dimension of media. All are concerned not so much with the success of particular messages as with the conditions for communication as such. Once noise has been defined as the main ideological function of contemporary media, one can begin to discern new strategies of resistance, strategies which extend to the omnipresent constitution of society through media and which embrace the festival of meaning beyond the closure of the cultural code. In the next chapter I will discuss the two strategies which I regard as having the most to offer to new social movements (in distinction from the individual artistic critic)—the critique of the consumer construction of social identities by social movement reinterpretations (strategy one) and the recovery of the conditions of speech as embodied action (strategy three).

CHAPTER 11

New Mediations

The critique of common sense of consumer society by the new social movements raises central issues for the relationship of discourse and society insofar as it is through such critical interventions that the identity of the social movement is itself constructed. While the critique of common sense begins from the content of expression, it is finally not limited to it since it is concerned with the reflexive construction of identity and, as such, addresses the identities proposed by the constitutive dimension of media. It is a kind of transitional category that begins from the content-orientation of most communication analyses but also, by way of the self-construction of identity, implicates and revises the primal scenes constituted by media of communication themselves. This chapter will thus undertake a detailed examination of the construction of identities through the resistance strategies of social movements.

The dominant conception of ideology-critique, one that has tended to isolate it from this focus on social action, has implicitly regarded ideology as a kind of frame "within which" social interactions occur. Ideology seems to come as a distorting influence from the macrosocial "framework" that is laid over microsocial interactions, as it were. A language-based perspective, to the contrary, has the virtue of focusing on the "ideologemes" (Volosinov), the particles or fragments from which a full-blown ideology is rhetorically *assembled*. It can bring the critique of ideology much closer to the ground, where it may enter into a productive relationship with social movements. Moreover, it serves to emphasize that ideology is not a simple "given," as it were, but is continuously being constructed and reconstructed in changing, and contested, contexts. Ideology is at its most effective where it is presupposed as common sense. This radicalized concept of ideology requires that its true-false formulation be supplanted by the concept of hegemony, which focuses on the effective power of ideas, rhetoric, rather than their truth-orientation. Hegemony refers to the role of ideas in constituting social groups, whereas ideology refers to the use of ideas made by constituted groups. The hegemonic power of common sense is perhaps most evident in what one might call the "obligatory preface," where an element of common sense must be acknowledged and bowed toward before one's own speech can be commenced. In the United States during the Persian Gulf War virtually every speaker, especially those critical of government policy, began by saying "I support our troops, but. . . ." The power of delegitimation that could be induced by suggesting that a speaker was endangering, or even not fully supporting, "our troops" was such that speakers anticipated and attempted to ward off this line of criticism from the outset. Common sense is rarely so visible, or its ideological implications as clear, but such obligatory prefaces indicate the wider significance of unstated assumptions. Social change thus must begin from an unsettling of established common sense and continues through its reformation.

One key aspect of this reformation is the forging of a discourse that both denounces a state of affairs and promotes action toward changing it. Feminism, in particular, has developed a substantial literature on the problem of the "silencing," or "marginalizing," of women's experience by patriarchal institutions. Gayatri Spivak has generalized this focus into an account of politics as the suppression of its constitutive marginality. "The prohibition of marginality that is crucial in the production of any explanation is politics as such, what inhabits the prohibited margin of a particular explanation specifies its particular politics."[1] The emergence of social movement politics originates from a process of *undiscounting* what is left aside by dominant explanations. The process of the disruption of common sense by social movements is now well underway and our current society is traversed by the rhetoric of consumer society, critical rhetoric emerging from movements, and counter-rhetoric in opposition to movements. In this chapter I discuss four different components of this rhetoric of common sense under the headings of equivalences, hierarchies, voicing/linking, and part/whole relations, but I will begin with an illustration of the problematizing of common sense.

In July 1991 Gwen Jacobs walked on the streets of Guelph, Ontario, without any covering on the top part of her body. She was arrested for "indecent exposure" and, in January 1992, found guilty and fined seventy-five dollars. Judge Bruce Payne rejected the notion that women have the same right as men to remove their shirts in public. The reasoning is interesting. He said, "the essence of the matter is that anyone who thinks male breasts and female breasts are the same thing is not living in the real world. . . . Her lawyer argued that her right to sexual equality under the Charter of Rights and Freedoms had been violated. A Crown prosecutor said that, unlike men's breasts, women's breasts can be sexually provocative."[2] Of course, it is crucial whose "real world" is being referred to here. There are three related distinctions built into this utterance: first, the biological basis of the gender distinction between men and women; second, the behavioral distinction between covered and uncovered; and, third, the erotic distinction between provocative and non-provocative. It might be diagrammed in this way:

men	women
uncovered	covered
non-provocative	provocative

The prosecutor's statement, which was accepted in the judge's verdict, consisted in setting up relations of equivalence between these three aspects in a dualistic mode: men's breasts can be uncovered because they are non-provocative, whereas women's breasts must be covered because they are provocative. Thus, the terms on the right side of the list are mutually implicatory, or equivalent, signs of the relationship—as are those on the left. The base-line assumption is that public activity should be legally certified as non-provocative, or non-erotic. The judgment gains its "common sense" through semiotic equivalences. Because it seems unlikely, or even ridiculous, that women's breasts would not be provocative, the judgment that women can, or must, be treated differently than men is sanctioned.

The first observation that can be made is that women's breasts are provocative—usually, though not exclusively—to heterosexual men. There is an implied viewer at the key moment of the semiotic chain, the moment that connects the two sets of equivalences to the base-line assumption that public behavior must be non-erotic. This assumption itself is a cultural formation and pertains to the Anglo-Saxon cultural basis of the legal system. If one is interested in unsettling this chain of equivalences, which was, after all, effective enough to back a legal decision that is part of the state policing of public behavior, one should look for weak points in the chain. Since the judgment was based on the "self-evidence" of the women's side, the weak points in the equivalences are likely to be found on the other side. The equivalence that implies that men's breasts are not provocative also contains a heterosexual man as the implied viewer. While some women may not find men's breasts provocative, it should be a fairly simple task to find some who do. Public testimony to this effect might demonstrate that it is not the case that provocativeness is the criterion for covering as the judge claimed. It only seems as if provocativeness is the criterion if the assumed male viewer is *not named*. In other words, the fact that the male viewer is assumed, rather than spoken and avowed, allows the criterion for covering to be presented in a misleading way. While it would be inadmissable to claim explicitly nowadays that women are, or should be, excluded from public life, the un-remarked equation of women's breasts with provocation implicitly contains such an assumption. This assumption becomes explicit when "provocativeness" is analyzed as a term containing an implicit reference to a viewer, the "provoked," which reveals that it is (primarily, or "normally") a relation to heterosexual men that is at issue.

Many linguistic terms contain such implicit references to a social relation that is not marked directly by the term itself. Such implicit references can often be brought out by the strategy of reversing the terms, as Anne Hansen did when she commented that, at the sight of men's chests, "women are expected to control the urge to catcall, grunt and to help themselves."[3] Such symbolic *reversals,* often utilized in humor and satire as well as political slogans, are an important component of language-based social criticism.

There is a weak point also in the equivalence assumed between non-provocation and revealing. The initial assumption here is that public behavior should be non-provocative. First of all, this is not always the case. With regard to the women's side of these equivalences, Anne Hansen has pointed out that strippers and topless dancers are not arrested[4]—though, it must be said, this behavior occurs in specified places where the exclusion of minors and the fact that entry is a personal decision means that such places are only "public" in an incomplete sense. Second, we might well think of some popular music performances as well—pertaining, as Mick Jagger well knows, not only to women. It seems that it is not that public behavior must be non-provocative, but that it may be so only in certain situations. The issue here is really the circumscription and licencing of public provocative behavior, since it is not the case that it is always disallowed. Uncovering these presuppositions should allow an explicit discussion of the cultural politics of such licencing. Also, putting this point together with one noted earlier, it is also implied that men are less likely to (be able to) restrain themselves than women. The provocation of women by bare-breasted men in public places does not seem to pose a problem for public order. This element, or ideologeme, clearly plays into larger ideological issues concerning gender and self-restraint, and the definition of emotion as uncontrollable, which are reinforced and reproduced by the public acceptance of the policing of clothing.

This analysis indicates that the semiotic chain of equivalences is weak at three points: the presumption that the public consists of heterosexual males, the presumed non-provocativeness of men's breasts, and the licencing of public provocation. If the judgment is to be delegitimated, social criticism can begin most effectively from these weak equivalences, leaving aside for the moment the strong ones which are rooted in the common sense that backs the judgment. Without the analysis of weak points, one could get caught in arguments that are unlikely to go anywhere because they are too close to the common sense they attempt to disrupt. One could argue, for example, that women's breasts are not provocative, or are so only when she wishes them to be. Anne Hansen, commenting on her own arrest at a July 18, 1992, topless protest in Waterloo, Ontario, argued as much. "Breasts are sexual, but only when a woman chooses to present them as such." Her fellow-protester Adel Arnold, however, said of male observers that she "can't control their minds."[5] Such a strategy seems unlikely to succeed since it shunts the argument toward the suggestion that the "author's viewpoint" (in literary terms), or the "viewpoint of the actor" (in sociological terms), is the ultimate adjudicator of social meaning. This is an untenable position, since meanings are intrinsically interpretable from a plurality of standpoints. The argument tends to get lost either in claiming a privileged standpoint or in sheer plurality if it is pursued in this manner. This is the ideological effect of the semiotic equivalences and their self-reinforcing character.

What is really at issue is the establishing of a public context in which the common sense licencing the prohibition is unsettled and an alternative context becomes plausible. This is what subsequent protesters achieved when their own charges for appearing topless were thrown out on the grounds that it was a political issue rather than a sexual or moral one.[6] The argument that the Canadian Charter of Rights and Freedoms (1982) guarantees women the same treatment as men prompts the rejoinder: the same rights apply only in the same circumstances, and these are not the same circumstances, and it was this qualification that won out in this case. It raises a larger question about the extent to which an argument for women's rights need commit itself to the "sameness" of men and women. Or, is it an issue of "different therefore equal" as Peggy Seeger's album cover had it? This larger issue obviously goes beyond the present example. Nonetheless, it may be surmised that an argument that rests its case on sameness (or, the irrelevance of differences) may tend to produce its own backlash since there are clearly situations in which sameness isn't applicable. Dislodging the certainty of the semiotic equivalences on the male side may serve to unsettle the common sense of the judgment more effectively than a statement of sameness that probably can be made questionable in many concrete cases.

This whole episode might serve to bring into question several key assumptions in the policing of public behavior. In particular, questioning the link between the public presumed as heterosexual males and the relative exclusion of eroticism from public life would be central to rethinking current sexual morality. There are gender issues, homosexual rights issues, and (cross-)cultural issues here. In a society which can no longer justify directly and unproblematically excluding women from the public realm, and in which multiculturalism is both daily reality and public policy, yet where traditional assumptions about who is entitled to the public domain have not lost their force, exposing the weakness of the equivalences embedded in common sense can open the possibility of social criticism and cultural politics.

It is clear from the above example that the rationale for treating women differently from men emerges not merely from the fact that there is a distinction between men and women, but from the embedding of this distinction within a field of signs whose organization—in this case as a chain of equivalences constructed from three dualisms—is manifested in the utterance. While it is theoretically possible that a dualism may be conceptualized as an equal and opposite tension as, perhaps, in the yin/yang of Chinese philosophy, a field of signs such as that described above inflects the dualism as a hierarchy. This hierarchical relation derives not simply from the disjunctive distinction but from the chain of equivalences that establish its meaning in use. Due largely to the influence of feminism as a social movement, the social construction of terms like "woman" and "man" is widely appreciated nowadays and plays a part in daily politics. The hierarchical organization of the field of signs can thus be elicited by looking at the social situation in which such an argument prospers.

What is the rhetorical force of arguing that a concept, or a reality, is socially constructed? The argument that a concept is socially constructed is most powerful when it occurs against the background of a taken-for-granted context which has been naturalized as common sense. To pick a key concept out from this background and to argue for its social construction functions to de-naturalize the context and to suggest that the given social reality can be altered. The argument that gender is socially constructed, for example, works best when it is generally assumed that the relations between men and women follow naturally from the sexual difference. In this context, the argument aims to de-naturalize the connection between sexual difference and gender relations. It may draw on anthropological and historical accounts in order to establish that gender relations are extremely variable across different societies and it may analyze the structuring of gender relations in contemporary society. The most basic strategy is thus to make a distinction between sex and gender. Sex is defined first, as it were, to refer to the cross-cultural and undeniable fact of the division of humans into two sexes. Gender is defined in relation to this as the plurality of forms that social arrangements of this division into two sexes may take. One admits nature and biology in a first step in order to displace them in a second step by emphasizing that no definite set of consequences follows from this admission. A third step points to the systematic structuring of gender relations in the context of social power in order to show that prevailing conceptions are not neutral but advantage men as against women.

The argument for the social construction of gender differences thus deploys a three-step argument in order to conclude with the suggestion that existing gender relations can be altered to suggest the promotion of more equitable relations between women and men. It unsettles a taken-for-granted context by arguing for the social construction of a key organizing concept that has previously been taken to be natural. Such an argument enables the taken-for-granted context to be *retroactively* stigmatized as ideological and named as "sexist." Sexist ideology can therefore be succinctly defined in terms of the naturalizing of the passage from sex to gender through three key factors: First, the picking out of sexual difference as the *salient* difference for social relations. Second, the presentation of this difference as a *binary opposition*—if not man, then woman; if not woman, then man. Both of these factors were operative in the example of topless behavior discussed above; they are the condition for the presupposed naturalness of the chain of equivalences. Third, this binary opposition is structured as an unequal relation in which the dominant side *monopolizes the generic "higher-level" category* "human."

In the previous example this structuring was evident in the assumption that the viewer in the public sphere is a male heterosexual, though it was unspoken and taken as simply a universal standpoint. This structuring of common sense is what deconstruction seeks to make evident by pulling it apart. This process of marking terms in everyday discourse infuses sexist ideology into the assumptions that constitute common sense. Thus, within sexist ideology "man" refers both to "not-woman" and "generically human." Consequently, "woman" counts as human only by qualification and in comparison to "man." In ordinary discourse this hierachical formation of the binary opposition is signaled by the use of a *marked category* in the case of the subordinate term, whereas the dominant term remains unmarked. Again, it is theoretically possible that a marked term may be an exception of any kind, even an approbative one, but, with regards to social definitions, the marked category is usually used to indicate that one is lacking in some necessary quality.

In fact, a negatively aligned marking can even occur when the explicit attention of a phrase is positively oriented. Franz Fanon specified this marking process in his discussion of responses to Aimé Césaire's poetry, such as André Breton's positively intended remark that "Here is a black man who handles the French language as no white man today can."[7] Césaire, even by those who acknowledged his brilliance, was qualified as a "black" poet. This serves to underline further the fact that we are discussing social usage here, not the intentions of individual speakers. Ordinary usage qualifies the terms "doctor" and "driver" by referring to a "woman doctor" or a "lady driver," whereas the unmarked terms are assumed to be men. This is the semiotic process which underlies the definition of the Other described by Simone de Beauvoir whereby "man represents both the positive and the neutral" and woman is "defined and differentiated with reference to man and not he with reference to her."[8] A term is thus marked not merely by its relational definition, which is inevitable in any identity defined within a system of signs, but by the *incomplete reciprocity* of the relational definition. There is also a relational definition between the terms man (as human male) and Man (as generically human). However, this relation is obscured by the use of the unmarked term "man" to cover both uses. The lack of marking thus also has an ideological effect through the *obscuring* and *displacing* of the relationality of the term "man." It may seem that "man" gets his identity simply and directly from himself, or "authentically." Alternatively, it may appear that he gets it through an immediate relation to human universality. In the first case, an unviable concept of identity as pure authentic self outside of relationship is produced. In the second case, relationality is recognized but displaced from the man-woman relation to the man-Man relation. Thus it seems that one could gain human self-identity without taking account of the division of humanity into two sexes and the consequent inability, or at least difficulty, of each one of us to directly experience the whole of human reality. Complete reciprocity of the terms would make directly evident this permanently problematic character of human universality.

Racist ideology works similarly in this respect. Skin color is selected as the central salient variable and the wide range of colors is narrowed to the binary relation white/not-white, or black. Whites are assumed to be directly and simply human and thus any achievements by whites need not be specially marked. In contrast, Jesse Jackson was marked as a *black*, or African-American, candidate for President of the United States—with the corresponding, but unexpressed, presumption that he was necessarily lacking in some unstated requisite for the job, or that he must represent only a "special interest" rather than the voters as a whole. This marking process has been noted by subordinate groups seeking to adjust their status and has led to a complex politics of marking and naming in social movements.

At this point I just want to note a structural similarity in the ideological formation when considered at a certain level of abstraction. It is through the marking of one side of a dualistic distinction that a hierarchical relation between them is reproduced in everyday life such that the relation of the unmarked term to the universal category is rendered unproblematic and apparently immediate, whereas the relation of the marked category is defined as non-universal, therefore mediated and questionable. From this perspective, it would be a mistake directly correlative to this dominant ideology to argue that women, black people, or any "marked" group themselves have an unmediated relation to human universality. Such an argument mimics and reproduces the ideological relation man-Man that is only apparently unmediated, but actually produced by the field of semiotic oppositions into which the term "man" enters. It is not a problem that all distinct human groups have a mediated relation to universality; it is a problem that one group apparently has a direct and unquestionable relation. It is the hierarchical inflection of the dualism that produces the derogation of the marked group. Thus, Fanon can say that racism, and indeed any such "ism," originates in the moment that I approach another with condescension, that is to say, when a hierarchy appears between two relational terms.[9]

Actually, no ideological field is sufficiently complex to work as a cultural formation with only one dualism. The initial example concerning "provocative behavior" required three inter-related dualisms, and this would seem to be the minimum required to construct a functioning ideological field. It is through the inter-relation of the related dualisms in an ideological field that one term of the predominant dualism is constructed as "higher" without being explicitly named as such. In contemporary discourse, it is no longer generally acceptable to claim directly that women are passive and domestic creatures, or that black people are unintelligent and capable of only physical culture. Such directly racist and sexist discourse is normally excluded from the public realm. In its place has arisen a more indirect formation in which the set of associations surrounding terms constructs a hierarchical relation anonymously, as it were. Hierarchical dualisms thus take on more complex features by the construction of a *discursive field* of sufficient complexity to allow enough debate and disagreement within it to obscure the limits of the field. A more complete account of the man/woman semiotic relationship might be diagrammed in this manner, to indicate the many terms to which "man" may be opposed:

man	woman	(as a sex/gender relation within humanity)
man	nature	(as human to nature)
man	boy	(as mature to immature)
man	mouse	(as strong to weak)

In each case, the specific meaning of the term "man" is derived from the term to which it is opposed. But, because all of these uses are culturally available, the general, or unqualified, unmarked, meaning of the term "man" hovers indiscriminately around each of the specific meanings which it may take on in a defined and hierarchical context. This unqualified meaning puts each of the terms to which it can be opposed into relationship with each other. Thus, woman is "like" nature, is "like" boy, is "like" mouse, and it is "better" to be "male," "human," "mature," and "strong." The exact character of this relationship is *undefined* precisely because it is derived from the discursive field of dualistic relations that are not named. However, the relationship is *evoked* by the use of any one of the terms. Thus, a specific meaning becomes hierarchically placed by virtue of the field in which it is used but the hierarchy is not named as such. It has become invisible to ordinary discourse, which may then pride itself on being non-sexist or non-racist while still evoking connotations with the same effect.

It is possible, of course, for more "theoretical" elaborations to pretend to define the "logical" relations between these terms. This is one way in which "philosophy," in the sense criticized by Marx and Nietzsche, gives an ideological apology for the cultural formations of common sense. This undefined relationship, based on the absent key term, allows a *slide* between the terms such that a weak man can be called a sissy, or weak "sister," women are seen as more connected to nature than men and as immature and emotional, like boys, in relation to them. Such slides between meanings characterize the implicit cultural content of terms like "woman." The ideological function occurs, not through the imposition of incorrect or distorted ideas, but through the shunting of debate into dead-ends within the ideological field rather than the exploration of its limits. To this extent, the analysis of the construction of an ideological field comes to the aid of a social movement by pressing at its limits. An analysis of language can concretize the critique of ideology by extending the capacity to engage in a politics of common sense by contesting the discursive functioning of ideologies. The implication for practical intervention with which such an inquiry concludes is by no means accidental. Variability across cultures, alongside processes of social structuring, combine to suggest the possibility of alternatives. Discourse theory is therefore, in the current terminology, "anti-essentialist" in that it suggests that there is nothing about gender relations, for example, that could in principle mark a limit to their variability and mutability.

Social movements begin from the perception that something key to the experience of their reference group has been left out of the prevailing discourse, the experience of an undefined and as yet vague "lack of fit." As this perception is given expression, it simultaneously undiscounts this now defined expression and denounces a "silencing" of the experience of the group in question. This process implies a conception of leadership as the voicing of the latent and inchoate desires of the group to which its rhetoric is addressed. The Spartacist leader Eugen Leviné, who was executed after the uprising in Munich in 1919, put it this way in his final speech to the court that condemned him: "leaders emerge from the masses, even if from a different milieu. They become leaders not because they are superior to the masses but only because they are capable of formulating what the masses themselves intuitively desire but cannot express for lack of formal education."[10] A large part of the activity of leadership, especially in the initial stages, is devoted towards naming the problem and exploring its implications. The classic statement of this within feminism is Betty Friedan's analysis of "the problem that has no name," as it was called in *The Feminine Mystique*.[11] It is present in other social movements too. For example, in the peace movement of the early 1980s the necessity of speaking out about one's fear of nuclear war, as a preface to overcoming that fear, was recognized.

This initial moment of a social movement, in which experience that has been left out of the prevailing discourse is legitimated and given expression, has often been called "making public"or "public-ation" because the initial moment of activism is a bringing of previously hidden "private" issues into the public realm.[12] However, there is a potential disadvantage in this terminology in that it seems to regard the problem as "already there" prior to the process of expression and naming. While one would not likely want to go so far as to say that the problem is *created* from whole cloth by its expression, as if the problem itself were a problem of language, nonetheless the naming process is active in a fundamental way: it *unifies* various previously unexpressed events under a single term and thereby allows them to be discussed together as instances of a (new) category, and it *names* these events specifically as a social *problem* in relation to a constellation of forces such that remedial *action* is implied. Thus, the active power of the language-ing process must be recognized. I think that the term "voicing" better captures this active process of a problematization and refiguration of common sense and has the added advantage of not buying into terminology rooted in the assumption of the separation of private and public spheres, which is precisely what the analysis wants to undermine.

For reasons similar to those that suggest that the identity of the speaker does not preceed the voicing, the identity of the addressees of the new speech also cannot be presupposed to simply exist prior to the voicing. The voicing discourse, in redefining the situation, calls a new social subject into being, a new subject from whom new activities and ways of seeing the world are demanded. Maurice Charland, for example, has analyzed the way in which the shift from the term "Canadiens français" to "Québécois" called forth an intensified identification with the Quebec state, as opposed to Ottawa, and rhetorically implied the sovereignty of this state. The new "peuple québécois" is not identical to the previous subject, but is constituted by the rhetoric itself.[13] In a similar vein, Karlyn Kohrs Campbell has pointed to the oxymoronic character of feminist rhetoric. The uniqueness of feminist rhetoric, she argues, lies in its mode of addressing an audience that, in a sense, doesn't (yet) exist.[14] My argument here, however, is that this is not unique to feminism, but is characteristic of contemporary social movements in general.

This active component of voicing in constructing the subjects to which it is addressed is often overlooked by social movements themselves; the new identity is often supposed to have been there, repressed but already formed, prior to the voicing that brings it out. For this reason, it tends to use a rhetoric of supression and domination rather than one of expression and identity-construction. Such an essentialism (whether "strategic" or not) derives from the hegemony of liberal individualist discourse such that a prior supression can readily yield a right to redress, whereas there is no liberal right to become someone new. The naturalizing of its addressee in social movement discourse obscures key elements of the process of social change. The focus on the language of social movements, and its role in the construction of social identities, has the advantage of pointing to this overlooked active function of movement rhetoric. Blindness to this function leaves such movements helpless in the face of competing articulations that serve to defuse and disorient their self-construction. Stuart Hall has analyzed the failure of the Left in the face of the re-articulations of Thatcherism that was produced, at least in part, by the presumption that it had a natural constituency.[15] Thus, one must conclude, the identity of social groups and the voicing of their perspective on the social world is a co-constitutive process. In other words, identity is constructed through a process of identification which selects and amplifies associations and makes comprehensible the plurality of identities by which any actor is traversed. To speak simply of "identity" runs the risk of naturalizing or essentializing a substantial identity within an "identity politics" in which what "I am" is static, closed, and unproblematic.[16] It is from this naturalization that some of the excesses of "identity politics" have come—the idea that "you can't understand me" because I'm female, black, etc. and thus the implication that we are each, finally, so different that no one can say anything about anyone else. This tendency pushes us toward a generalized solipsism not unlike that of consumer society, rather than the discourse politics of plural identities that social movements open up. The present investigation attempts to clarify the dynamics of the process of identification.

Voicing sets into motion a rhetorical process in which can be discerned four parts: First, it makes clear that which was previously only a vague dissatisfaction. Second, it makes open to the public, in a way that allows sharing and discussion, what was previously unexpressed and thus not clearly formulated as a problem. These two aspects of voicing indicate why poets often play an important role in the early stages of a social movement. Third, clear and public expression defines an opponent and a goal, which makes social action oriented to altering institutions possible. Fourth, a counter-response from those targeted as the opponent is brought into being. This dialectic tends to continue, until the dissatisfaction that brought the social movement into being is resolved, one may presume, through reciprocal rhetorics that influence each other. Michael McGee has shown how ordinary discourse contains terms, which he calls "ideographs," whose meanings are interpreted in the context of contesting versions of the social world, and which occur in "clusters" that call forth related meanings of surrounding terms.[17] While the initial response to black power in the United States was to attempt to beat and shoot them back into place, it has now been replaced with a rhetoric of gradual progress through "affirmative action." Nowadays, at least within advanced industrial societies, hegemony works much more by domesticating and absorbing criticism than by repressing it—what we used to call "cooptation." Oppositional movements are redefined as "countercultures" by the dominant discourse, and especially by the mass media, by stripping the movement of its aim of transforming the dominant society and presenting it as a lifestyle option that can exist within contemporary society. Once it has become articulated, this dialectic between a social movement and the society as a whole sets up a social distinction between those who identify with the movement and those who do not. Thus, the debate over what the movement *is,* that is, how it will be *defined,* is also the contest over who will associate themselves with it and therefore, in the long term, the chances of success. As Alberto Melucci suggests, politics has shifted from the actions of stable groups to actors with a "prophetic function" who "fight for symbolic and cultural stakes, for a different meaning and orientation of social action" so that the life and identity changes of social actors today can be linked to a project of social change tomorrow.[18]

Voicing, and the dialectic that it generates, leads to a related process that Ernesto Laclau and Chantal Mouffe call articulation, or *linking.*[19] Linking refers to the relationship of a developed social movement to other movements and forces in the society. To the extent that it gains influence, a social movement is pressed to articulate a perspective on the whole of society, to generalize and sometimes even to depart from the particular voicings from which it emerged. Thus, the relation between feminism and the peace movement, or feminism and the politics of race, to name only two examples, is a matter for contemporary debate—a debate of considerable significance for whether such social movements can ally in such a way as to alter fundamentally the dominant discourse of society as a whole.

While it is tempting to see such social movements as linked through their opposition to contemporary society, there is no pre-established harmony here—witness, for example, the conflict between feminism and some sectors of the ecology movement over abortion, and between feminists and African-Americans over the politics of affirmative action in the United States. Also, feminism has often succeeded to the extent that it has embraced the dominant liberal individualist ideology compatible with consumer capitalism. This is a fate common to many of the social movements originating from the 1960s. Nonetheless, there is no pre-established antagonism between social movements either. These examples are meant to indicate that the attempt to form a new hegemony through a politics of linking is fraught with difficulties that depend on the definition of the social movements in question—a definition which is constantly changing through the dialectic set into motion by voicing. A link between, say, feminism and the ecology movement can be forged only by embracing (or at least implying) specific definitions of feminism and ecology. Eco-feminism, which has achieved this link, depends upon characterizations of "feminism" and "ecology" which are debatable within their separate camps.

While the object that social movements oppose may seem abstractly identical—our contemporary society—different definitions of this society are coagulated in their voicings. Voicing a previously unexpressed dissatisfaction implies a characterization of the society as a whole such that it performs this exclusion. Feminism opposes patriarchy; ecology opposes industrial society; socialists oppose capitalism; black power opposes racism; multiculturalism opposes the continued dominance of the elite Anglo culture. These different definitions of the dominant society originate in specific social demands, imply different programs for action, and propose different conditions under which the claim of the social movement might be satisfied. In this sense, a social definition is *indexed* to its conditions of origin.

Differences in characterization are developed and mutated in the practical politics of linking, and it is a task for contemporary social theory to explore the implications of the different definitions. There is one demystifying contribution that social theory can provide in this context: Every social definition contains the seeds of a future exclusion. Or, to put it somewhat differently, there is no concrete social definition that is purely and simply universal. "Society" is always a contested site whose meaning is in principle unstable and whose present stability operates through exclusions. The specific situation that Madhu Kishwar encountered as a third world woman that made it impossible for her to call herself a feminist,[20] can be addressed, and perhaps ameliorated, through a politics linking feminism and imperialism, though the linkage between the two sometimes makes this difficult—"the specific structure of domestic work in Latin America is a clear case where class oppression supercedes gender oppression."[21] But while amelioration is possible, the formation of the word "feminism" in the context of a middle class movement in advanced capitalist society cannot simply be set aside.[22] Such situations, in general, where words crucial to an emancipatory struggle in one context become aspects of oppression in another, are unavoidable.

Discourse theory makes this especially evident with its focus on the *performativity* of a social definition, which refers back to the one who performs and the social location from which the definition emerges. It is for this reason that Gayatri Spivak connects the very idea of politics to such exclusions. If a definition of society is sufficiently concrete to connect to the specific demands of social movements—such as gender inequality, ravages of industrial society, class exploitation, racism, etc.— it cannot at the same time be universal enough to avert future exclusions. For this reason, self-criticism cannot be a luxury in social movements; it is essential to keep them from reproducing exclusion. The actor who situates him/herself unproblematically within one movement's definition of the social world is, from this perspective, potentially as dangerous as someone who accepts the dominant hegemony, since that unproblematic situation implies a reductionism of all social issues to the formulation proposed by one movement. If this is so, it implies that the "subject" of contemporary social change needs to be both committed to an "identity" stemming from a specific definition and also profoundly aware of the partiality of that identity. Such a subject needs its "other" and knows itself in this need.

The capacity of voicings to construct new social identities sets up a dynamic relation between parts and wholes in social movements. Karlyn Kohrs Campbell has pointed out that there is a duality inherent in feminism due to the fact that, on the one hand, it must assert the irrelevance of gender to certain positions and activities (in order to argue that women should gain access to domains from which they have traditionally been excluded), whereas, on the other hand, it must affirm gender (in order to argue for the positive social contributions made in the traditional domains open to women). This duality engenders a tension between arguments that appeal to the universality of humans and those that pertain to the difference of women.[23] It might be tempting to try to resolve this tension between particularity and universality; however, attempting to do so would be self-defeating. To opt for a straightfor-wardly universalist rhetoric would undermine the voicing that lies at the basis of feminism. Voicing emerges from particular concerns, concerns which in the case of feminism are unique to women, and—though it is the case that subsequent linking requires an entry into a universalist dis-course—this particular component cannot be abandoned without cut-ting off the basis of the initial social criticism. Since women have been excluded *as women* from certain social domains, they must voice their experiences as women in order to insert them into the social discourse.

Thus, this tension between particular and universal is better inter-preted in a temporal manner. First, there must be a voicing of women's experience; then the question of its (relation to) universality becomes pertinent. Once feminism as a social movement is articulated enough to enter into the rhetoric and counter-rhetoric of social movement and social hegemony, however, the appeals to particular and universal dimensions co-exist as distinct "moments" of the rhetoric. The tempo-ral character of this part/whole tension originates in the previously noted fact that social movement discourses are rhetorics of change which constitute their addressees as the new subjects that they address. This has been best theorized in the feminist practice of consciousness-raising, but it is not limited to it.[24] Similarly, the ecological movement must appeal to an audience capable of becoming different from those who they presently are in consumer, industrial capitalism. International solidarity movements must appeal to an audience for whom the suffer-ing of those far away is/becomes as the suffering of those close at hand. Social movements, virtually by definition, require a rhetoric of change, and that change is in part a change in the subjects to whom it is addressed. A social movement speaks in such a way as to require that those who hear become part of the movement, make changes in them-selves, and assert these new identities in opposition to the dominant way of being. A temporal demand is thus intrinsic to the speech.

The particular/universal tension is thus ineradicable and in a more developed politics the two moments co-exist as different elements of a single rhetoric. In order for particular experience to be voiced it breaks with the dominant hegemony which is proffered as universal. Of course, this doesn't mean that it "really" is universal, or "the same," for every-body—if it were there would be no need for social movements. A dom-inant hegemony, however, has a place for everyone in the sense that one is "fitted into" the dominant social structure by a rationale (whether explicit or, usually, at least partially hidden). In this sense, it claims uni-versality and the first moment of a social movement must be to puncture this claim. It is punctured by showing that there is something left out—that the claimed universality is only apparent. This is done with an assertion of particularity through voicing that I have termed "un-discounting."

One main linguistic strategy used to supplement voicing at this moment of particularity is the symbolic reversals mentioned above, whereby it is shown that what applies to blacks doesn't apply to whites, or women to men, etc. This may lead to "apparent reverse racism" if it is not understood that the intended audience for the speech is the denigrated group.[25] It is not intended as a universal discourse and others only "overhear," as it were, the construction of a group identity by revealing and exploiting the fault-lines of the dominant hegemony. This phenomenon leads to complex misunderstandings and counter-uses at times. For example, meaning reversal seems to require a caricature of the "mainstream" which may indeed function as a "reverse" racism if it is taken literally. It may also lead to a situation, common enough today, in which everyone wishes to evacuate the mainstream, insisting on some difference as important, leaving the "us" of the mainstream without a basis for commonality. This is also complicated by the fact that, largely under the influence of the mass media, stable cultural groups are disintegrating and it is possible for almost any group to "overhear" the statements of another, even if intended privately. Such a postmodern discursive situation calls for an "ethics of difference," in which a common language for assertions of difference reworks universality without conferring an advantage (hierarchy) on any one difference within the field. At the point of symbolic reversals the immediate and long-term goals of social change seem fused. As Campbell says, there seems to be no option to be reformist because of the construction of a new identity with radical implications.[26]

As the movement develops, however, the new identity takes on definition. There are defined audiences that can be regarded as "feminist," "environmentalist," etc. and the movement's rhetoric is, in part, oriented to this constituency. Thus, its appeal rests on a previously defined identity and is less radically oriented toward its construction. At this point, the movement must be placed in relation to other claims, stemming both from other movements and from key players in the establishment, pressed by other actors on the scene. There arise simultaneously the necessity of a universalist component to the rhetoric and, with this problematic of universality, the emergence of a distinction between universality and particularity that brings in a distinction between reformism and radical change. It is in this second moment that there emerges the possibility of a definition of a new universality, or to phrase it from the other side, of an exit from the previous hegemony. The two stages of social movements, which we may call *reversal* and *exit*, are rooted in the temporal structure of social movements and the tension between particularity and universality that this entails. In a word, it is a deconstructionist two-step. All of this follows from the fact that social movements must produce the social identities to which they appeal.

The preceding overview of the contributions that discourse theory can make to the analysis of social movements indicates that the new intellectual perspective is tied to certain assumptions about the character of society. To argue that social distinctions have been *socially constructed* in a hierarchical manner suggests that they can be practically and theoretically *deconstructed* and ends by opening the possibility of *transformative action*. It is my claim, however, that discourse analysis by itself cannot adequately address the question of action. Let us begin by noting that nothing positive can be said about the alternatives to be promoted on the basis of the discursive analysis alone. If one wants to say, for example, that relations between women and men, between races, or between cultural groups, *should* be more equitable and, if one wants to design strategies to pressure for this change, the selection of "equality" as the characteristic to be promoted comes from a source external to the discourse. Neither cultural variability nor the systematic structuring of gender by power suggest, by themselves, that equality—either greater equality or complete equality—is indeed possible or desirable. Deployed in this manner, discourse analysis has the character of an intellectual strategy: It is a theoretical means to suggest the possibility of alternatives, but the alternatives themselves enter by another door. They are either assumed at the outset or chosen after the analysis terminates, not part of the theoretical work itself.

Let me be clear on this point. I am not saying that this external relation is a "bad thing" and that one should somehow try to avoid the postulates from which alternatives might be designed, or that discourse theory is somehow irrevocably tainted as a result. I am only pointing out that the designing of alternatives is theoretically distinct from the analysis of language use and that, to that extent, the theory and practice of discourse analysis is dependent on another theoretical discourse which it assumes, attempts to serve, but cannot justify within its own terms. I will call that theoretical discourse, for the sake of brevity, ethics—understanding that it is inseparable from politics and economics.

Since alternatives have the character of an empty space to be filled in with an unknown but crucially important theoretical investigation, discourse theory contains a *transcendental illusion* which it can neither properly recognize nor definitively exorcize. In using Kant's terminology here I am suggesting that the illusion comes from the same source that he analyzed: the concepts are used beyond the range of their applicability, where they can only generate contradictory perspectives that are incapable of resolution. "We therefore take the subjective necessity of a connection of our concepts, which is to the advantage of the understanding, for an objective necessity in the determination of things in themselves."[27]

The transcendental illusion in the case of gender relations is that they are infinitely malleable and that social intervention is potentially all-powerful—that gender can be designed in any way that we choose. Or, to put it somewhat differently, that sexual difference has no implications whatsoever for social organization. As Kant also points out, revealing this illusion will not dispel it.[28] It is interesting to note that this illusion is the mirror-image of the "naturalist" ideology that gender relations are direct consequences of the sexual difference.

To state this point in a more general way, the transcendental illusion endemic to discourse theory is that its subject-matter is presented in the inquiry to appear as infinitely alterable and to suggest that deliberate interventions encounter no limits in constructing the subject-matter according to the inquirer's desires. Its source is clearly in the very advantage of discourse theory, for revealing the rhetorical construction of social identities such that they are seen to be non-natural and therefore capable of transformation. The only adequate response to this illusion that accompanies all language-based inquiry is to recognize it as a limited theoretical strategy.

Let us determine this limitation more precisely by considering again the structure of analyses that reveal the social construction of hierarchical dualisms that was sketched above. The argument of discourse theory proceeds by *denying* the relevance of sex in order to open up possibilities for intervention in the social construction of gender. The question about the limits to this intellectual strategy comes down to the status of the first category which is mentioned, and postulated as outside of discourse, in order for its *relevance to be denied*. The source of the transcendental illusion is precisely here: discourse theory supposes that an initial concept can be mentioned solely to deny its relevance to the subsequent discourse. But, of course, it is this initial mentioning and denial that gets the argument concerning what is socially constructed going. The initial move is *structuring* and the gesture of denial is not accidental but characteristic of the intellectual strategy. Clearly, the definition of sex as "outside" the gendering social formation is itself discursively accomplished by the rhetorical intervention. It is not "really" natural, as it were, any more than any concept or word can be really natural. My point is that the definition of the first category is rhetorically constructed in such a manner (i.e., mentioned and denied) that its formation cannot be thematized within the subsequent discourse. The field of a specific discourse analysis is structured in this way by its originating rhetorical formation.

A simpler example may make the point more forcefully. Food functions in all societies as a carrier of social meaning, status, and ritual. In order to investigate the discursive structuring of the meaning of food in a given context, the alimentary function of food must be "mentioned and denied." Clearly, food does nourish, but the meaning circulations that can be analyzed by language use about food are not restricted to claims about nourishment. In fact, the point is even stronger: claims to "nourishment" are themselves rhetorically structured within the knowledge claims of both a scientific and traditional sort within the available discursive field. Thus, the first category is, in a certain sense, discursively constructed; but, it is constructed in a specific way that excludes it from further discursive analysis.

I am arguing that a discursive field is opened up by a rhetorical intervention that is not analyzable within the discursive field that is thus opened up. It is the point of a *deconstructive* analysis to show this "hidden origin" that inheres in any discursive field. To put the point most directly, food is a carrier of social meaning, but it is not *just* about meaning. Food also nourishes. Thus, the point that I am making here does not rely on any conception of a non-discursive realm that might be contrasted with rhetorical constructions. The present argument fully accepts the discursive turn of the human sciences. The point refers to the *self-limitation of the field of any given discursive analysis.* All of human society is thoroughly formed by language use and symbolic meaning. Nonetheless, human society is not *only* symbolic meaning and, consequently, discourse analysis is a limited intellectual strategy. Not all of ethics is encompassed in rhetoric. The initial rhetorical move that I have called "mentioning and denial" structures the subsequent inquiry to serve a project of intervention and social change, about which it nevertheless can say nothing—and thereby implicitly supposes it to be unlimited. The issue of the first category of the "mentioned and denied" unravels the whole question of the rootedness of the concepts and categories in experiences which might constrain their mutability. We might refer in a general way to these experiences that escape discourse theory as the instituted, embodied history which I have developed the theory of primal scenes to elaborate.

This issue has surfaced in contemporary uses of discourse theory, though it has not been theorized in the fashion presented here. One evidence of this is the way in which discursive de-naturalizing critiques may be utilized while simultaneously other social categories are regarded, or left un-analyzed, as "natural." While "women," "black" or "of color," can be shown to be socially constructed categories, "white men" might be assumed to be a natural category as if it were any more obvious to whom this equally socially constructed category might pertain. There is a tendency to constrain the apparently limitless mutability to which social constructionism gives rise by naturalizing a limit at an (assumed to be) unmovable point. This tendency stands in for an ethics, in the sense that it provides the practical orientation that gives direction and purpose to a discursive critique, though it does not articulate its basis.

I have mentioned only one example that pertains to the main emphasis of the examples discussed above, it may be that all social movements need to engage in some such naturalizing due to their orientation to action. Gayatri Spivak has argued that all discursive criticism takes this form, that practical intervention requires a "strategic essentialism" that posits one term as essential or natural even though theoretically it is known to be socially constructed.[29] I do not see how this could be interpreted as an adequate theoretical response, though it is certainly descriptive of a certain tendency of current discursive criticism. On the theoretical level, the notion of strategic essentialism seems to be an admission that the theory with which one is operating is inadequate as an account of the practical interventions which it stimulates. Nonetheless, however adequate one judges this account to be, it indicates the issue to which I am pointing: that the infinite mutability to which discourse theory points is useful in criticism but not sufficient as an orientation of social action (including the strategic selection of targets for criticism). Even if one wants to avoid the direct articulation of an ethics toward which my argument points, one is forced to coin a concept that stands in for an ethics of embodied history at key points in the theory.

The limits to social construction thus pertain to the conceptual distinction which gets its argumentative strategy going. This may be sex and gender, skin color and race, and so on. As long as such a distinction can be meaningfully drawn, social constructionism can be deployed in order to open a space for social change. *Whether* such a distinction can be meaningfully drawn depends upon the prior taken-for-granted context from which discourse theory draws its rhetorical force. This leads to the question: Can a society understand all its major orienting themes as discursively constructed? Or, what happens if everyone understands everything as socially constructed through discourse? This is probably an impossible situation. But asking the question in this way does allow us to see that the rhetorical force and intellectual strategy of discourse theory would be abolished thereby. So let us ask this question in a more meaningful way: At what point does the perspective of discourse theory arise? Discourse theory must be analyzed not only as an intellectual standpoint but also as a social phenomenon in its own right with a precise historical location. It not only addresses the possibilities and difficulties of our time but also exemplifies them. The argument that a given concept is constructed in discourse is a constitutive part of the process of social change. It occurs after the possibility for changing a given set of social relations has been grasped by some part of the population, but before this possibility has been widely accepted in the society as a whole. In this context, it gains its rhetorical force by contributing to the increasing dissemination of the possibility of social change and increasing sophistication of the analysis and critique of the dominant ideology.

The de-naturalizing of common sense is a process of making questionable the constitutive practices of a society. It occupies a mediating role in that it does not institute the initial impetus to change nor is it capable of carrying through to see change accomplished. Discourse theory thus occurs in a society in transition with regard to the credibility of its fundamental assumptions—at a moment in which the old values have ceased to hold sway and new ones have not yet caught on. This situation requires a particular role for intellectuals—understanding the "intellectual" function in the widest Gramscian sense as the articulation of leadership—in destroying the old world and elaborating a vision of the new. It is at this point of the self-construction of identity that the content-orientation of rhetorical interventions discovers the invention of primal scenes in media of communication.

The tendency of postmodern consumer society toward the loss of mediation is contested by the practice of the new social movements and their strategies for reintroducing mediations. While this may occur through the strategy of constructing identities through discursive strategies (strategy one) as discussed above, it may also pertain to the communication media themselves that are used in the discursive strategies—strategy three. From this latter perspective, we can begin to characterize both the information revolution and consumer society as postmodern culture, and to address that component of the embodied history made possible by primal scenes, that, as I have argued thoughout, is always external to a purely content-oriented discourse theory.

A crucial element of the emergence of new social movements over the last thirty years is due to the failure of both sides of the traditional alternative of "reform or revolution" with respect to the issue of systemic change. The traditional problem with the perspective of reform is simply that, in reforming the bureaucratic consumer capitalist system, the goals of the reformist movement are incorporated back into the system to strengthen it without altering its fundamental characteristics. The traditional revolutionary critique of reform has some validity in this respect.

The problem with the revolutionary alternative is somewhat different. At least under some historical circumstances the revolutionary option has been exercised successfully. The problem is that there is a tendency to reproduce in the new revolutionized system certain key features of the previous system. To generalize, the actually existent socialist societies did not achieve the integration of economic and political freedom that Marx projected, but rather have achieved the suppression of political participation in the name of economic planning (although it is clear that communist economic planning is not a superior economic system to that of capitalism in important respects, in any case).

Intelligent critics in the Marxist tradition have analyzed this problem with revolutionary transformation. Gregory Bateson has, though in a less nuanced fashion, also pointed to the tendency of revolutions initiated by those dominated within a system to reproduce the fundamental characteristics of the system.[30] Nevertheless, the reformist alternative also faces a similar problem—that of strengthening the given system. Thus, inheritors of both revolutionary and reformist traditions now face the key issue of how to achieve systemic change without reproducing in a new (and perhaps diabolical form) unwanted features of the previous system. The Marxist tradition, encompassing both revolutionary communism and social democratic reformism—which are the two main Marxist alternatives of the twentieth century—has failed to resolve this problem. In the nineteenth century, the unity and continuity of reform and revolution could be assumed. In the twentieth century, we are faced with a darker unity: neither revolutionary or reformist options seem capable of achieving fundamental systemic change. This analysis is not a statement of historical inevitability, but rather the statement of a *problem* that must be confronted by any self-aware contemporary effort at transformation of the system of bureaucratic, consumer capitalism. The revolution or reform alternative poses the issue of social change *either* at the systemic, universal level *or* the particular, intra-systemic level. For historical reasons dependent on the breakdown of nineteenth-century Marxism, the alternative became intervention in the present system at the level of the whole or that of the part. Both sides of the argument assume that the relevant choice is between the whole and the part.

In contrast, I want to suggest that the key question facing social change at the present time is rather "mediation"—that is the mediation *between* whole and part. The political practice of the new social movements—for example, ecology, anti-nuclear, anti-racist, feminist, peace, regional, and national movements—is precisely to intervene at this "middle" level of mediation. The slogan "Think globally, act locally," which has been so effective in this context, begins to make this clear by pointing out that there must be both universal and particular elements in political intervention. Nevertheless, the present suggestion is that it is really the *interaction* between the global and the local that is key. The mediation between global and local is the strategic point for contemporary political intervention. Insofar as this mediation is understood as taking multiple forms, the system is also characterized in a plurality of ways. It is understood as an *environment* (in Husserlian fashion) rather than as either an empirical aggregate or a rationalist totality. It is at this point that the possibility of systemic change that does not reproduce key features of contemporary domination emerges. However, since totality is not understood as a determinate whole in Hegelian fashion, the project of social transformation is not a project of system-transformation as a whole as it was for Marxism. The multiple characterizations each imply transformation of the whole *in some pervasive aspect* but the whole itself is neither characterized positively nor changeable toward another determinate system.

As Laclau and Mouffe have argued, the key political issue in the new social movements is the transformation of relations of subordination into relations of antagonism.[31] For example, in the current industrial order, nature is normally subordinated to human interests. Similarly, in patriarchy women are subordinated to men. With the arising of a new social movement, the normally subordinated relations of nature and women are experienced as antagonistic to the dominating terms of humanity and men. This process of transformation into antagonism brings the normal order into question. Notice that the order *as a whole* becomes questionable though it is questioned *from a particular angle*. The Marxist tradition was "essentialist" in the sense that it attempted to see these multiple sources of critique as expressing an underlying class contradiction. It is characteristic of the new social movements that this explanation is rejected and the plurality of critiques is neither reduced to an underlying unity nor subsumed under a higher genus—which would render the specificity of the antagonism irrelevant. Accepting the multiplicity of critiques requires rethinking the mediation between universal and particular, since the critique is both directed toward a specific, irreducible aspect of the system (nature, women) and directed toward the system as a whole. Rather than discovering an "underlying" or "higher" unity of these movements, the political issue becomes mediation "across" planes of antagonism—or, in the term developed previously, as a translation of one antagonism into another. Thus, I will next address the dual aspects of mediation between particular and universal as *environment* and between multiple planes of antagonism as *translation*.

In the twentieth century capitalist societies have pursued unbridled economic self-interest which has led to the massive political-economic power of multinational corporations while communist societies have subordinated individuals to the state. In other words, the liberal conception of an alternative between private self-interest and the social good has been realized in a diabolical fashion in the duality between two world social systems. The inability to reconcile individual and society in a higher unity has now been proven by historical development or, precisely, it has become political folly, with foreseeable dangerous effects, to advocate a reconciled unity of individual and society. Both "alternatives" tend toward the concentration of power in the hands of a few.

Where can a critical conception arise in this situation? Is one thereby thrown back into the classic liberal opposition between individual and society? It is true that, if one abandons the notion of a "unity" between individual and society, one must be confronted with two separate discourses—a discourse of individual interest and self-protection alongside a discourse of social responsibility—but everything depends, at this point, on how one conceives of this "alongside." Liberal ideology asserts that they are necessarily in opposition; it is this tension that supplies the motive power of contemporary bureaucratic, consumer, capitalist society. The practice of the new social movements indicate that there is another possibility. It is this new possibility that can be given a theoretical foundation in the notion of "mediation" suggested in the focus on a "medium" of communication. While part two of this book suggested that contemporary consumer society is characterized by a loss of mediation, the present part indicates that social movements have become sources for the introduction of mediation into the code of contemporary society and that they can be productively investigated with the notion of a medium of communication.

This perspective implies a thorough rethinking of the political and epistemological basis of modern thought, which can be introduced through the observation that the two discourses of self-interest and social responsibility, though different and often incompatible, nevertheless overlap at key points. If we imagine them as a Venn diagram, they would be two separate circles which overlap over a certain area. This area—where one can pursue one's own welfare while at the same time furthering the overall social good—is very small in both contemporary capitalist and communist societies. The liberal conception of their opposition is rooted in powerful social forces that are aligned in that manner. In this situation, the expansion of the realm of mediation is a political intervention designed to increase to the maximum the "overlap" between individual self-interest and social responsibility. It does not imagine a reconciliation between them in the sense that it does not expect a third circle to encompass both of them or, what would amount to the same thing, the two circles overlapping to such an extent that they become almost identical. Nevertheless, to the extent that the area of compatibility *between* individual self-interest and social responsibility can grow, there is an increasing possibility of social change at the systemic level which will not reproduce in a future system the key characteristics of the present system.

This is the only possible location for post-liberal and post-Marxist attempts to found communities based on democratic participation and decision-making. In short, the political problem of our time is how to make arrangements so that one can experience the activities that further one's own welfare in daily life as expressions of a more encompassing social good. But understanding the mediation performed by communication through the three concepts of environment, translation, and reflexivity goes much farther in theorizing the perspectives opened up by the new social movements than simply suggesting the expansion of the intermediate realm of "overlapping." "Mediation," understood in this way, is not defined in relation to some supposedly "unmediated" experience. Rather, it is concerned with the *establishing of connection*—with the "in-between" or "intentionality" of experience whereby a relation is constructed between an identity and its world. This theory of mediation unsettles and rethinks the particular-universal relation as it has been understood in modern philosophy and politics.

The emergent alignments of the new social movements practically engage this rethinking. Ecology and feminism, for example, are both more universal than the nation-state, and are extremely particular concerns centering on the well-being of one's own body. The new terms for these emergent relationships, such as person-planet and global-local, are attempts to think this new particular-universal relation through. They engage the component of an identity in relation to its environment in the outline of comparative media theory previously sketched. As I suggested, there is another dimension to mediation in this context—mediation "across" the multiple planes of antagonism.

Culture consists of continuous translation between a plurality of media of communication. Each medium mediates culture as a whole by providing an explicitness to that culture and mediating its past with its future state. The argument for mediation suggests that a given state of culture consists of given *delays* in this translation process—where translation "in" exceeds translation "out." The attempt to stop translation, to imagine a *total* delay, is to imagine the modern *reconciliation* of individual and society that has gone sour. At present we can see these delays as points of intervention where more possibilities of mediation across different antagonisms lurk. This approach is a theorization of the post-liberal, post-Marxist, pluralist political strategy of the new social movements.

The idea of delay and mediation invokes the reverse possibility of rapid translation out, and slow translation in, by a medium of communication. This begins to theorize the conception of reflexivity required by the previous components of environment and translation, allowing possibilities of greater representation and the possibility of fewer attempts at unification. Some such strategy is necessary to avoid the tragic consequences of both reformist and revolutionary politics in the twentieth century, and, even more to the point, the fateful *dichotomy* of reformist versus revolutionary politics. Mediation through comparative media theory is an attempt to think the multiple planes of critique as particular-universal determinations of the environment and as translations across these environments.

This new concept of reflexivity as a *transversal* accomplishment of thematization from a ground is the justification for the claim that social movements invent and insert reflexivity into the consumer code and thereby open possibilities for social transformation. These movements can still be called "emancipatory" in the sense that they aim to rid society of an endemic inequality, but there are necessarily a plurality of movements whose mutual relations are complicated. One must, therefore, let go of the key assumption of modernity that there is a single social contradiction, thus a single emancipatory movement, and therefore a linear direction of progress in history insofar as it approximates this utopia. A plurality of emancipation movements implies a multidimensional approach to history, the abandonment of the notion that it may progress, and a loosening of the many utopias from history. There could never be a final state that satisfied them all; not only in fact, but in principle. But, unlike many postmodern writers, I still call these movements "emancipatory" due to their struggles to redefine society and remove oppression. The plurality of movements leads to a politics of hegemony, of a necessary plurality within a new type of unity.

CHAPTER 12

Discourse and Identity

New mediations are introduced into postmodern consumer society by the resistance strategies of social movements. This chapter builds upon this argument in order to develop a conception of articulation theory as an appropriate social and political theory, focused on the process of communication, for the criticism engaged in by social movements.

Insofar as humans are not simply determined into a "natural" and unchanging social order, their participation requires that a particular social location be coordinated with the social order as a whole. This coordination relies on relationships based on understanding, affective interactions and desires—in short, the establishment of meaning. To this extent, social order relies on the circulation of meaning for its legitimation and social change requires an intervention in this circulation. The rhetoric of order or change is thus not simply a coercive one, which would imply that all participation in social bonds has been broken and can only be maintained through the threat of violence, but is, above all, a construction of meaning. As Weber pointed out, following Trotsky on this point, the modern state maintains itself through a monopoly on the means of violence,[1] but the question remains as to when these means can be "legitimately" used, without escalating the disintegration of the social meaning–fabric—which would, in turn, escalate the use of violence.

The more fundamental question was posed in the mid–sixteenth century by Etienne de la Boettie in his *Discourse on Voluntary Servitude*: "the powerful influence of custom is in no respect more compelling than in this, namely, habituation to subjection."[2] Since the king is only one man, what ensures that even his lieutenants will obey him? The rhetoric of meaning that (dis)establishes social order cannot be simply opposed to violence, but underlies even the use of violence and determines when, to what extent, and to what effect the means of coercion can be employed. Clearly, then, this rhetoric is always imbued with power—not only externally, due to the social position of the one who speaks (which is established in the social field as a whole), but also internally, as the power of a given speaking to (de)legitimate elements of the meaning-fabric and contribute to the (re)arranging of social order. It is the interplay between these external and internal dimensions of a given discourse that constitutes its contribution to the (de)legitimation of the social order. Every intervention in the circulation of meaning derives its power from the specific intervention in relation to the context of already existing discourses.

The concept of articulation focuses on this relation between discursive intervention and the context, or field, of discourses. It incorporates, and attempts to develop, a conception of power that is not limited to the disjunction or consensus (convergence) between different interests, but is directed toward the more fundamental level of intersubjective meaning. As Charles Taylor says, "convergence of belief or attitude or its absence presupposes a common language in which these beliefs can be formulated. . . . Much of this common language in any society is rooted in its institutions and practices; it is constitutive of these institutions and practices."[3] The concept of articulation is concerned with the politics of common sense in which discursive interventions modify the field of power. Thus, legitimations of the social order succeed, not so much by repressing already formulated alternatives, but by preventing their formulation or, later, by recuperating formulated alternatives within the dominant articulation and thereby, of course, changing their meaning. The latter move is what we used to call co-optation. In the contemporary configuration of the field of common sense, the articulation of alternatives by new social movements must continually struggle with their de- and re-articulation, in which the mass media play a key role.

The concept of articulation has become central to recent critical cultural studies. It is rooted in the history of Marxist theory and politics and refigures the relationship between theory and praxis. The concept of hegemony emerged in Russian Social Democracy and became the center of the work of Antonio Gramsci through an increasing expansion of the realm of contingent specific circumstances, to which the Marxist theory of historical development had to be adapted to attain practical relevance for political action. In articulation theory, the significance of the realm of contingent hegemonic relations is radically reinterpreted so as to undermine the background of the logic of historical development against which it emerged. Totality is understood as a diversity of locations unified through a leadership, rather than as a Hegelian process of internal and pervasive development or as a structuralist framework which admits of various substitutable contents. In contemporary articulation theory a figure-ground shift takes place: Articulation theory is the form that hegemony takes when it has ceased to be the thematic concern against a presupposed background of historical logic and has itself become the background against which any historical figures emerge. This radicalization of the problematic of hegemony centers the "logic of contingent relations" which is extended to the entire social field. Put in another way, the activist component of ideological intervention is conceived to be an inherent limit to any theoretical totalization, and therefore any historical logic, such that the unity of any social form is achieved through a political intention (rather than preceding it) and is therefore always a partial unity articulated against alternatives. As we will see later, this figure-ground shift is not only the necessary condition for the emergence of the concept of articulation, but also needs to be understood as a key component of the concept itself.

Understood even in this provisional manner, it is clear why the concept of articulation is central for the practice of cultural criticism: Communication is understood, not merely as a reflection of something underlying it, but as an active component (perhaps *the* active component) in the construction of social reality. From within Marxist theory, articulation theory offers a departure from the base-superstructure model which places cultural dynamics at the center of theoretical and political praxis. For cultural critics, it offers a connection to wider social and political criticism. For political activists, it offers a serious reflection on the everyday struggle for meaning in which they are engaged that surpasses such terms as "bourgeois ideology," which are simply dismissive and practically useless unless they can be compared to an existing revolutionary subaltern ideology.

In all of these phrasings of this intellectual shift, communication becomes central to the process of meaning-making in a culture and thereby to the possibilities of political intervention. Moreover, these advantages of articulation theory converge in finally according due significance to the new social movements that have been the main forces for social change in advanced capitalist societies in the post-war period, and which cannot properly be understood if they are reduced to expressions of an underlying class contradiction. Struggles over the definition of common sense have been key in the ecology, anti-nuclear, anti-racist, ethnic, feminist, sexual liberation, regionalist, nationalist, and other movements. These are, in large part, struggles over the process of "normalization" by which the (de)legitimation of movements for social change takes place and in which language plays a key role. It is of primary importance to move forward with any concepts that can clarify these struggles in a manner that will help us to pass beyond their mere enumeration. They need to be understood together through some (as yet unclarified) notion of "totality," but not reduced to expressions of an underlying (class) unity. In this sense, communication issues are central to the agenda of movements for social change.

Here, I want to argue for one main criticism of the concept of articulation as developed by Laclau and Mouffe and utilized by Stuart Hall, and develop a corollary of it. I claim that the "elements" of an articulation are not satisfactorily theorized by these thinkers, with the exception of the negative comment that they are not the "moments" of a logical totality. With respect to the relation of elements and the discursive field, I will suggest that this relation should be understood as a theme-background relation as developed in the phenomenological tradition. Articulatory practice not only forges a linkage, but also focuses on, or highlights, selected elements through the phenomenon that was described as "voicing" above. This foregrounding of selected elements allows them to become leading moments in the equivalences forged between moments of different articulations. A corollary of this critique is that the notion of articulation is situated more effectively at the point of political action—which is explicated through the notion of "particularity."

The theory of articulation in its contemporary form begins from Ernesto Laclau's book *Politics and Ideology in Marxist Theory*, which was first published in 1977. Laclau's critique of the Marxist reduction of all social phenomena to class position and his alternative theory of articulation has been extended into cultural studies by Stuart Hall.[4] A discussion of the appropriation of the problematic of articulation in British cultural studies will allow the introduction of this critical point: the "elements" of an articulation must be understood as thematizations from a taken-for-granted background.

British cultural studies originated at the intersection of the two traditions of structuralism and culturalism—associated in Britain with the work of Raymond Williams and Edward Thompson. The latter emphasizes the experience of individuals and classes as constitutive of the social totality whereas the former insists on the thorough mediation of any subjective experience of immediacy by the totality of the social structure. In the terms of international Marxism, these two traditions are most marked in the divergence between Gramsci's problematic of hegemony and Althusser's structuralism. Despite this divergence, British cultural studies attempted to mediate these two key poles of Marxist theory in a manner that enabled concrete investigations. In British Marxism, the monumental historical work of Edward Thompson, *The Making of the English Working Class*, emphasized the notion of "experience," understood as the interaction of consciousness with the conditions of life.[5] Despite the rejection of Thompson's formulation as an "expressive totality" (due to the structuralist influence), it formed the basis for the appropriation of Gramsci's concept of hegemony—which Hall has described as "the inventory of traditional ideas, the forms of episodic thinking which provide us with the taken-for-granted elements of our practical knowledge, [that Gramsci] called . . . 'common sense.'"[6]

It is through this intellectual route that the experiential component entered the concept of articulation, though it has never been theoretically accounted for to the same degree as structuralism, even while this experiential component has usually dominated both the choice of problems and the rhetoric of presentation. A fuller theoretical treatment requires the inclusion of concepts adequate to theorizing the "immediacy" of experience that are best developed in the phenomenological tradition. In short, there is a hidden proximity between the emphasis on subjectivity, experience, and decision in Thompson's historical writing, Gramsci's concept of hegemony, and the phenomenological tradition.

Hall's formulation of a cultural politics of common sense introduces the component of the taken-for-granted into the concept of articulation. When understood as constitutive of common sense, ideology is most effective precisely when it is invisible, when it has come to form the unquestioned basis *from which* people argue, rather than the explicit conclusions that they *argue toward*. As Hall puts it, "it is in and through the systems of representation of culture that we 'experience' the world: experience is the product of our codes of intelligibility, our schemas of interpretation. . . . Here we are most under the sway of the most highly ideological structures of all—common sense, the regime of the 'taken for granted.'"[7] In explaining his usage of the concept of articulation, Hall has pointed to two distinct meanings that are built into the concept.

In England, the term has a nice double meaning because "articulate" means to utter, to speak forth, to be articulate. It carries that sense of language-ing, of expressing, etc. But we also speak of an articulated lorry (truck): a lorry where the front (cab) and back (trailer) can, but need not necessarily, be connected to one other. The two parts are connected to each other, but through a specific linkage, that can be broken. An articulation is thus the form of the connection that *can* make a unity of two different elements, under certain conditions. It is a linkage which is not necessary, determined, absolute and essential for all time.[8]

While the first sense of expressing has a clear affinity with the notion of thematization, it is the post-structuralist notion of "linkage" developed by Laclau that has come to dominate the definition and use of the concept of articulation.[9] The dominant component in the definition emphasizes that an articulated cultural unity links components which do not necessarily belong together, but whose connection is forged in the activity of articulation itself. This component is very similar to Michael McGee's notion of the "ideograph," whose meaning is established by the "cluster" of terms in which it operates.[10]

But, beginning from the above definition by Hall, one may say that articulation is also *enunciation*, the activity of "putting into words" that is involved in the notion of thematization. Before elements can be linked together they must be focused on, brought into the light, from a more global, undifferentiated, and presupposed background. These two aspects of the concept of articulation need to be distinguished and conceptually clarified: the *thematization* of elements from the undifferentiated background of interconnected presuppositions and *combination* of these distinct elements. Thematization is a prior activity in which the anonymous interconnected field of assumptions pre-existing the articulatory activity is selectively focused on to yield distinct elements. Subsequently, combination of these elements achieves a specific discursive formation that then enters into common sense. Common sense itself can be understood as the totality of these discursive formations, including their inter-relationships, subsisting at any given spatio-temporal nexus and awaiting further articulation.

The activity of thematization which produces elements can thus be understood as a relationship between a taken-for-granted background and a focused-upon theme. This productive focusing captures the primary, and neglected, sense of articulation as an uttering, a bringing-forth into language. Alfred Schütz's phenomenological sociology examined this process of selective focusing as a process of determining "relevances" for orientation in the common-sense world. In his words, "the selective function of our interest organizes the world in both respects—as to space and time—in strata of major or minor relevance. From the world within my actual or potential reach those objects are selected as primarily important which actually are or will become in the future possible ends or means for the realization of my projects, or which are or will become dangerous or enjoyable or otherwise relevant to me."[11] Thus, we may say that the totality of discursive formations that constitute common sense are given their distinctive organization by a system of relevances interwoven with the conduct of practical life. Common sense is always *this* sense, here and now, and this particularity of its formation is constituted through thematization.

Despite the primacy of thematization, the later activity of combination can influence the productive process of thematization. The linkage of a prominent element with a less prominent one tends to transfer the prominence, or relevance, and with it, shall we say, the "strength" of thematization. But this transfer cannot itself produce a theme; even if a combination of a key ideological term like "freedom" with a relatively minor element like buying tennis shoes can serve to transfer and effect an association that makes buying tennis shoes, or even a specific brand of tennis shoes, more significant; it cannot accomplish the isolation and characterization of the element of "buying tennis shoes" in the first place. This element is pre-given to the activity of combination as the product of a thematization in the economic sphere that has separated out this kind of shoes from all others. Thus, the linkage of elements derives a great deal of its efficacy from the prior process of thematization.

While thematization and combination function in an inter-related manner in the articulations that constitute common sense, the exclusive focus on the latter, such as is characteristic of British cultural studies, tends to obscure the manner in which a given articulatory practice not only recombines elements inherited from the previous formation, but focuses on and puts into circulation elements that had no existence in the previous formation. An articulation can function to silence certain experiences which still function within the assumptions of common sense. This is one of the main characteristics of ideology—it "anonymizes" certain elements of common sense which nevertheless do not entirely disappear. A re-articulation which combats such silences will indeed forge linkages with other competing but subaltern articulations. But it also does something else in the activity of thematization: It focuses on new elements; it slices up experience in new ways; it gives voice to the world. This giving voice is itself a fundamental aspect of articulation because it indicates where articulation cuts into the anonymous fabric of presuppositions.

Thematization and combination, the two components of articulation, are related to each other as poetry and rhetoric. There is the initial expression of a meaning in which the inchoate background is disclosed—which, in the context of new social movements, I have called "voicing"—and there is the preserving and extending of this known theme—which was called "linkage" or "rhetoric." The initial expression is poetry which, as Heidegger has elucidated, is at the origin of language where the world is brought forth into human experience.[12] In rhetoric, the given experience of the world is commemorated and made known to a wider cultural formation.[13] The thematizing aspect of articulation is a speaking-forth-the-world which involves both disclosure and preservation and forms the cultural unity of a social identity. There is no identity, or experience, prior to this productive activity. Thematization is a determining of relevances for which we may use the term "expression" as long as it is understood as a *cultural* concept without the assumption of an initial mental internality that must be brought outside. The activity of thematization is assumed, and even occasionally described, by Hall and in cultural studies generally, but it is never theorized as such. Richard Johnson approximates the same concept and describes it as "public-ation," but this term carries too much baggage in implying separate social spheres and wrongly assumes the explicit pre-existence of elements prior to their thematization.[14] This crucial absence means that there can never be a satisfactory account of the origin of the elements and, consequently, a sufficiently *critical theory* of common sense. In order to account for this absence, we will have to recall the origin of the concept of articulation in the work of Ernesto Laclau that is the basis for its development in British cultural studies.

The introduction to Ernesto Laclau's *Politics and Ideology in Marxist Theory* gave a general formulation of the concept of articulation. The book consists of four essays that intervene in key disputes in the Marxist theory of ideology—dependency and underdevelopment in Latin America, the specificity of politics and the role of the state, fascism, and populism. The last three of these debates touch on an identical underlying issue: the extent to which features of political life have an independence from the economic and class forces toward which Marxist theory routes its explanations. With respect to populism, for example, Laclau points to "*the relative continuity* of popular traditions, in contrast to the historical discontinuities which characterise class structures." Marxist theory has failed to solve the issue of the class adherence of populism—which can take either a fascist or socialist direction—because it has failed to see that "popular traditions do not constitute consistent and organized discourses but merely *elements* which can only exist in articulation with class discourses."[15] The problem requiring explanation shifts with this crucial reformulation. Rather than attempting to discover the *essential class ascription* of populist politics, the task becomes to explain the *specific conjuncture* of forces which articulate populism in either a right or left direction in a specific case.

The first essay in the book, which is a critique of Andre Gunder Frank's theory of dependency, centers on the concept of "mode of production" itself. Confronted with alternative analyses of Latin American societies, Laclau suggests a distinction between "economic system" and "mode of production" that, again, radically refigures the debate:[16] "The concept of 'world capitalist system' is therefore the nearest approximation to the concrete which a merely economic analysis permits, and . . . it cannot be *derived* from the concept of 'capitalist mode of production' but must be *constructed* by starting from the theoretical study of possible articulations of the different modes of production."[17] Thus, it is not possible to derive salient features of the current world system directly from the mode of production. Rather, it is the specific character of the *linkage*, or combination, of modes of production that characterizes the world system. This is a more fundamental critique of the Marxist base-superstructure model than that contained in the other three essays. While they indicate limitations to the derivation of the political superstructure from the base and suggest a certain autonomy of elements and their combinations from economic determination, this argument suggests that the economic base itself is a unity only insofar as it is constructed by an articulation of more fundamental elements (modes of production). In the Introduction Laclau generalizes these points by pointing out that the four essays demonstrate that there are two ways in which the theoretical debates he discusses have become confused: Either there is a failure to respect the proper level of theoretical abstraction, usually by substituting more concrete empirical determinations; or, there is a denial of the specificity of the subject-matter, and its reduction to another, supposedly more fundamental, one. His critique of Marxism thus focuses on the consequences of the failure to theorize adequately "abstraction" and "specificity." On this basis, Laclau develops a full-blown theory of articulation which focuses on the *elements* of a socio-economic unity and the *linkage* whereby they are forged into such a unity.

The introduction begins with Plato's allegory of the cave and thereby links the theory of articulation to the social function of philosophy. Philosophy breaks up, or disarticulates, the connotative and evocative links of common sense, purifies theoretically their inherent meanings, and then rearticulates them as purely logical links. This dual movement has two related consequences: First, the purification of concepts dissolves the ideological identification of concepts with specific social forms. For example, "those concepts which defined for the bourgeoisie the abstract conditions of any possible society, lost their necessary articulation with the concrete forms in which those conditions were locally materialized."[18] Philosophy functions as critical of the established order by measuring the given reality in relation to ideal determinations. Second, this critical practice is intertwined with a corresponding rationalist illusion that the whole of reality can be reconstructed in a logical and necessary manner. While common sense forms an interconnected whole absorbing every possible meaning through external links with all other meanings, philosophy claims to rearticulate a similar all-encompassing system, but exclusively through inner logical links between meanings. According to Laclau, the progress of Marxist theory has been hindered by both the connotations of common sense and essentialist rationalist paradigms, due to its inadequate understanding of the relation between these two poles—or, we might say, a failure to resolve its relation to philosophy. On the one hand, connotative meanings from political practice have been inserted into theoretical discourse uncritically. On the other hand, when theory purifies common sense it often falls prey to the rationalist illusion of constructing a system of essential internal logical relations.

The paradigmatic logical relation in Marxism is class reductionism—the idea that any element of social or political life is a necessary outgrowth of an underlying class contradiction. Thus, the twin errors in Marxist theory of reduction to common sense and rationalism reinforce each other in class reductionism, which is really another way of saying that the base-superstructure metaphor is characteristic of Marxism as such. If the various elements of political life have no necessary class ascription, then even less do the elements of cultural life generally. But this is emphatically not to say that these elements are independent of politics. Rather, the cultural and ideological sphere forms the common-sense assumptions that enter into explicit political views and positions. Thus, the political sphere is expanded into a cultural politics of common sense, but this is no longer posed through the fixation of cultural elements to any necessary class belongingness, but rather through the mode of articulation of these elements into a cultural unity. It is the cohesion of elements and the overall hegemonic intent of this cultural unity that defines its political component.

Some of the implications of the first critical point that was introduced above through the discussion of British cultural studies—distinguishing poetic expression from rhetorical linkage—can be clarified on the basis of this full-blown account of articulation by Laclau. Let us pinpoint carefully the error that is involved in describing articulation solely in terms of linkage, or combination, of elements, and thereby missing the activity of thematization. The error consists in taking the elements that are a *result* of the dearticulating activity of theoretical criticism to be simply there, that is, given prior to the thematization.[19] This is a form of objectivism insofar as it anonymizes the (dearticulating) activity of theory and presents its results as simple givens. In short, failure to account for thematization leads to the error of empiricism, which wrongly takes the experienced everyday world to be a plurality of elements, rather than an articulated whole organized through relevances appearing as common sense. Since one of the main purposes of Laclau's first theory of articulation was to account for the role of theory in the (de)construction of common sense, this must be reckoned a key internal failure. The tendency to rediscover empiricism, which is the polemical complement of structuralism, indicates that the theory of articulation has not (yet) escaped the metaphysical oppositions it attempted to undercut. This problem is a motive for the later development of the theory of articulation by Laclau in collaboration with Chantal Mouffe.

We must differentiate three levels of inquiry: the prior process of thematization (poetry), the intermediate level of linkages (rhetoric), and the historical level of transition between different epochs. But this critical revision can only be developed further through an analysis of the later theory of articulation developed by Laclau and Mouffe, in which the notion of element is clarified by distinguishing it from a "moment" of an articulated unity. *Hegemony and Socialist Strategy*, co-authored by Ernesto Laclau and Chantal Mouffe, develops the theory of articulation in a manner that follows out the consequences of Laclau's earlier work and transforms a theoretical development within Marxism into a post-Marxist political theory of "radical democracy" based on contemporary discourse theory. Laclau introduced the term "elements" of political ideologies in *Politics and Ideology in Marxist Theory* in order to supplant reductionism back to class origin and instead to orient toward the effectivity of a combination of these elements in an articulation. In the later work, this aspect is developed further through the distinction between "elements" and "moments" of a cultural unity, which allows Laclau and Mouffe to understand the social field as constructed through *antagonism*. This notion of antagonism allows them to specify under what conditions a given social difference becomes experienced as oppressive or exploitative and, moreover, to extend such analysis beyond the terrain of class to the other antagonisms specified by the new social movements—struggles over the meaning of nation, race, sex, nature, and so forth. In each case, a given social difference, such as superpower-country, nation-region, white-black, male-female, humanity-nature, is given the inflection of an antagonism due to an effect emerging from the outside, or limit, of the social difference in question. The crucial contribution of this work is thus its rethinking of the Marxist notion of class struggle by investigating the conditions under which a social identity experiences a block to its realization. The point of political action is understood as constitutive of the social field, rather than as a circumscribed domain within it. A formulation of this issue in general terms is important because, without it, studies of the construction of social identities focus simply on their plurality and heterogeneity—thereby becoming an apologetic pluralism. A critical theory, however, is concerned with the *differential* effects of power and the consequent *prevention* of the realization of social identities.

The articulation of a given cultural meaning is achieved through discursive practice oriented to linking what, in a slight shift of terminology, Laclau and Mouffe now call the various "moments" of a discourse. The identity, or meaning, of these moments within the given articulation is modified, or defined by, the particular character of the linkage established in each case. An "element," on the other hand, is defined as a "difference which is not discursively articulated."[20] Articulatory practice, therefore, can be defined as the transformation of elements into moments.

> We now have all the necessary analytical elements to specify the concept of articulation. Since all identity is relational— even if the system of relations does not reach the point of being fixed as a stable system of differences—and since, too, all discourse is subverted by a field of discursivity which overfows it, the transition from "elements" to "moments" can never be complete. The status of the "elements" is that of floating signifiers, incapable of being articulated to a discursive chain. And this floating character finally penetrates every discursive (i.e. social) identity.[21]

Elements must be conceived as pre-existing the discursive formations into which they are articulated, since articulation is not a creation from nothing but a practice of linking. Moreover, the transformation of elements into moments can never be complete since this would misinterpret the articulated discursive identity as a rationalist totality accomplished exclusively through mediation by logical relations. In consequence, any social identity must be understood as temporary and partial, sustained only through a continuous articulatory practice that succeeds in repulsing alternative articulations which would dearticulate the given identity.

The key implication of this distinction (and relation) between elements and moments is the dynamic reformulation it allows of the notion of "antagonism." Without this term, articulation theory would bear no important relation to the Marxist tradition. Consequently, they distinguish "subordination" from "domination."[22] The former refers to any unequal social relation, whereas the latter refers to the same unequal relation experienced as "injust," "insufferable," "exploitative," (or some equivalent term). An articulated set of social relations interpellates social differences in relations of subordination, such as lord-serf, capitalist-worker, white-black, man-woman, humanity-nature, and so forth. The Marxist question is: Under what conditions do such relations of subordination become experienced as relations of domination, or oppression, and give rise to struggles directed at their transformation? In other words, what occurs when relations of difference become experienced as antagonistic? Within an articulated cultural unity, relations of difference are "moments" and experienced as normal. But since the transition from elements to moments is never complete, there is always the possibility of dearticulating these moments from this cultural unity into elements—which can, of course, enter as moments into a new articulation.

It is at this point of dearticulation of moments into elements that antagonism arises, that the social difference is experienced as "not necessary and capable of being transformed"—what I called above *un-discounting*. Laclau and Mouffe reject the possibility of theorizing antagonism as occuring between positive social identities because such identities are understood as constituted by their articulation within a discursive formation. They exist "positively" only as a relations of subordination within a given articulation. In their words, "[b]ut in the case of antagonism, we are confronted with a different situation: the presence of the Other prevents me from being totally myself. The relation arises not from full totalities, but from the impossibility of their constitution."[23] A relation of antagonism thus implies a relation to a negativity, to the "outside" of the given discursive formation. It is this relation outside that transforms the internal relation of subordination into a relation of domination. Since society is not understood to be a *given totality* (whether expressive, rationalist, or empiricist) but as an articulated social unity, antagonisms can be said to point to a "limit of the social," its inability to be fully present to itself. Thus, power must be understood, not as a conflict between constituted social identities, but as operative in the formation of identities themselves—their prevention, their temporary unity, and their dissolution, in relations of antagonism with other identities.

The limit of the social attains a presence within the discursive formation by an operation that Laclau and Mouffe designate as "equivalence." They give the example of a colonized country in which differences of dress, language, skin color, and customs become equivalent, or substitutable, as evidence of the oppressiveness of the dominant power and remark that "[s]ince each of these contents is equivalent to the others in terms of their common differentiation from the colonized people, it loses the condition of differential *moment*, and acquires the floating character of an *element*."[24] This common differentiation should not be understood as various expressions of an underlying essentially antagonistic relation, which would be to revert to the positivity of the social that they criticize, but as the *construction* of equivalences that, through the antagonism, articulate the relation colonizer/colonized as domination, rather than as just a subordination. We may notice that the example in this case does not do the full duty that the theory requires. Actually, they speak of the dominant power being "made evident" in these different contents,[25] but this misleading phrase is indicative of a problem which will allow me to draw out a corollary of my first critical point: If it cannot mean essential underlying relations of power which express themselves in various forms, as the phrase seems to imply (but which would be incompatible with their entire approach), then the issue is exactly how this cultural unity of "the dominant power" is constructed, and their terminology avoids this posing of the question.

To clarify that this key issue of antagonism has not been well enough illuminated by Laclau and Mouffe, let us instead refer to a dominated, but not colonized, country like Canada in which, we may say, the dependent relations between Canada and the United States are "like" the relations of labor and capital, which, in turn, are "like" the relations between Quebec and the federal government, "like" relations between men and women, and "like" relations between humanity and nature. This collection of similitudes, or equivalences, is not pre-given but constructed in the practical politics in which one and/or more of them is at issue. In each case, it is by no means self-evident that the best way to push one of these causes is by alliance with the dominated part of another social difference. Why not ally oneself with a dominant power in another discourse? And, of course, in the practical politics of the last thirty years—both in Canada and elsewhere—such alliances have indeed occurred. Feminism, to pick just one example, has been most "successful" where it has allied itself with the business mentality and possessive individualist notions of equality. To assume from the outset that one subordinated social difference, when it is experienced through antagonism as a domination, is in any "natural," or predictable, sense drawn to alliance with other subordinate sectors, is a remnant of exactly the Marxist essentialism that Laclau and Mouffe criticize.

Let me finally say it clearly: The standpoint of the subordinated is not an epistemologically privileged one, though it is crucial politically. This certainly does not mean, however, that the question of how to ally various social identities experiencing themselves as dominated is not a fundamental issue for contemporary radical politics. Laclau and Mouffe suggest, or assume, that this project can be formulated solely through the notion of equivalences—with rhetorical linkages and without poetic voicing. The present analysis claims that it also requires some theorizing of the expression of the particular domination experienced in a given social difference and thus requires poetry also. Moreover, this prior cultural expression must also be placed within a conception of the social formation as a "whole," as an "epoch" characterized by a pervasiveness of the experience of domination—though this is to anticipate my second critical point, which will be discussed below.

An antagonism, in Laclau and Mouffe's analysis, is constructed through the articulation of likenesses between various social differences. The construction of such equivalences is the assembling of a chain of substitutions in which each term stands as a metaphor for the others. Politics in the new social movements involves such a practice of metaphorical linkage. For this reason hegemony is fundamentally metonymical.[26] The metaphoric equivalences, once established, are triggered by any one of them. Any part is displaced to all equivalent parts, and confirms the whole. This is true of articulations whether one broadly labels them either "status quo" or "progressive." Equivalences thus transform the moments of different discursive formations into floating elements which are not confined to any given formation since they tend to substitute in other formations. Such floating elements are the condition for the emergence of the problematic of hegemony in modern society—"a field criss-crossed by antagonisms and therefore sup-pose[s] phenomena of equivalence and frontier effects."[27] But if we are not to simply presuppose the form that such equivalences may/should take—even to the point of assuming that the dominated relations have something in common—we must also focus on the constitution of spe-cific antagonisms in the phenomenon of expression.

The construction of the equivalences that constitute antagonism requires an articulating subject. Clearly, this subject cannot pre-exist the articulation since its identity is formed through the equivalences (inte-rior to it); likewise, it cannot be entirely formed within the articulation since its construction is a discursive practice, that therefore requires an initiating action (exterior to it). "If the exteriority supposed by the artic-ulatory practice is located in the general field of discursivity, it cannot be that corresponding to two systems of fully constituted differences. It must therefore be the exteriority existing between subject positions located within certain discursive formations and 'elements' which have no precise discursive articulation."[28] It is this exteriority which becomes the "'experience' of the limit of all objectivity" within a discursive for-mation that achieves "a form of precise discursive presence" as an antagonism.[29] The floating elements upon which articulatory practices operate are constructed by a chain of equivalences within the general field of discursivity.

The totality of a certain discursive formation within this field is con-stituted by a negativity; it *is not* what is beyond the limit of its equiva-lences. This is termed, by Laclau and Mouffe, a transformation of lim-its into frontiers.[30] The frontier is thus the limit of a discursive formation (what it includes) transformed into a negation (what it excludes) by the construction of floating signifiers through articulating equivalences between discourses. In order to characterize the "form of presence" which this negation assumes, the term "experience" is utilized relatively often[31] and is probably ineradicable from a discourse concerning social change, but it is always put in quotation marks—which implies a dis-tancing that probably is due to the structuralist origins of their work. Nevertheless, it is significant that in certain contexts, and especially the transformation of social subordinations into antagonisms, it is unavoid-able. One would think that the task should be to abandon this embarass-ment with one's language and to further the concept of articulation through a conceptualization of the experiential component that neces-sarily arises at this point. In this context Laclau and Mouffe state that antagonism cannot be apprehended by language—which they under-stand, following Saussure, as a system of differences—since "language

only exists as an attempt to fix that which antagonism subverts. . . ."[32]
But this only serves to indicate the insufficiency of their conception of
language (a structuralist-Wittgensteinian amalgam).[33] Language is not
only a system of differences, and a rhetorical practice, but more fundamentally language-ing—the making known of the world through poetry.

The relation of interiority and exteriority of the subject to the articulation is, as was indicated at the outset of this chapter, the core of the
power of any given articulation. However, Laclau and Mouffe attempt
to *reduce* interiority to exteriority; they investigate linkage but not
thematization. Consequently, properly theorizing the power of articulation requires the utilization of the notion of "expression" as making-
known that was introduced as our first critical point in connection with
the extension of Laclau's earlier concept of articulation into British cultural studies. To re-state this point: the relation of elements and the discursive field should be understood as a theme-background relation as
developed in the phenomenological tradition. Articulatory practice not
only forges a linkage, but also focuses on, foregrounds, selected elements. This poetic sense of articulation as expression, of putting into
words, is prior to rhetorical linkages. The making-known of selected elements allows them to become leading moments in the equivalences
forged between moments of different articulations. It provides the theoretical basis for the expressive *difference* between the subordination-
domination articulated by one social movement and that of another.

As the fundamental component of hegemonic struggle, an "element" is in the process of transformation into moments of various articulations, but this process is incomplete due to the competition between
articulations. Thus, it has a floating character which consists of not
appearing outside a discursive formation, rather appearing inside many,
but in a situation of partial transformation into moments. The identity
of this element is thus of a peculiar character. If it appeared outside an
articulation (which it does not), it would be a positivity. If it were totally
inside a given articulation (which it isn't), it would be simply a moment.
In this case, it would be a pure absence signifying the impossibility of
equivalences, i.e., the total externality of articulations. In short, an element only appears as itself within a field of competing discourses, as an
expressed theme in relation to a background field, on the one hand, and
in polemical opposition to the rejected Hegelian mediation of moments
into a purely logical totality, on the other. There are thus two senses of
the term "element," or, better, two ways in which the term "element" is
used in Laclau and Mouffe's theory of articulation. First, an element is
prior to its articulation into a moment of a discursive formation, and

needs to be brought forth into language by poetry. Second, an element is constructed from moments of various articulations through the rhetorical elaboration of equivalences. But this temporal terminology may be misleading. It is rather that an element exists in a field of tension; it is a nodal point in a "space" crisscrossed by competing meanings. This meaning-tension tends to fall into (moment) or away from (element) the temporary unity of an articulated totality. In theorizing in this manner, the theory of articulation seeks to put itself at the point of political action, but, as we have indicated above, it does so only with respect to forging equivalences between existent movements, not with respect to the poetic expression of domination itself.

The aspect of articulation that I have called thematization, or poetry, situates the theory of articulation more precisely at the point of political action. Laclau and Mouffe's denial of sutured totality is a valid response to the diffusion of political effects, which is to destablize every given whole and to demonstrate that it only appears as a unity under conditions of continuous re-articulation in the face of de-articulations. But in order to approach more closely the point of politics, we may begin by noting that the denial of "necessity" to articulatory linkages is of relatively little use to any social identity attempting to *forge a specific articulation* in a situation of antagonism. While it is no doubt the case that political articulations have often falsely presented themselves as "necessary" in order to achieve hegemony, it is nevertheless the case that it is not usually a purely logical "necessity" that is meant. Moreover, the assertion of contingency amounts to only a bare assertion of the possibility of an alternative articulation. It is of no help in deciding which articulation to project and thereby which equivalences to forge, which depends upon the resources enabled by the expressive poetic component of articulation. The consequences of a polemical denial of necessity rebounding simply to the "contingency" which is its complementary metaphysical opposition is as likely to lead to a self-satisfied (or, even, violent) assertion of one's own contingencies as a skeptical social critique of contingent social domination.[34] The point, here as elsewhere, is to struggle toward concepts that encourage a thinking that exits from this sort of rebounding—which, as fashions change, will rebound back to another assertion of "necessity" soon enough.

The point of political intervention requires a distinction between contingency and "particularity." These are not complementary metaphysical opposites, as are contingency and necessity. Rather, "particularity" refers to the elements of an articulation as they are actively embraced *in the process of poetic expression*—that is to say, at the very point where a given articulation comes into being. "Particularity" is a term used by George Grant to refer to a non-universal element of social life that cannot be regarded as merely contingent by the social identity which is expressed in it because it is the indispensable condition for the apprehension of more universal dimensions of human life.[35] Thematization of elements raises them from the contingency of an anonymous background to particular elements conferring identity. The construction of particularity through articulation is an anticipation of homecoming, a construction of a world in which the non-universal elements to which identities are attached become hegemonic. In a world of leaky totalities, political action is not aided, and perhaps is diffused, by an assertion that it is pervaded by contingency. This is not false, it is merely the assertion of a truth inherited from previous political action—it is an effect, an afterthought. Enacting is a positing, both an expression and a linkage, that proposes a way of viewing the world. One cannot assert the contingency of an articulation in the same moment that one enacts it. The point of politics itself involves in its practical embodiment the assertion that the proposed articulation is not merely contingent, though neither can it claim necessity. Political action can, in contrast, claim particularity, which involves a new formation of the part/whole relationship based on the phenomenological notion of thematization. Particularity involves a step back from the relation between contingency and universality to the *conditions under which* a specific being might apprehend a universal good. This regressive step back is made necessary by the absence of authoritative origin. To those situated within them, the struggles of the new social movements and the new identities forged within them are particular, neither necessary nor contingent. They bring into focus new expressions of identity which do not have a similar claim on other identities, but which must be defended nonetheless. We are in the realm here not of reason but of love and hate, suffering and joy, wherein attachment to particulars resides.

The construction of equivalences between these particulars cannot reduce this specificity of attachment and, in this sense, Laclau and Mouffe's term "equivalences" is marred by the term contingency.[36] The elements within the new social movements can never become strictly equal, even in a temporary fashion, since this would reduce the specificity of the antagonisms. Laclau and Mouffe's political theory of radical democracy contains within itself the ghost of the Marxist claim to universalize all struggles in that of the proletariat, though now as an articulated unity aiming at hegemony. The real political point now is a "difference in unity," a new relation of part and whole, that is not well served by a simple polemical denial of the whole and an assertion of equivalence between parts.

The "likeness" we find in different struggles can never predominate over the expression of difference. If metaphor is the process of forging equivalences, and metonymy the ideological triggering of a whole hegemonic articulation by any part, then the new social movements require also anti-metonymy as a counterpart to metaphor. While there may be no ultimate literality of expression, anti-metonymy can undo the displacements toward hegemonic universality, by means of a "regression" [*Rückgang*] toward the specific concrete particularity—the "condition under which," without which metaphor equivalents become substitutions. The expression of the part in the midst of the dissolution of the whole field permeated by equivalences is the constitution of particularity. I have argued that the politics of the social movements is indeed characterized by the metaphoric construction of equivalences, as Laclau and Mouffe suggest—rhetoric—but that it is also characterized by a more fundamental thematizing component which, in an anti-metonymical, "regressive" move, expresses the particularity of a cultural identity and its experience of domination—through a voicing, or poetry. The theoretical basis for this argument is the phenomenological interpretation of the notion of the "element," from which the theory of articulation was developed, as a thematization from a non-thematically presupposed background which is instituted by a primal scene of communication.

CHAPTER 13

Conclusion

I have argued for a convergence of phenomenological philosophy with a certain tradition of communication studies that focuses on the medium of communication. From the literature on media of communication, I singled out the work of Harold Innis as particularly significant. From phenomenology, I rejected Husserl's explicit analyses of communication, and began instead from the key concept of institution. "Institution" is a specific form of "constitution" that opens a cultural form through the "bias" inherent in a medium of communication. Comparative media theory is thus an inquiry into a mode of intentionality. The name "comparative media theory" applies to the synthesis of these two traditions in a coherent philosophy of communication which implies both further inquiry into overlapping areas of contemporary philosophy and empirical studies into contemporary and historical complexes of communication media.

The comparative media theory approach to the study of communication takes seriously the central paradox of communication: while every communication is oriented to the transmission of information, or sense-content, it also expresses the phenomenon of communication as such—which pertains to the very formation of subjectivities in a culture such that transmission can take place. Moreover, a theory of communication is both an enunciation and a theory of enunciation. As such, it must address its own self-referential constitution. The three parts of this book elaborate this constitutive paradox of self-reflexive constitution: part one describes the essentials of comparative media theory, part two describes its point of origin in consumer society, and part three pinpoints the rupture of the consumer code by social movements whereby reflexivity emerges. They answer the questions: *what* theory? why this theory *now*? and, how/why does one *become aware* of this phenomenon now?

The thesis proper to communication studies, in the context of the philosophy of human sciences, is the constitution of perception, social relations, institutions, and thought by media of communication. This requires a turn away from the sense-content, meaning, or information of a message toward the manner of formation of the message by the medium itself. This turn toward "materiality" can, however, be misunderstood if it is taken to refer to a merely physical externality, or "dead materiality." Communication media must be understood as extensions of the living human body such that the entire complex of media forms is a culture constituted by living expressions of a way of life. Thus, contrary to Husserl, communication is not marked by a subjective intention to communicate through a mark. Rather, communication is a constitutive characteristic of the world we inhabit. Whether it be the tracks of animals or marks on a computer screen, communication is what makes cultural subjects of us. Proximally and for the most part, it calls us, we do not use it, insofar as we dwell within an already-instituted opening.

To speak of primal scenes, the instituting of an opening, one must be approaching its *Endstiftung*, or completion. Social movements are the signs of this completion insofar as they (re)discover the perennial possibility of reflection in a situation of a consumer code whose completion—self-referentality, self-confirmation, and closure—tends to short-circuit reflection entirely. Social movements thus contain possibilitities of enlightenment and emancipation. Though, given that there are a plurality and multi-directionality of these possibilities, they cannot be unified into a supposedly necessary historical project to become human emancipation *tout court*. They illuminate our condition, point to paths onward, but they are not strong enough to institute a new primal scene. To the extent that this possibility of enlightenment becomes actual, we do not simply live within a communicative form but can engage new projects of instituting.

Media of communication constitute primal scenes, a complex of which defines the culture of a given place and time, an epoch of Being. This cultural complex is the extended body of the social identities that compose it. When one thematizes the process of communication, one abstracts one element from this complex against the background of an unthematized Gestalt whole that is the cultural complex minus its thematized element. This necessary abstraction defines the analysis of communication as a part-whole, or inside-outside, relation. The part, a primal scene of communication such as speaking or writing, not only can be analyzed thematically for its own characteristics, but also non-thematically manifests horizonally the whole cultural complex.

This horizonal manifestation is the means whereby the analysis of a particular medium of communication reveals the meaning and potential of communication as such. Each primal scene manifests the transcendental constitution of human being through communication. In this sense, every communication is a doubling. It is a particular communication within a cultural form, but it is also a manifestation of the cultural form as such, insofar as it can be understood on the model of this primal scene. Every expression horizonally manifests expression as such. This non-thematic manifestation of communication as such escapes the cultural complex that defines an epoch of Being. Such open-ness, as open-ness, is the limit of communication. We may find it in those components of social life that resist closure and which open human identity to its possibility of reflexive self-constitution, but this possibility itself emerges at the border of human culture, the region where the sacred begins. Since it alone enters this region without belief or armor, philosophy hovers on the skin of humankind.

Notes

Chapter 1

1. Michel Foucault, *The Order of Things* (New York: Vintage, 1973), pp. 318–322, and Edmund Husserl, *The Crisis of the European Sciences and Transcendental Phenomenology*, trans. David Carr (Evanston: Northwestern University Press, 1970), pp. 178–186. Foucault's later work tries to avoid this doubling through a return to "practice," though this is an unlikely solution since it tends to find the same duality concealed in practice. See on this point Hubert L. Dreyfus and Paul Rabinow, *Michel Foucault: Beyond Structuralism and Hermeneutics* (Chicago: The University of Chicago Press, 1983), especially chapter 9.

2. Compare Edmund Husserl, *Die Krisis der Europäischen Wissenschaft und die Transzendentale Phänomenologie* (The Hague: Martinus Nijhoff, 1976), pp. 74–75, 386, to *The Crisis of the European Sciences and Transcendental Phenomenology*, pp. 73–74, 378.

3. Edmund Husserl, *The Crisis of the European Sciences and Transcendental Phenomenology*, pp. 354. Cf. *Die Krisis der Europäischen Wissenschaft*, p. 366.

4. Maurice Merleau-Ponty, *Themes from the Lectures at the College de France 1952–1960*, trans. John O'Neill (Evanston: Northwestern University Press, 1970), chapter five, and "Indirect Language and the Voices of Silence" in *Signs*, trans. Richard C. McCleary (Evanston: Northwestern University Press, 1962), p. 59. Claude Lefort, *Democracy and Political Theory*, trans. David Macey (Minneapolis: University of Minnesota Press, 1988), pp. 10–12, 217.

5. Martin Heidegger, "The Origin of the Work of Art" in *Poetry, Language, Thought*, trans. Albert Hofstadter (New York: Harper and Row, 1971), p. 62; cf. "Der Ursprung des Kunstwerks" in *Holzwege* (Frankfurt am Main: V. Klostermann, 1950), p. 50.

6. Edmund Husserl, *The Crisis of the European Sciences and Transcendental Phenomenology*, p. 72. Cf. *Die Krisis der Europäischen Wissenschaft*, p. 73.

7. Aristotle, *The Rhetoric and Poetics of Aristotle*, trans. W. Rhys Roberts and Ingram Bywater (New York: The Modern Library, 1954), pp. 27, 61.

8. Ibid., pp. 31–32.

9. Kenneth Burke, *A Rhetoric of Motives* (Berkeley: University of California Press, 1950), especially pp. 55–58, 19–23.

10. Hans Blumenberg, "An Anthropological Approach to the Contemporary Significance of Rhetoric" in *After Philosophy: End or Transformation?*, ed. Kenneth Baynes, James Bohman, and Thomas McCarthy (Cambridge: MIT Press, 1987), p. 437.

11. This point has been made by many contemporary writers using different vocabularies. See in this connection, Charles Taylor, *The Malaise of Modernity* (Toronto: Anansi, 1991), p. 33, and *Multiculturalism and "The Politics of Recognition"* (Princeton: Princeton University Press, 1992), pp. 32–34; Richard Rorty, *Contingency, Irony, and Solidarity* (Cambridge: Cambridge University Press, 1989), pp. 10–16, 41, 75. Ernesto Laclau and Chantal Mouffe suggest that as a consequence of this point the term representation could be replaced with the concept of articulation in *Hegemony and Socialist Strategy* (London and New York: Verso, 1985), pp. 58, 65.

12. Marx and Engels, *The German Ideology* in *The Marx-Engels Reader*, ed. Robert C. Tucker (New York: W. W. Norton, 1978), p. 158, and Friedrich Nietzsche, *The Gay Science*, trans. Walter Kaufmann (New York: Vintage, 1974), p. 198.

13. Michel Foucault, *The Archeology of Knowledge*, trans. A. M. Sheridan Smith (London: Tavistock, 1972), p. 38.

14. J. L. Austin, "Performative-Constative" in *The Philosophy of Language*, ed. J. R. Searle (Oxford: Oxford University Press, 1971).

15. See John R. Searle, "How to Derive 'Ought' from 'Is'," *Philosophy Today*, no. 1, ed. Jerry H. Gill (New York: MacMillan, 1968).

16. Ernesto Laclau and Chantal Mouffe, "Post-Marxism Without Apologies" in Ernesto Laclau, *New Reflections on the Revolution of Our Time* (London and New York: Verso, 1990), p. 100.

17. Ludwig Wittgenstein, *Philosophical Investigations*, trans. G. E. M. Anscombe (New York: MacMillan, 1989), part 1, number 2.

18. Many articulations of the discursive stance remain trapped within this discursive/extra-discursive dualism and thus do not achieve a genuine concept of "discourse." Stuart Hall, for example, refers to a distinction between the discursive and the extra-discursive, without implying any distinction of levels between (extra-)linguistic and discursive as do Laclau and Mouffe. He thus enters into the intractable problem of how one can speak meaningfully about the extra-discursive, a question that is not resolvable in these terms. See, for example, Stuart Hall, "The Toad in the Garden: Thatcherism Among the Theorists" in *Marxism and the Interpretation of Culture*, ed. Cary Nelson and Lawrence Grossberg (Urbana and Chicago: University of Illinois Press, 1988), pp. 51–52; "Encoding/Decoding" in *Culture, Media, Language*, ed. S. Hall, et. al. (London: Hutchison, 1980), pp. 131–132; and "On Postmodernism and Articulation: An Interview with Stuart Hall," edited by Lawrence Grossberg, *Journal of Communication Inquiry* 10, no. 2 (Summer 1986): pp. 56–57.

Chapter 2

1. See, for example, Jean-François Lyotard, *The Postmodern Condition: A Report on Knowledge*, trans. Geoff Bennington and Brian Massumi (Minneapolis: University of Minneapolis Press, 1984) and David Harvey, *The Condition of Postmodernity* (Oxford: Blackwell, 1989). Habermas rejects the postmodern turn precisely because of this emphasis on locality and particularity—in short, the rejection of Enlightenment ideals—in *The Philosophical Discourse of Modernity*, trans. F. Lawrence (Cambridge: The MIT Press, 1987). The position articulated in this book accepts the turn to locality but argues, against the main tendency, that the historical epoch can be simultaneously theorized. It thus takes up a position distinct from both sides of this debate which is made possible by the theorization of the materiality of forms of expression that I have derived from Harold Innis.

2. A more thorough account of Innis's work that takes into account his earlier work on the political economy of dependency and relates this work to his theory of communication has been presented in chapter 3 of my *A Border Within: National Identity, Cultural Plurality and Wilderness* (Montreal and Kingston: McGill-Queen's Press, 1997).

3. H. A. Innis, *The Press: A Neglected Factor in the Economic History of the Twentieth Century* (London: Oxford University Press, 1949), p. 5.

4. Harold Innis, *Empire and Communications* (Toronto and Buffalo: University of Toronto Press, 1972) p. 7.

5. See, for example, *Empire and Communications*, pp. 7, 26–28.

6. Marshall McLuhan, *Understanding Media* (New York: New American Library, 1964).

7. Don Ihde, *Technics and Praxis* (Dordrecht: D. Reidel, 1979) and *Existential Technics* (Albany: State University of New York Press, 1983).

8. See "A Plea for Time" in Harold Innis, *Bias of Communication* (Toronto and Buffalo: University of Toronto Press, 1973), p. 76. Orality is also counterposed to "mechanized" in *The Press*, p. 4, and "A Critical Review" in *Bias*, p. 190.

9. *The Press*, p. 4.

10. *Empire and Communications*, p. 9.

11. "Industrialism and Cultural Values," in *Bias*, p. 132.

12. *Empire and Communications*, p. 9.

13. Ibid., pp. 24, 44, 90, 100; *Bias*, pp. 4, 35–36, 50, 100. This account of the contrast of writing and orality also relies on Walter Ong, *Orality and Literacy* (London: Methuen, 1982).

14. At this point we may ask a question. Is oral society as stable as it seems? Or does it appear so because it consumes its past? Innis has suggested that orality has a time bias, a stability through time even though it is very local in space. Could it be that oral society simply does not preserve the memory of its instabilities? That it stabilizes in time by forgetting, not memory? Also, in reflecting on this question, how could we know oral society as it is, as distinct to how oral society appears to us? In short, how can we answer the reflexive question of appraisal that underlies Innis's work?

15. "A Plea for Time," in *Bias*, p. 76.

16. *Empire and Communications*, p. 56. This analysis of interaction between different media as creating the potential for reflexive awareness is expanded in Marshall McLuhan's conception of "media hybrids" as the source of creative energy. See Marshall McLuhan, *Understanding Media: The Extensions of Man* (New York: Mentor, 1964), pp. 57–63.

17. See *Empire and Communications*, pp. 115, 170.

18. I have made such an argument in chapter 7 of *A Border Within: National Identity, Cultural Plurality and Wilderness*.

19. Gayatri Spivak, "Can the Subaltern Speak?" in *Marxism and the Interpretation of Culture*, ed. Cary Nelson and Lawrence Grossberg (Urbana and Chicago: University of Illinois Press, 1988).

20. "The Problem of Space," in *Bias*, p. 105. This conception is even more central in the work of McLuhan. See, for a selected statement of this pervasive theme, *Understanding Media*, p. 81.

21. *Bias*, pp. 61–62.

22. This is a large literature. Let me mention here only Samir Amin, *Eurocentrism*, trans. Russell Moore (New York: Monthly Review, 1989); Edward W. Soja, *Postmodern Geographies: The Reassertion of Space in Critical Social Theory* (London and New York: Verso, 1989); and Frederic Jameson, "Cognitive Mapping" in *Marxism and the Interpretation of Culture*, ed. Cary Nelson and Lawrence Grossberg (Urbana and Chicago: University of Illinois Press, 1988).

23. Edmund Husserl, *The Crisis of the European Sciences and Transcendental Phenomenology*, trans. David Carr (Evanston: Northwestern University Press, 1970), *passim*.

24. This book follows out the re-evaluation of the concept of civilization further with emphasis on the contemporary cultural configuration of consumer capitalist societies. If, however, further radical questions are asked about the colonialist and imperialist institution of such societies, an even more radical questioning of the concept of civilization is required—with regard to the conquering and/or marginalization of aboriginal societies, for example. This book does not extend the critique this far, precisely in order to focus clearly on the internal dynamics of consumer capitalist societies.

Chapter 3

1. Harold Innis, *The Bias of Communication* (Toronto and Buffalo: University of Toronto Press, 1973), p. xvii.

2. Jack Goody and Ian Watt, "The Consequences of Literacy" in *Literacy in Traditional Societies*, ed. Jack Goody (Cambridge: Cambridge University Press, 1968), pp. 28–29; see also Jack Goody, *The Logic of Writing and the Organization of Society* (Cambridge: Cambridge University Press, 1986).

3. Claude Leví-Strauss, *Myth and Meaning* (Toronto and Buffalo: University of Toronto Press, 1978), p. 15.

4. Eric Havelock, *Preface to Plato* (Cambridge: Harvard University Press, 1963), *Origins of Western Literacy* (Toronto: Ontario Institute for Studies in Education, 1976), *The Muse Learns to Write* (New Haven and London: Yale University Press, 1986); F. M. Cornford, "The Invention of Space" in *Essays Presented to Gilbert Murray* (London: Allen and Unwin, 1936).

5. Marshall McLuhan, *Understanding Media: The Extensions of Man* (New York: Mentor, 1964); Walter Ong, *Orality and Literacy* (London: Methuen, 1982); James W. Carey, *Communication as Culture: Essays on Media and Society* (Boston: Unwin Hyman, 1988).

6. For a wide collection, see Hans Ulrich Gumbrecht and Ludwig K. Pfeiffer, eds., *Materialities of Communication* (Stanford: Stanford University Press, 1994).

7. Edmund Husserl, *The Crisis of the European Sciences and Transcendental Phenomenology*, trans. David Carr (Evanston: Northwestern University Press, 1970), p. 161; *Die Krisis der Europäischen Wissenschaften und die Tranzendentale Phänomenologie* (The Hague: Martinus Nijhoff, 1976), p. 164.

8. Ludwig K. Pfeiffer, "The Materiality of Communication" in *Materialities of Communication*, p. 1.

9. Karl Marx, "Theses on Feuerbach" in Robert C. Tucker (ed.) *The Marx-Engels Reader* (New York: W. W. Norton, 1976), pp. 144–145.

10. Harold Innis, *The Bias of Communication*, p. xvii.

11. Harold Innis, *Empire and Communications* (Toronto and Buffalo: University of Toronto Press, 1972), pp. 5, 7, 11.

12. Eric Havelock, *Preface to Plato*, p. xi.

13. While I cannot address the institutional aspects of this issue here, it may well be that the rhetoric of oscillation is rooted ultimately in the institutionalization of specialized inquiry in the contemporary university, state and corporate structure and the problems that this poses for the allocation of resources, on the one hand, and the difficulties of wider intellectual discussion, on the other.

14. Harold Innis, *Empire and Communications*, p. 9.

15. Edmund Husserl, *The Crisis of European Sciences and Transcendental Phenomenology*.

16. Ernesto Laclau, *Politics and Ideology in Marxist Theory* (London: Verso, 1982), p. 70; Ernesto Laclau and Chantal Mouffe, *Hegemony and Socialist Strategy* (London and New York: Verso, 1985), p. 105. I have defended a version of transcendental phenomenology that can address these issues in *(Dis)figurations* (London and New York: Verso, 2000).

17. Gregory Bateson, "Form, Substance and Difference" in *Steps to an Ecology of Mind* (New York: Ballantine Books, 1972).

18. Gregory Bateson, "From Versailles to Cybernetics" and "The Roots of Ecological Crisis" in ibid.

19. Edmund Husserl, *Crisis*, p. 184.

20. Ludwig Landgrebe, "The Life-World and the Historicity of Human Existence," *Research in Phenomenology* (1981): p. 134.

21. Gregory Bateson, "Conscious Purpose versus Nature" in *Steps*.

22. Laclau and Mouffe, *Hegemony and Socialist Strategy*, p. 146, ft. 16. See Aron Gurwitsch, *Phenomenology and the Theory of Science* (Evanston: Northwestern University Press, 1974), chapter 10, and my discussion in *Technique and Enlightenment: Limits of Instrumental Reason* (Washington: University Press of America and Centre for Advanced Research in Phenomenology, 1984), pp. 35–38.

23. Marshall McLuhan, *Understanding Media*, p. 69; *The Gutenberg Galaxy* (New York: Mentor, 1969), p. 27.

24. Gregory Bateson, "Cybernetic Explanation," "Conscious Purpose and Nature," and "Pathologies of Epistemology" in *Steps*.

25. Eric Havelock, *The Muse Learns to Write*, pp. 24–29.

26. Ibid, pp. 105–116; Eric Havelock, *Preface to Plato*, pp. 208–210.

27. Plato, *Republic*, ed. Edith Hamilton and H. Cairns (New York: Pantheon, 1966), pp. 742–744, 507b–509b.

28. See, for the philosophical intuition of cosmological order, *Republic*, 518c, 540a, 585a–586a, 611a–612d; *Phaedo*, 90a–d; *Seventh Letter*, 433b.

29. Heidegger described poetry as the "projective saying of world and earth" in "The Origin of the Work of Art" in *Poetry, Language, Truth*, trans. Albert Hofstadter (New York: Harper and Row, 1975), p. 74. This Heideggerian conception of poetry has been developed into a conception of rhetoric as the institution and confirmation of human dwelling in the world by Ernesto Grassi in *Rhetoric as Philosophy* (University Park and London: The Pennsylvania State Press, n.d.) and Michael J. Hyde in "Rhetorically, Man Dwells: On the Making-Known Function of Discourse" in *Communication* 7 (1983). My preference here is to reserve poetry for institution and rhetoric for ceremonial confirmation. But this conception of poetry, even as developed into rhetoric, contains a mystifying temptation for misunderstanding language due to the loss of its material component. My appropriation of Innis's work attempts to remedy this mystification of Heideggerian origin.

30. These few lines bounce too lightly over the history of phenomenology in its discovery and reformation of regressive thinking. However, this is not the place to discuss the continuation and difference between Husserl's concept of "dismantling" [*Abbau* and, later, *Rückgang*], Heidegger's concept of the step back" [*Rückgang* and *Destruktion*], and Derrida's concept of deconstruction. Such an inquiry would turn this into another book entirely.

Chapter 4

1. Ludovico Geymonat, *Galileo Galilei*, trans. S. Drake (Toronto: McGraw-Hill, 1965), and Karl Marx, *Capital*, Vol. 1, part four, trans. Ben Fowkes (New York: Random House, 1977).

2. Edward G. Ballard, *Man and Technology* (Pittsburgh: Dusquesne University Press, 1978), p. 194.

3. Jurgen Habermas, "Technology and Science as 'Ideology'" in *Toward a Rational Society*, trans. Jeremy J. Shapiro (Boston:Beacon Press, 1970), *passim* and p. 96; Jurgen Habermas, *Theory and Practice*, trans. John Viertel (Boston: Beacon Press, 1973), p. 286, ftn. 4; Hans-Georg Gadamer, "Theory, Technology, Practice: The Task of the Sciences of Man," *Social Research* 44, no. 3 (Autumn 1977); and Hannah Arendt, *The Human Condition* (Chicago: University of Chicago Press, 1973). See my critique of this dualism as a standpoint for the analysis of contemporary technology in *Technique and Enlightenment: Limits of Instrumental Reason* (Washington: Center for Advanced Research in Phenomenology and University Press of America, 1984), pp. 99–118.

4. See Max Horkheimer, *Kants kritik der urteilskraft als bindeglied zwischen theoretischer und praktischer philosophie* (Stuttgart: Verlag von W. Kohlhammer, 1925); Hans-Georg Gadamer, *Truth and Method* (New York: Crossroad, 1975); and Ian Angus, *Technique and Enlightenment: Limits of Instrumental Reason*, pp. 99–118.

5. Ian Angus, *Technique and Enlightenment: Limits of Instrumental Reason*, p. 142.

6. See, for a more complete account of the phenomenological concept of the world, Edmund Husserl, *The Crisis of European Sciences and Transcendental Phenomenology*, trans. David Carr (Evanston: Northwestern University Press, 1970), pp. 103–189, and Martin Heidegger, *Being and Time*, trans. John Macquarrie and Edward Robinson (New York and Evanston: Harper and Row, 1962), pp. 91–148.

7. Karl Marx, "Economic and Philosophical Manuscripts of 1844" in *The Marx-Engels Reader*, p. 75.

8. Edmund Husserl, *The Crisis of European Sciences and Transcendental Phenomenology*, p. 5.

9. See Ian Angus, *Technique and Enlightenment: Limits of Instrumental Reason*, pp. 135–148.

10. See Ian Angus, *George Grant's Platonic Rejoinder to Heidegger: Contemporary Political Philosophy and the Question of Technology* (Lewiston and Queenston: Edwin Mellen, 1987), pp. 105–114.

11. Raymond Williams, "Means of Communication as Means of Production" in *Problems of Materialism and Culture* (London: Verso, 1980), p. 53.

12. G. W. F. Hegel, *Phenomenology of Spirit*, trans. A. V. Miller (Oxford: Oxford University Press, 1979), p. 111.

13. Ibid., p. 118.

14. Charles Taylor, *The Malaise of Modernity*, p. 46, and *Multiculturalism and "The Politics of Recognition,"* p. 26.

15. This position is pervasive in Marx's work from beginning to end but, for one example, see Karl Marx, *Capital*, Vol. 1, part four.

Chapter 5

1. Edmund Husserl, *Logical Investigations*, trans. J. N. Findley (London: Routledge and Kegan Paul, 1970), p. 280; German edition, *Logische Untersuchungen*, Vol. 2, part 1 (Tübingen: Max Niemeyer, 1968), p. 37.

2. Ibid., p. 284; German edition, p. 42.

3. Ibid., p. 269; German edition, p. 23.

4. Ibid., p. 270, emphasis removed; German edition, p. 25.

5. Ibid., pp. 270 (second emphasis added) and 274; German edition, pp. 25, 29.

6. Ibid., p. 273; German edition, p. 28.

7. *Logical Investigations*, p. 276; German edition, p. 32. Jacques Derrida's account of Husserl begins from precisely this point, suggesting that expression is "really" a form of indication and that scientific discourse is "really" another form of the association of ideas. See *Speech and Phenomena*, trans. D. Allison (Bloomington: Indiana University Press, 1973), p. 21; cf. J. Claude Evans, *Strategies of Deconstruction* (Minneapolis: University of Minnesota Press, 1991), p. 37. My argument here, though it covers some of the same terrain as Derrida's writing, does not require the collapse of Husserl's distinction, but only that the basis for communicative interaction be distinguished from scientific discourse—and this is thoroughly consistent with Husserl's work at this point. My later argument, that Husserl's account of communication is erroneously founded on a distinction between communication as a transfer of meaning-content and expression as the formation of a meaning-content, is also made by Derrida, but in a way that attempts to impale the distinction, rather than use it to open a new area of inquiry. See *Speech and Phenomena*, pp. 37–38; cf. Evans, *Strategies of Deconstruction*, pp. 32–36. My account, and critique, does not require the acceptance, nor even consideration, of Derrida's thesis that Husserl's theory incorporates a phonocentric myth—a myth of the self-presence of consciousness to itself in speech.

8. *Logical Investigations*, p. 273; German edition, p. 29.

9. Ibid., p. 273; German edition, p. 28.

10. For a detailed discussion of this larger claim, see my *(Dis)figurations* (London and New York: Verso, 2000).

11. *Logical Investigations*, p. 277; German edition, p. 33.

12. Ibid., p. 278; German edition, p. 35.

13. René Toulemont, "The Specific Character of the Social According to Husserl" in *Apriori and World*, ed. and trans. W. McKenna, R. Harlan, and L. Winters (The Hague: Martinus Nijhoff, 1981), p. 229, emphasis added.

14. Edmund Husserl, *Cartesian Meditations*, trans. Dorion Cairns (The Hague: Martinus Nijhoff, 1969), p. 132; German edition, *Cartesianische Meditationen und Pariser Vorträge* (The Hague: Martinus Nijhoff, 1973), p. 160. Edmund Husserl, *The Crisis of the European Sciences and Transcendental Phenomenology*, trans. David Carr (Evanston: Northwestern University Press, 1970), p. 188; German edition, *Die Krisis der Europäischen Wissenschaft und die Transzendentale Phänomenologie* (The Hague: Martinus Nijhoff, 1976), pp. 191–192.

15. *Logical Investigations*, p. 270; cf. German edition, p. 24.

16. Ibid., pp. 313, 315; German edition, pp. 79, 81.

17. G. W. F. Hegel, *Phenomenology of Spirit*, p. 60.

18. V. N. Volosinov, *Marxism and the Philosophy of Language*, trans. L. Matejka and I. R. Titunik (Cambridge: Harvard University Press, 1973), p. 99.

19. Ibid., pp. 95, 103, 106.

Chapter 6

1. Friedrich Pollock, "State Capitalism: Its Possibilities and Limitations," in *The Essential Frankfurt School Reader*, ed. Andrew Arato and Eike Gebhardt (Oxford: Blackwell, 1978), p. 73.

2. Jean Baudrillard, *The Mirror of Production*, trans. Mark Poster (St. Louis: Telos Press, 1975), pp. 121, 127.

3. Henri Lefebvre, *Everyday Life in the Modern World*, trans. Sacha Rabinovitch (New York: Harper & Row, 1971), pp. 111, 112, 116–117.

4. Ferdinand de Saussure, *Course in General Linguistics*, trans. Wade Baskin (New York: McGraw-Hill, 1966), pp. 67–68.

5. Claude E. Shannon and Warren Weaver, *The Mathematical Theory of Communication* (Urbana: The University of Illinois Press, 1962), p. 5. This model was, of course, extremely influential in forming the new field of communication studies as well as more popular views about the nature of communication. See, for example, David K. Berlo, *The Process of Communication* (New York: Holy, Rinehart and Winston, 1960), p. 72 and Roman Jacobson, "Clos-

ing Statement: Linguistics and Poetics" in *Style in Language*, ed. Thomas A. Sebeok (New York: The Technology Press of MIT and John Wiley and Sons, 1960), p. 353.

6. G. W. F. Hegel, "The English Reform Bill" in *Hegel's Political Writings*, trans. T. M. Knox (Oxford: Clarendon Press, 1964), especially pp. 328–330.

Chapter 7

1. Jean-François Lyotard, *The Postmodern Condition: A Report on Knowledge*, trans G. Bennington and B. Massumi (Minneapolis: Minneapolis University Press, 1984), p. 5.

2. Marshall McLuhan, *Understanding Media: The Extensions of Man* (New York: Mentor, 1964), pp. 64–65.

3. S. Serafini and M. Andrieu, *The Information Revolution and Its Implications for Canada* (Hull: Supply and Services Canada,1980), pp. 21–22.

4. *Planning Now for an Information Society* (Hull: Supply and Services Canada, 1982), especially pp. 47–48, 49, 61–62.

5. Walter Ong, "African Talking Drums and Oral Noetics" in *Interfaces of the Word* (Ithaca and London: Cornell University Press, 1977).

6. Ibid., p. 118.

Chapter 8

1. Raymond Williams, "Means of Communication as Means of Production" in *Problems in Materialism and Culture* (London: Verso, 1980), p. 53.

2. Raymond Williams, *Television: Technology and Cultural Form* (New York: Schocken Books, 1975), chapter 1.

3. Ibid., pp. 126–130.

4. Ibid, pp. 20–29.

5. Ibid., pp. 25–27.

6. Ibid., pp. 13–14.

7. Ibid., p. 29.

8. Ibid., pp. 28–29.

9. Ibid., pp. 78–118.

10. Marshall McLuhan, *Understanding Media: The Extensions of Man* (New York: Mentor, 1964), pp. 49, 294ff.

11. Jacques Derrida, *Of Grammatology*, trans. Gayatri Chakravorty Spivak (Baltimore and London: The Johns Hopkins University Press, 1976), p. 215.

12. Ibid., p. 304. Italics removed.

13. Marshall McLuhan, *Understanding Media*, p. 47.

14. Ibid., p. 52.

15. Raymond Williams, *Television*, pp. 147–152.

16. This suggests that Husserl's discovery of the "stream of internal time-consciousness" marks him as a/the "founding" postmodern philosopher. While this is certainly not a widespread reading of Husserl, I think that it is not without justification. I have developed this view of Husserl in *(Dis)figurations* (London and New York: Verso, 2000).

17. Ibid., p. 64.

18. Jean Baudrillard, *Simulations*, trans. Paul Foss, Paul Patton, and Philip Beitchman (New York: Semiotext(e), 1983) pp. 199–120.

19. Jean Baudrillard, *In the Shadow of the Silent Majorities*, trans. Paul Foss, Paul Patton, and John Johnson (New York: Semiotext(e), 1983), p. 6.

Chapter 9

1. Karl Marx and Friedrich Engels, *The Communist Manifesto* in *The Marx-Engels Reader*, ed. Robert C. Tucker (New York: W. W. Norton, 1976), p. 476.

2. Walter Benjamin, "The Work of Art in the Age of Mechanical Reproduction" in *Illuminations*, ed. Hannah Arendt (New York: Schocken Books, 1969), pp. 222, 239–241. Benjamin's account of the audience is taken from Brecht, see *Brecht on Theatre*, trans. John Willett (New York: Hill & Wang, 1964), pp. 44, 50, 56.

3. Max Horkheimer and Theodor Adorno, *Dialectic of Enlightenment*, trans. John Cumming (New York: Herder and Herder, 1972), pp. 129–130.

4. Walter Benjamin, "Work of Art," pp. 232ff., 235ff. Theodor Adorno, "Letters to Walter Benjamin" in *Aesthetics and Politics* (London: Verso, 1980), p. 122. Adorno wrote his essay "On the Fetish Character of Music and the Regression of Hearing" precisely to document audience regression as against the expectations of Benjamin. This essay is reprinted in *The Essential Frankfurt School Reader*, ed. Andrew Arato and Eike Gebhardt (Oxford: Blackwell, 1978).

5. Benjamin, "Work of Art," p. 218.

6. Ibid., p. 224, cf. p. 230.

7. Jacques Derrida, "Structure, Sign and Play in the Discourse of the Human Sciences" in *Writing and Difference*, trans. Alan Bass (Chicago: University of Chicago Press, 1978), p. 278ff.

8. Horkheimer and Adorno, *Dialectic of Enlightenment*, p. 145–146.

Chapter 10

1. Claude E. Shannon and Warren Weaver, *The Mathematical Theory of Communication*, (Urbana: The University of Illinois Press, 1962), p. 109.

2. Jean Baudrillard, *In the Shadow of the Silent Majorities*, trans. Paul Foss, Paul Patton, and John Johnson (New York: Semiotext(e), 1983), pp. 43–44.

3. Sheldon Wolin, "What Revolutionary Action Means Today" in *Dimensions of Radical Democracy: Pluralism, Citizenship, Community*, ed. Chantal Mouffe (London: Verso, 1992), p. 250.

4. Ibid., p. 251.

5. Gregory Bateson, "Cybernetic Explanation" in *Steps to an Ecology of Mind* (New York: Ballantine Books, 1972).

Chapter 11

1. Gayatri Chakravorty Spivak, *In Other Worlds* (London and New York: Rotuledge, 1988), p. 106.

2. *Globe and Mail*, 18 January 1992, p. A4.

3. *Vancouver Sun*, 21 November 1992.

4. Ibid.

5. *Vancouver Sun*, 21 November 1992 and 25 November 1992.

6. *The Province*, 4 March 1993, p. A18. Hansen's conviction was quashed in an appeal to the Supreme Court of Ontario in 1996.

7. Franz Fanon, *Black Skin/White Masks* (Weidenfeld: Grove Press, 1967), p. 39.

8. Simone de Beauvoir, *The Second Sex*, trans. H. M. Parshely (New York: Random House, 1970), pp. xv–xvi.

9. Franz Fanon, *Black Skin/White Masks*, p. 33.

10. From the speech by Eugen Leviné before the court prior to his death sentence, included as an appendix to Rosa Leviné-Meyer, *Leviné, The Spartacist* (Glasgow: The University Press, 1973), p. 210.

11. Betty Friedan, *The Feminine Mystique* ((New York: Norton, 1983), chapter one.

12. Seyla Benhabib, "Models of Public Space: Hannah Arendt, the Liberal Tradition, and Jurgen Habermas" and Mary P. Ryan, "Gender and Public Access: Women's Politics in Nineteenth-Century America," both in *Habermas and the Public Sphere*, ed. Craig Calhoun (Cambridge: The MIT Press, 1992); Richard Johnson, "What Is Cultural Studies Anyway?," *Social Text* 16 (1986–87).

13. Maurice Charland, "Constitutive Rhetoric: The Case of the Peuple Québécois," *Quarterly Journal of Speech* 73, no. 2 (1987).

14. Karlyn Kohrs Campbell, "The Rhetoric of Women's Liberation: An Oxymoron," *Quarterly Journal of Speech* 59 (1973).

15. Stuart Hall, *The Hard Road to Renewal* (London and New York: Verso, 1988).

16. See Ian Angus, *A Border Within: National Identity, Cultural Plurality and Wilderness* (Montreal and Kingston: McGill-Queen's Press, 1997), pp. 11–27, 105–118.

17. Michael Calvin McGee, "The 'Ideograph': A Link Between Rhetoric and Ideology," *Quarterly Journal of Speech* 66, no. 1 (1980).

18. Alberto Melucci, "The Symbolic Challenge of Contemporary Movements," *Social Research* 52, no. 4 (1985).

19. Ernesto Laclau and Chantal Mouffe, *Hegemony and Socialist Strategy* (London and New York: Verso, 1985) p. 87.

20. Madhu Kishwar, "Why I Do Not Call Myself a Feminist," *Manushi* 61 (1990).

21. Ofelia Schutte, "Philosophy and Feminism in Latin America," *The Philosophical Forum* 20, no. 102 (1988–89): p. 73.

22. Karlyn Kohrs Campbell, "Feminism and Femininity: To Be or Not to Be a Woman," *Communication Quarterly* 31, no. 2 (1983).

23. Ibid., p. 102. See also Gayatri Chakravorty Spivak, *In Other Worlds*, p. 144.

24. Campbell, "Feminism and Femininity," pp. 104–106, and Iris Marion Young, "Abjection and Opression: Dynamics of Unconscious Racism, Sexism

and Homophobia" in *Crises in Continental Philosophy*, ed. Arleen B. Dallery, and Charles E. Scott with P. Holley Roberts (Albany: State University of New York Press, 1990).

25. Richard B. Gregg, A. Jackson McCormack, and Douglas J. Pederson, "The Rhetoric of Black Power: A Street-Level Interpretation," *Quarterly Journal of Speech* 55 (1969).

26. Campbell, "The Rhetoric of Women's Liberation," pp. 77–78.

27. Immanuel Kant, *Critique of Pure Reason*, trans. Norman Kemp Smith (Toronto: Macmillan, 1965), p. 299.

28. Ibid.

29. Gayatri Chakravorty Spivak, *In Other Worlds*, p. 206.

30. Gregory Bateson, "Conscious Purpose Versus Nature" in *Steps to an Ecology of Mind* (New York: Ballantine Books, 1972).

31. Laclau and Mouffe, *Hegemony and Socialist Strategy* (London and New York: Verso, 1985), pp. 122–134, 164–171.

Chapter 12

1. Max Weber, "Politics as a Vocation" in *From Max Weber*, ed. and trans. H. H. Gerth and C. Wright Mills (New York: Oxford University Press, 1976), p. 78.

2. Etienne de la Boettie, *Discourse on Voluntary Servitude*, trans. Harry Kurz (Montreal: Black Rose, 1975), p. 60.

3. Charles Taylor, "Interpretation and the Sciences of Man" in *Understanding and Social Inquiry*, ed. Fred R. Dallmayr and Thomas A. McCarthy (Notre Dame: University of Notre Dame Press, 1977), p. 120.

4. Stuart Hall, "The Problem of Ideology—Marxism without Guarantees," *Journal of Communication Inquiry* 10, no. 2 (Summer 1986): p. 39; "On Postmodernism and Articulation: An Interview with Stuart Hall," ed. Lawrence Grossberg, *Journal of Communication Inquiry* 10, no. 2 (Summer 1986): p. 53; *The Hard Road to Renewal* (London: Verso, 1988), p. 10.

5. Stuart Hall, "Cultural Studies: Two Paradigms" in *Media, Culture and Society*, ed. J. Collins, et al. (London: Sage, 1986), p. 39.

6. Stuart Hall, "The Rediscovery of 'Ideology': Return of the Repressed in Media Studies" in *Culture, Society and the Media*, ed. M. Gurevitch, T. Bennett, J. Curran, and J. Woollacott (London: Methuen, 1982), p. 73. See also "Culture, the Media, and the 'Ideological Effect'" in *Mass Communication and Society*,

eds. J. Curran et al. (London: Edward Arnold, 1977), pp. 332–334 and "Gramsci's Relevance for the Study of Race and Ethnicity," *Journal of Communication Inquiry* 10, no. 2 (Summer 1986).

7. Stuart Hall, "Signification, Representation, Ideology: Althusser and the Post-Structuralist Debates," *Critical Studies in Mass Communication* 2, no. 2 (June 1985): p. 105.

8. Stuart Hall, "Gramsci's Relevance for the Study of Race and Ethnicity," p. 53.

9. Stuart Hall, "Signification, Representation, Ideology: Althusser and the Post-Structuralist Debates," pp. 113–114, ftn. 2; "On Postmodernism and Articulation: An Interview with Stuart Hall," pp. 53, 56; *The Hard Road to Renewal*, pp. 9–10; "Cultural Studies: Two Paradigms," p. 45. The influential studies *Learning to Labor* by Paul Willis and *Subculture: The Meaning of Style* by Dick Hebdige focus on the aspect of linkage when defining the term and its genealogy, but also utilize the notion of the taken-for-granted in undertaking their empirical studies. See Paul Willis, *Learning to Labor* (New York: Columbia University Press, 1981), pp. 60, 77, 120, 139, and Dick Hebdige, *Subculture: The Meaning of Style* (London: Methuen, 1979), pp. 11, 13, 19, 91.

10. Michael Calvin McGee, "The 'Ideograph': A Link Between Rhetoric and Ideology," *Quarterly Journal of Speech* 66, no. 1 (1980).

11. Alfred Schütz, "On Multiple Realities," *Collected Papers*, Vol. 1., ed. Maurice Natanson. (The Hague: Martinus Nijhoff, 1971), p. 227. In personal conversation Hall has admitted the influence of Schutz in developing his conception of the taken-for-grantedness of common sense and also that his failure to achnowledge this influence was due to the high profile of structuralism in British debates throughout the 1970s. In addition, early in his career Hall taught a seminar on Sartre's *Search for a Method*.

12. Martin Heidegger, "The Origin of the Work of Art" and ". . . Poetically Man Dwells . . ." in *Poetry, Language, Thought*, trans. Albert Hofstadter (New York: Harper and Row, 1971).

13. Michael J. Hyde, "Rhetorically, Man Dwells: On the Making-Known Function of Discourse," *Communication* 7, no. 2 (1983).

14. Richard Johnson, "What Is Cultural Studies Anyway?," *Social Text* 16 (1986–87): p. 67.

15. Ernesto Laclau, *Politics and Ideology in Marxist Theory* (London: Verso, 1982), pp. 166–167.

16. This debate also took place in Canada in the 1970s, but without any satisfactory resolution. Laclau's intervention, by way of contrast, became very significant for subsequent Latin American politics. One important political task

for Canadian socialist theory, one that would link it directly to recent Latin American struggles, is the development of the theory of articulation with respect to Canada-U.S. relations. Concretely, this would mean a re-articulation of the work of Harold Innis with current Marxist theory. The Marx-Innis debate in the 1970s, since it did not achieve the level of rethinking of Marxism represented by Laclau's work based in Latin America, largely degenerated into a useless polemic between a so-called nationalist "synthesis" without theoretical foundation and a Marxist orthodoxy of independent capitalist development that totally ignored the specific features of Canadian political economy explained by Innis. I have addressed this task in *A Border Within: National Identity, Cultural Plurality and Wilderness* (Montreal and Kingston: McGill-Queen's Press, 1997), pp. 43–48.

17. Ernesto Laclau, *Politics and Ideology in Marxist Theory*, p. 43.

18. Ibid., p. 8.

19. Ian Angus, *Technique and Enlightenment: Limits of Instrumental Reason* (Washington: Center for Advanced Research in Phenomenology and University Press of America, 1984), p. 53.

20. Laclau and Mouffe, *Hegemony and Socialist Strategy* (London and New York: Verso, 1985), p. 105.

21. Ibid., p. 113.

22. Ibid., pp. 154, 124.

23. Ibid., p. 125.

24. Ibid., p. 127.

25. Ibid.

26. Ibid., p. 141.

27. Ibid., pp. 135–136.

28. Ibid., p. 135.

29. Ibid., p. 122.

30. Ibid., p. 143.

31. Ibid., pp. 104, 122, 125, 126; cf. 146, ftn. 16.

32. Ibid., p. 125.

33. I can only assert, and not defend, at this point an alternative position with respect to the philosophical question of the nature of language. This position centers on "world-disclosing expression," which has been expressed in the text through the notion of poetry as a primal scene, and can be developed theoretically through reliance on Husserl, Heidegger, and Walter Benjamin. One may

remark also that the question of whether the whole cultural world can be adequately understood through language depends primarily on the notion of language that one adopts.

34. The consequences of a polemical denial of necessity rebounding simply to its complementary metaphysical opposition, "contingency," are abundantly clear in Richard Rorty's *Contingency, Irony, and Solidarity* (New York: Cambridge University Press, 1989), though it would be too far afield to document them here. Such a rebound is as likely to lead to a self-satisfied (or even violent) assertion of one's own contingencies as a skeptical social critique of contingent social domination.

35. Actually, Grant uses both "particularity," and, more often, "one's own," which is his rendering of Heidegger's *Eigentlich*, usually translated into English as "authenticity." See George Grant, *Technology and Empire* (Toronto: Anansi, 1969), pp. 23ff, 73ff. See my discussion and extension of this concept in *A Border Within: National Identity, Cultural Plurality and Wilderness*, pp. 155–169.

36. I have pursued this criticism in more detail in *(Dis)figurations* (London and New York: Verso, 2000), chapter three.

Index